THE JEWISH INTELLIGENTSIA AND RUSSIAN MARXISM

THE JEWISH INTELLIGENTSIA AND RUSSIAN MARXISM

A Sociological Study of Intellectual Radicalism And Ideological Divergence

Robert J. Brym

SCHOCKEN BOOKS · NEW YORK

First published by SCHOCKEN BOOKS 1978

Copyright © Robert J. Brym 1978

Library of Congress Cataloging in Publication Data

Brym, Robert J   1951 –
   The Jewish intelligentsia and Russian Marxism.

   Bibliography: p.
   Includes index.
   1. Jews in Russia—Politics and government.
2. Socialists, Jewish—Russia.   3. Russia—
Politics and government—1894–1917.   4. Socialism
in Russia.   I. Title.
DS135.R9B86   301.45′19′24047   77–14724
ISBN 0–8052–3685–6

Manufactured in Great Britain.

Contents

List of Figures

Preface

This monograph is a sociological study of the recruitment of Jewish intellectuals to four Marxist political parties — Bolshevik, Menshevik, Bundist and Poalei-Zionist — in turn-of-the-century Russia. Through an examination of biographical and historical sources, it isolates the structural forces which radicalised intellectuals and led them to diverse ideological viewpoints.

Unlike many students of the subject I have not sought to employ an explanatory framework which emphasises the structural 'rootlessness' or cultural 'alienation' of intellectuals. Quite the contrary. The thrust of this study is (to paraphrase an expression used by George Homans in a quite different context) aimed at bringing intellectuals back in to society. We can, I submit, learn a good deal more about the behaviour of intellectuals by examining their mutable social connections than by assuming their isolation from social structure. Specifically, the following chapters seek to demonstrate that ideologies are shaped and reshaped by (a) intellectuals' shifting occupational ties in changing social structures; and (b) their learning and relearning of culture patterns associated with different positions in society.

During the two and a half years it took to arrive at this conclusion I incurred a large number of debts, both personal and intellectual. An earlier version of this study was written as a University of Toronto Ph.D. thesis and my advisors, Professors Irving M. Zeitlin, Stephen Berkowitz and Dennis Magill offered many valuable criticisms of the preliminary drafts. I was exceedingly fortunate to have on my examination committee three scholars who wrote perceptive critiques of my work: Professors T. B. Bottomore, Anatol Rapaport and Jack Wayne were instrumental in forcing me to clarify a number of primitive ideas. It was partly due to Professor Bottomore's kind assistance and encouragement that the thesis was revised and published. I also profited from conversations and/or correspondence with Professors Robert Johnson, J. Douglas House, Henry Tobias, Charles Woodhouse, Austin Turk, Clinton Herrick, Ezra Mendelsohn, Jacob Schatzmiller and Isaac Levitats; and fellow graduate students Gail Sarginson, Barry Edginton and Karen Anderson. Gayle Kerbel and Sophie Brym helped immeasurably by taking my mind off this project from time to time. And it was largely because my father, Albert, my late uncle, Kalman, and I met in Tiberias that the puzzle I have tried to solve here first presented itself to me. Although all these people are complicit in having shaped my thinking, I alone bear full responsibility for whatever weaknesses may be found in this study.

I also want to thank the Canada Council for the financial assistance which enabled me to take my Ph.D. degree; the staffs of the YIVO Institute, the Zionist Archives and Library, the Bund Archives, the interlibrary loan department of the Robarts Library, University of Toronto; and the editors of the *Journal of Social History* and the *Scottish Journal of Sociology*, who granted me permission to use material from two previously published articles (Brym, 1977a; 1977d).

This study is dedicated to my parents.

St. John's, Newfoundland, Canada R. B.
23 April 1977

Note: Transliteration was an enduring problem in the preparation of this study. Early on I decided not to use available formal systems because of the confusion which could result from the fact that phonetic equivalents are often rendered differently for different languages. In order to achieve a higher level of standardisation, transliterations are by and large phonetic. Some inconsistencies will, however, be found since I have attempted to retain widely accepted spellings, especially for proper nouns.

1 Theoretical Prospectus

That then is the intelligentsia; its members were . . . held together solely by ideas.

Nicolas Berdyaev

In 1903 Minister of the Interior Plehve rank-ordered the four most serious issues plaguing the Russian Empire: the agrarian problem, the Jewish question, the intellectual radicalism spawned by the school system and the condition of the working class. In terms of historical significance the subject matter of this book requires little justification, for Russian-Jewish Marxist *intelligenty*[1] stood at the intersection point of these four problems. They forged the ideologies of Labour Zionism, Bundism, Menshevism and, to a much lesser degree, Bolshevism. They were both products and key architects of socio-historical changes which permanently altered the texture of social life in Russia, the Middle East and therefore the world.

It is precisely for this reason that one must be careful not to exaggerate their role. Historians of revolutionary Russia have done us a considerable disservice by focusing undue attention on 'great men' in their explanations of events. Lenin, Trotsky and other *intelligenty* loom large in accounts of the Russian revolution; the worker and peasant often disappear from sight as we make our way through the web of political intrigue and ideological conflict in which the intelligentsia was entangled. Who else but an historian of Russia could have entitled a book *Three Who Made a Revolution?* To be sure, there were 'great men' among the intelligentsia. (Witness Trotsky's claim in his *History of the Russian Revolution* that the events of 1917 would never have occured but for Lenin.) And *intelligenty*, whether great or mean, undoubtedly represented a more powerful force in Russian radical politics than did, say, their American or French counterparts. (As is evidenced by the relatively high ratio in Russia of *intelligenty* to workers and peasants in party organisations.) But the fact remains that *mass* unrest played the major role in weakening and finally toppling the old regime: Plehve, more than most historians, recognised that the foundations of the Empire were being undermined more by working class and peasant discontent than by intellectual dissent. A rough indication of this is provided by Fig. 1, which tabulates the occupations of Russian radicals from the 1860s to the early years of the twentieth century. Based on information contained in a multi-volume biographical dictionary and police statistics on political arrests, the table suggests that (a) over time, the

Fig. 1. Occupational Distribution of Russian Radicals, 1860–1903 (%)

occupation	year			
	1860–9 (n = 1,256)	1870–9 (n = 5,664)	1884–90 (n = 4,307)	1901–3 (n = 7,796)
student	61 ⎫ 71	52 ⎫ 65	25 ⎫ 36	10 ⎫ 21
professional	10 ⎭	13 ⎭	11 ⎭	11 ⎭
worker, artisan	1 ⎫ 1	16 ⎫ 21	16 ⎫ 23	47 ⎫ 56
peasant	0 ⎭	5 ⎭	7 ⎭	9 ⎭
other, unknown	28	14	41	23
	100	100	100	100

Source: Compiled from data in (Leykina-Svirskaya, 1971: 309, 313–14, 317).

intelligentsia's weight in the revolutionary movement decreased as rapidly as the workers' and peasants' increased; and (b) by the time of the 1905 revolution *intelligenty* constituted only a minority of Russian radicals.

Nor should one overstate the importance of Jews in the intelligentsia, as some writers do.[2] There were, in the first place, probably more Jewish liberal intellectuals than Jewish *intelligenty* in Russia. Moreover, the intelligentsia was comprised of three (or perhaps four) groups, only one of which was Jewish. Until the late 1870s the overwhelming majority of *intelligenty* was recruited from the nobility, which is why we possess information on a mere seventeen Jewish *intelligenty* before that decade (Cherikover, 1939: 79). By the late 1870s, *raznochintsy* — literally, men of 'various [non-noble] ranks' — had become predominant. Fig. 2, based on the smattering of numerical data we possess on the subject, hints at this. Jewish intellectuals were now radicalised in increasing numbers, but it was only in the early years of the twentieth century that they came to form a

Fig. 2. Social Origins of Russian *Intelligenty*, 1840–87 (%)

origin	year			
	1840–55 (n = 50)	1855–69 (n = 143)	1870–5 (n = 191)	1878–87 (n = 365)
nobility	82	64	52	49
raznochintsy	18	36	48	51
	100	100	100	100

Sources: Compiled from data in (Avakumovic, 1959: 183; Brower, 1975: 42; Brym, 1977d).

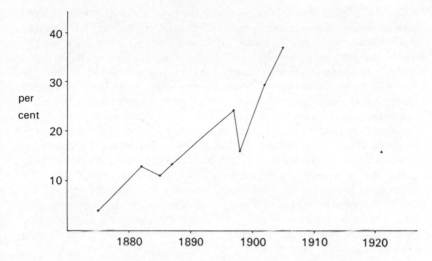

Fig. 3. Jews as a percentage of Russian Radicals, 1875–1905 and 1921–2

Sources: Compiled from data in (Avakumovic, 1959: 182; Dinur, 1957: 114; Greenberg, 1944–51: vol. 1, 149; Mosse, 1968: 148; Nedava, 1972: 143).
Note: See Technical Appendix.

plurality of *intelligenty*. And as Fig. 3, again derived largely from police statistics on political arrests, suggests, before 1917 their numerical ascendance appears to have been checked by the influx of a fourth group: the children of non-Jewish workers and peasants (Mosse, 1968).

If these comments serve to adjust our sense of proportion it becomes all the more necessary to justify this book on intellectual grounds. Much effort has been expended on studying the Russian intelligentsia. How much can yet another piece of research hope to add to our stock of knowledge? If knowledge means information, the answer is: 'Only a little'. If knowledge means the *organisation* of information (Bierstedt, 1974: 133–49), the answer is (I hope): 'A good deal'. Many of the facts contained in this study are already known to experts in the field. But by using and constructing sociological theory in the course of my research I have sought to arrange these facts in ways which deepen our understanding of intelligentsias in general and Russian-Jewish Marxists in particular. Some general theoretical remarks are thus called for at the outset.

In a justly famous essay written nearly half a century ago, Karl Mannheim suggested that intellectuals in the modern world are members of a 'relatively classless stratum which is not too firmly situated in the social order' (1954 [1929]: 154). Most students of the nineteenth-century Russian intelligentsia have, perhaps unwittingly, agreed. In fact, Russian *in-*

telligenty of the last century are generally regarded as having been afflicted with an *extreme* case of classlessness (see Berdyaev, 1960 [1937]; Billington, 1966; Malia, 1961; Raeff, 1966a; cf. Brower, 1967). They were (so the traditional account goes), recruited from various classes and, by entering an educational system which pumped them full of western ideas, became divorced, in both a structural and a cultural sense, from their class roots. Moreover, the intelligentsia, born of 'rootlessness' and raised in a state of 'alienation', had no functional role to play in Russian society: *intelligenty* originated as, and remained 'superfluous men'. This predicament (the accepted argument continues) had at least two important consequences. First, an existence outside the major classes of society ensured that ideas in general would exercise an uncommonly high degree of influence over the behaviour of intellectuals. Second, it meant that Russian intellectuals were unusually prone to accept and propound *radical* ideas: to be transformed into *intelligenty*. Bertram Wolfe, who states the case with characteristic incisiveness, is worth quoting at length here. The members of the Russian intelligentsia were, he writes,

> held together, neither by a common social origin and status, nor by a common role in the social process of production. The cement which bound them together was a common alienation from existing society, and a common belief in the sovereign efficacy of ideas as shapers of life. They lived precariously suspended, as in a void, between an uncomprehending autocratic monarchy above and an unenlightened mass below . . . They anticipated and supplied in advance the requirements of a world that was too slow in coming into being, and sought to serve a folk that had no use for their services. In the decaying feudal order they found neither scope nor promise; in the gross, timid, and backward mercantile bourgeoisie neither economic support nor inspiration; in the slumbering people no echo to their ardent cries (1948b: 33).

If Russian *intelligenty* were rootless, alienated, functionally superfluous and therefore easily swayed by ideological currents and remarkably susceptible to radicalism, then how much more true this was of the Jews among them. Conventional sociological wisdom locates the Jew in a 'marginal' social position during the early stages of capitalist development: a 'man on the margin of two cultures and two societies' as Robert Park put it in his classic statement of the problem (1928: 892). Having been insulated from contact with Gentiles in the pre-capitalist era, Jews were absorbed into European society only in the nineteenth century—and then only slowly and incompletely. Jewish and European culture thus met and fused in the Jewish mind. Rootlessness thereby promoted an unusually high degree of intellectual fecundity (cf. Deutscher, 1968; Veblen, 1943 [1934]; Weber, 1952 [1917–19]: 206–7); and the slow pace of absorption served to radicalise Jewish intellectuals in disproportionately large numbers. Robert Michels, who followed this line of reasoning, located the chief reason for the Jewish *intelligent*'s 'predominant position' in working class parties in

> the peculiar position which the Jews have occupied and in many respects still occupy. The legal emancipation of the Jews has not (in Germany and eastern Europe) been followed by their social and moral emancipation . . . Even when they are rich the Jews constitute, at least in eastern Europe, a category of persons excluded from the social advantages which the prevailing political, economic and intellectual systems ensure for the corresponding portion of the Gentile population . . . For all these reasons, the Jewish intelligence is apt to find a shorter road to socialism than the Gentile (1962 [1911]: 247–8; also 1932: 118).

In a word, middle-class Jewish intellectuals were, because of their disadvantaged position, marginal to the middle class and were therefore transformed into radical 'men of ideas' *par excellence*. Like Vilfredo Pareto before him and a host of social scientists and historians after, Michels argued that intellectual radicalism varies inversely with the degree to which intellectuals are attached to the middle class. Variously referred to as the theory of 'class marginality', 'interrupted elite circulation', 'structural blockage' or 'status inconsistency', this view has informed investigations of intelligentsias for decades (see Pareto, 1935 [1916]; Brinton, 1938: 78; Gurr, 1970: 144; Hughes, 1949; Lenski, 1954; Lipset, 1971 [1950]: 233–4; Lipset and Zetterberg, 1956; Mannheim, 1956: 145; Shils, 1962).

The argument fits the facts admirably well, which is why I adapt it to the study of the Russian-Jewish intelligentsia. But it is not without its problems, which is why I seek to place it within a broader explanatory framework. Consider for a moment the following implications of what I would prefer to call the 'marginality theory of the intelligentsia': (a) It is a central tenet of the Sociology of Knowledge that ideas are somehow 'related' to the social positions of their adherents. If, however, we assume that *intelligenty* are divorced from social structure it becomes exceedingly difficult (if at all possible) to use the insights generated by the Sociology of Knowledge in studying *intelligenty*. How can we claim that one's social position 'determines' one's ideas or even that there exists an 'elective affinity' between structure and consciousness when the objects of investigation are not firmly rooted in society and therefore have no socially-derived interests? A classless *intelligent* certainly cannot have class interests, so is it not reasonable to assert that he puts 'cultural considerations above social' (Parsons, 1963: 4) and 'ideals before interests' (Malia, 1961: 9)? (b) This further implies that, in studying *intelligenty*, we had best attend to problems of culture. If, for example, the 'qualities which made [the

Russian intelligentsia] what it was, belonged to the moral and intellectual order' (Frank, 1959: 100), then it would seem advisable to restrict our attention to the ways in which major ideological currents shaped its members' attitudes and actions. This is in fact what most students of the subject have done. The result: we know a great deal about the beliefs and values of Russian *intelligenty*, but little about their social origins and next to nothing about their social organisation, the mechanisms by which they were recruited to various political parties, and so forth. (c) Ultimately, cultural analysis has led us to engage in what Max Weber would have called the 'sympathetic understanding' of the motivations of *intelligenty*. Unfortunately, the price paid for this perfectly valid exercise has been excessively high for, as Charles Tilly (1963–4) points out, the *verstehende* method draws attention away from comparative analysis. We may understand perfectly well the unique *psychological* drives which prompted some Russian *intelligenty* of the 1870s to become Bakuninists, others Lavrovists and still others Tkachevists. But we have no idea if there were *social* differences among these groups which produced diverse patterns of motivation in the first place.

If, following Abraham Kaplan (1964), we liken theories to searchlights, we may raise at least two questions concerning the marginality theory of the intelligentsia: What is the intensity of its beam? How wide an area does it illuminate? The intensity appears to be adequate, for there is abundant evidence, some of which is discussed below, attesting to a strong, positive correlation between intellectual radicalism and class marginality. The trouble is that the beam is too bright, emits rays too narrow, leaves too much in the dark, and therefore blinds us to such comparative, structural problems as the one addressed by this study—why Russian-Jewish Marxists split into four, ideologically distinct groups.

In contrast to the marginality theorists, I assume that rootlessness is a variable, not a constant. The advantage of my assumption is not that it allows us to explain better, but that it allows us to explain more: not just the process of radicalisation but, in addition, the process of ideological divergence. Just how rootless were Russian-Jewish, Marxist *intelligenty*? How did their connections or lack of connections with major social groups (classes, ethnic communities) vary over time? To which groups were which *intelligenty* attached or unattached? What repercussions did their changing social ties have on their ideological views? These are the main questions which will occupy us in the following chapters. I shall seek to demonstrate that the ideologies of the *intelligenty* I examined were produced largely by the patterns of social mobility they experienced through changing social structures over time. Social structures evolve. So do intellectuals' careers. Match the two processes and, I submit, we can learn more about why intellectuals may become radicals and support a diversity of parties on the left than marginality theory can teach us.

Before turning to some methodological issues it must be emphasised that not just intellectual radicalism, but also radicalism among workers, peasants and farmers has been explained by the formula: rootlessness produces deprivation which, in turn, leads to discontent. (For a review of some of the literature, see Leggett, 1968: 62–75; for an application to the Russian case, see Haimson, 1964.) The argument as applied to workers, peasants and farmers has come under increasing attack over the past decade or so (see Brym, 1977b; Duncan, 1974; Lodhi and Tilly, 1973; Snyder and Tilly, 1972; Tilly, 1964; 1974; 1976 [1964]; Tilly *et al.*, 1975). From a theoretical point of view the justification for this book should therefore be plain: I have sought to add to the ongoing critique of marginality theory by assessing its weaknesses in explaining the behaviour of what is generally regarded as the most rootless group of all (*intelligenty*) and the most rootless element within that group (Jews).

In order to substantiate my argument I collected data from memoirs, biographies and biographical dictionaries on 207 Marxist *intelligenty* (operationally defined as members of the Bolshevik, Menshevik, Bundist and Poalei-Zionist parties with at least secondary education who joined the revolutionary movement while not employed as manual workers) born in European Russia (excluding Finland and Poland) before 1891. All 207 received at least their pre-university education in the Empire and had at least one Jewish parent. The sample was not, nor could it have been randomly selected since there exists no sampling frame which lists all members of the relevant population. This places obvious limits on the confidence with which one may regard my findings. I only suspect, but do not know that many of my arguments apply to all Russian radicals or even to all Russian-Jewish Marxists at the turn of the century. I am, however, certain that the claims made in the following chapters are valid for all Jewish *intelligenty* of primary, and many of secondary importance in the early histories of the four parties because they are included in my sample. The substantive propositions I advance are, moreover, historically specific. However, it is my impression that the *general* theoretical orientation of this study has considerable relevance to the study of intelligentsias in other times and/or places; and from time to time I make comparative observations to this effect.

There is nothing mysterious about the number 207. Following the Glaser and Strauss (1967) method for constructing 'grounded theory' by means of 'theoretical sampling' procedures, I stopped collecting data when I could with considerable confidence reject many of the hunches and hypotheses entertained in the early stages of research and accept those which form the study's theoretical framework. For example, Lewis Feuer (1969; 1972) has argued that age and radicalism vary inversely due to the operation of a generalised Oedipus complex in periods when authority is being eroded. This hypothesis was rejected after computing the average dates of birth of about 100, and then about 200 *intelligenty* in the four parties because the results (Brym, 1976: 14; also 1977c) indicated that the hypothesised relationship did not obtain at either point. This led me to expect that it would not hold if similar computations were made on, say, 300 cases. On the other hand, it became apparent after collecting data on about 100, and then about 200 cases that marginality theory offered a credible explanation for radicalism because, at both points, the posited relationship held and adding more cases would probably have involved an increment in the amount of data at my disposal but little new information. Thus, the advantage of theoretical sampling is that it permits one to construct theory well-grounded in data and therefore unmarred by that perennial sociological problem of excessive abstractness. Its disadvantage is that one cannot be certain of the theory's exact range of applicability because the sample on which it is based is non-random. If it is kept in mind that the object of this study is principally to *construct*, rather than *test* theory, the advantage clearly outweighs the disadvantage.

The data I collected on mobility patterns are analysed in Chapter 3, the consequences of these patterns for ideological allegiance in Chapter 4. Chapter 5 summarises the threads of argument which bind the study together. However, before explaining why Jewish intellectuals were radicalised and came to support conflicting ideologies, it will be necessary to examine certain changes which occured in the Russian class structure and the Jewish community up to 1905. In order to gain a clear understanding of later developments our starting point must antedate the 1905 revolution by nearly 700 years.

2 Class and Ethnic Structure to 1905

Vee es kristelt sikh, azoy yidelt es sikh.

Yiddish folk-saying[1]

A. The Jewish Community in Pre-capitalist Poland

West of the Elbe river, feudalism began to break up in the thirteenth century. To the east, 'feudalism'[2] began to crystallise in the fourteenth (Blum, 1957). During this period Jews first entered eastern Europe in significant numbers[3] — a fact which is neither fortuitous nor without its parallels in nineteenth-century Russia.

This can best be appreciated if we first note that the Jews were located not so much 'within' as they were 'between' the estates of the European feudal order. Although prone to generalise well beyond the limits of historical accuracy,[4] many sociologists — including Karl Marx (1971 [1867–94]: vol. 3, 330; 1972: 25–41), Max Weber (1952 [1917–19]: 336–55; 1961 [1927]: 151–2, 263–5), Georg Simmel (1971) and Howard Becker (1950: 109–13) — have hit upon the most striking fact concerning the Jews in medieval northern Europe: while lord and serf derived their existence from the land, the Jew subsisted by virtue of his position as a commercial intermediary.

Why then did the Jews migrate eastward? Largely because serfdom did. The Jews' economic functions were attuned to a form of labour organisation disappearing in the west (whence they were expelled) and becoming entrenched in the east (where they were eagerly accepted [Boswell in Reddaway *et al.*, 1950: vol. 1, 105, 155] or perhaps even invited [Balaban, 1960]). Serfdom implies decentralised extraction of tribute, not state-directed taxation; management of estates by agents of the landlord, not by agriculturalists themselves; money-lending, not banking; the acquisition of scarce goods more through trade than domestic production. And these were the roles which Jews performed, first in the west, then in the east: according to the most sophisticated, but inevitably rough estimate, approximately 85 per cent of the Jews in mid-fourteenth-century Poland were engaged in estate management, tax and toll collecting, money-lending and trade (Weinryb, 1972: 58–70).[5] So employed, Jews were bound to come into conflict with certain estates while coming under the protective wing of others. This was hinted at by a Latin saying of the time, which informs us that Poland became 'the heaven of the nobleman, the purgatory of the citizen, the hell of the peasant, and the paradise of the Jew' (Ginzberg, 1928: 13).

That royalty and the large landowners were their chief guardians can be seen in the special privileges granted the Jews. In 1264 Prince Boleslav the Pious of Kalish granted them a charter which demonstrated that he was 'anxious to secure for the Jews such conditions as might enable them to benefit the country by their commercial activity'. The enactment was formulated in consultation with 'the highest dignitaries and the representatives of the estates' (Dubnow, 1916–20: vol. 1, 47). In 1344, Casimir the Great ratified the charter and extended its operation from Great Poland to the entire kingdom. In return for the performance of commercial functions the Jews were permitted to erect separate political, judicial, administrative and educational institutions.

Because the Jews were the immediate agents used by landowners to extract surplus from the peasantry, they were deeply despised in rural Poland. But the chief opponents of the Jews were to be found in the cities. The monopolistic tendencies of medieval production encouraged the view among the burghers that the Jews represented a great competitive threat. Fearful of rivals, the guilds rejected aspiring foreign artisans, while the patriciate sought to curtail the activities of foreign middlemen. It was here that the 'main source of anti-Semitism in Poland' originated (Mahler, 1946: 147). Little wonder that opposition to the Jews increased as the Polish bourgeoisie grew.[6]

But in the sixteenth century the landowning nobility developed at the expense of the bourgeoisie (and royalty) into the most powerful force in Polish society. The hegemony of the magnates having been established, an expansion to the east began. Poland had just entered the world market (Malowist, 1958; 1959; 1966). Prices were rising (Burke, 1972). Increasing agricultural production thus became the principal aim of the landowners and colonising the eastern frontier the principal means:

> The magnates and particularly some lesser noblemen acquired large estates (latifundia) on which they founded new villages, towns, and a few cities. They enticed peasants, Jews, Armenians, and some urban elements from the western part of Poland or from abroad to settle in these places by granting them several years exemption from *corvée* as well as other civic benefits (Weinryb, 1972: 108).

It was in these new, noble-controlled settlements that the Jews were to find, for a time at least, a sanctuary far removed from the vicissitudes of *bürgerlich* and ecclesiastical opposition.

With the growth of serfdom there began the so-called 'Golden Age' of

Polish Jewry, usually defined as the period extending from the beginning of the sixteenth to the middle of the seventeenth centuries. Their population increased from 10,000 – 12,000 in the year 1500 to 150,000 – 170,000 in the year 1650 as a result of further migration from the west and a relatively low mortality rate which was due to affluence and freedom from military service (ibid.: 114 – 16).

In the sixteenth, and especially the seventeenth centuries there emerged a large artisan stratum within the Jewish community. By 1800 artisans constituted perhaps 12 per cent of the Jewish labour force (Leshchinsky, 1928: 30; Weinryb, 1972 [1934]: 93 ff.). The widespread participation of Jews in crafts demands serious revision to the thesis advanced by some Marxists (e.g., Leon, 1970 [1946]) that Jews in pre-capitalist Poland formed a *class* of commercial intermediaries. However, a close examination of their evolution and social organisation reveals that the artisans represented, in Jacob Katz's words, 'a social appendage to the body of merchants, lessees, and money-lenders' (1962: 58). This fact is of considerable importance in assessing the structure of the Jewish community.

The social location and resultant 'stranger' status of the Jewish community afforded only particular types of opportunities for employment in crafts. The community's intermediate position buttressed the maintenance of distinct religious customs which, in turn, required the provision of goods deemed necessary for religious practice. Moreover, merchants demanded the production of goods which, although of a non-religious character, serviced their activities. The impetus to manufacture garments and prepare foodstuffs, to mint coins and produce gold and silver decorations derived from this internal demand.[7]

As early as the fifteenth century, external demand also played a role in encouraging the growth of artisanry. As a result of the extraordinary position of the Jewish community as a whole, opportunities emerged for producing goods for royalty, the magnates, and even some serfs. As large consumers the noblemen and the Crown sought to mitigate the monopolistic practices of indigenous craft associations. The most effective means by which this could be accomplished was to encourage competitors to undermine the guilds. As 'strangers', Jews were excellent tools for such designs. In addition, their structurally-determined ability to 'wander' to new eastern settlements placed Jews in contact with peasants in need of some consumer goods (Wischnitzer, 1965: 206 – 52).

Nor do internal and external sources of demand exhaust the list of forces leading to the growth of Jewish artisanry, for the expansion of opportunities in the production of craft goods was matched by declining opportunities in the mercantile sphere due to the stirring of the Polish middle class. Thus, the Warsaw Diet in 1643 fixed rates of profit for native Christians at 7 per cent, for foreigners at 5 per cent, and for Jews at 3 per cent (Dubnow, 1916 – 20: vol. 1, 99; also Balaban, 1930: 169 – 80). Such legislation was bound to drive Jews out of mercantile activities.

These, then, were the principal forces — all of which derived from the intermediate social location of the Jewish community as a whole — which led to the emergence and growth of Jewish artisanry.

Artisans were socially tied to the Jewish community in a number of ways. First, just as the small merchant was very often dependent on the larger merchant for credit, the artisan might obtain credit or the tools of his trade from his more affluent co-religionists. For example, the sable and marten pelts and expensive equipment necessary to make fur coats had to be supplied by the well-to-do, who also sold the finished product to noblemen (Wischnitzer, 1965: 226). Second, as we have seen, the commercial strata served as the most important market for many of the artisans' products. These credit, employment and market ties were probably the most important sources of community solidarity: they bound artisan to merchant and ensured that the former would be no better integrated into the surrounding Gentile world than the latter. (As we shall see below, these linkages also ensured that the artisan's economic well-being depended upon what those at the top of the commercial ladder did with their capital.) In addition, a third factor prevented even those artisans who were free of such ties from being absorbed into non-Jewish society: artisans were often employed in repair and mending work — crafts which coincided to a considerable degree with the role of peddler. Due to this 'occupational pluralism', the craftsmen employed in these lines of endeavour displayed the same sort of marginality *vis-à-vis* Gentile society as the merchant. This is why Werner Cahnman writes that in 'a structural view . . . the existence of a Jewish artisan class is not contradictory to the theory which characterises the Jews as a "marginal trading people". The Jewish artisan . . . shares in the intermediacy of the trader's social position and role' (Cahnman, 1965: 208).

In light of the above discussion, it is clearly impossible to designate the Jews in feudal Poland a class, in the Marxist sense of the term, since they displayed *diverse* relationships to productive resources. But neither were the Jews an ethnic group — at least, not in the generally accepted sense of a group of persons who share certain cultural standards and historical experiences and therefore a sense of peoplehood (Francis, 1947; Lieberson, 1970; Vallee *et al.*, 1968 [1961]). Such a designation would be even more out of place since the community derived its solidarity not just from any cultural/historical uniformity but, fundamentally, from its peculiar structural location and the social ties between strata discussed above.

Fortunately, several recent discussions of the social roots of ethnic identity enable us to overcome these conceptual difficulties (see esp. Cohen, 1969; 1974a, 1974b; Howard and Wayne, 1976; also Glazer and Moynihan, 1965; Hall, 1971; Hechter, 1974; Yancey *et al.*, 1976). Increasingly, students of the subject are beginning to realise that ethnicity is a political phenomenon which enables relatively endogamous networks of persons, who may be socially differentiated, to control specific sectors of an economy. Medieval Polish Jewry fits well into this definition of an ethnic community. Members of the community were socially differentiated (merchants, artisans, etc.); they did form a social network (bound by employment, credit and market ties); they did proscribe exogamy; and they did erect political and other institutions in order to enhance their ability to control mercantile and related activities. The importance and usefulness of this definition will become apparent only when our discussion reaches the nineteenth century, for we shall see that once persons were detached from this network their ethnic identity began to weaken and that this had a considerable impact on their ideological views. For the moment, however, it will be necessary to turn to some general developments in neighbouring Russia.

B. The Decline of Serfdom and the Development of Capitalism in Russia

In Poland, the growth of serfdom was encouraged by the fact that a strong nobility wished to take advantage of rising prices in the world market for grain during a period of time when the ratio of land to labour was relatively high. Russia also had a strong nobility and, like Poland, suffered from a scarcity of labour. But centralisation of power, territorial expansion and internal commerce, rather than foreign trade, provided the incentive to fetter peasants to the land in Russia. In the fifteenth century the isolated and economically self-contained estates of that country were being transformed into a unified money economy by the Moscow state. The growing market and the demands made by the state led the principal consumers of commodities, the rural lords, to desire more money. They achieved their aim through the ever more brutal exploitation of the peasantry.

Surplus was extracted from the peasantry by two methods: *barshchina* (forced labour) and *obrok* (payment in kind or in money). The former method was predominant in the fertile, 'black soil' region of Russia where agriculture was widespread. In the less fertile, 'non-black soil' region, *obrok* was the more common mode of surplus extraction.

In the seventeenth century, the *barshchina* system involved, on the average, the cultivation of one *desyatina* (about 2.7 acres) of owner's land in exchange for the peasant's use of three to four *desyatinas*. By the middle of the eighteenth century, the serf was forced to increase his obligation to the point at which he worked one *desyatina* of the owner's land for each *desyatina* of his 'own'. Legislation enacted in 1797 restricted *barshchina* work to three days per week, but by the nineteenth century it was not uncommon to see peasants working five or six days per week on the lords' land. In Tula province some landowners even enforced labour on Sundays, arguing that it would be 'a sin for a Christian to work for himself on a holiday' and thereby forcing the peasant to harvest his own meagre allotment at night (Lyashchenko, 1949 [1927]: 312 – 13). Nor did agricultural labour exhaust the peasant's obligations. In addition to tilling his master's soil the peasant was required to do various kinds of construction work, transport produce to the market and make small 'contributions' to the welfare of the landowner in money or in kind.

The *obrok* system, under which the master found it more profitable to allocate land to the peasant in exchange for payments in kind or cash, also became more of a burden to the peasant over time. Thus, in the 1760s *obrok* amounted to one or two rubles per person; but by the first decade of the nineteenth century it reached thirty rubles — an increase of 3,000 per cent in the space of half a century (ibid.: 315 – 16).

This growing 'squeeze' on the Russian peasantry was a manifestation of the increasing inefficiency of the feudal system, of the fact that feudal class relationships hampered the growth of productivity.[8] Both the growing urban population and the foreign market — the latter of which became particularly important when the English Corn Laws were abolished in 1846 — demanded the enlargement of grain production. After the 1870s, Russia persistently supplied as much as one-quarter to one-third of total world grain exports (Falkus, 1966: 416). The landowner, anxious to increase his revenue, could in principle meet this demand by either increasing the productivity of his labourers or by simply increasing the acreage under cultivation and more ruthlessly exploiting the peasant. But the very institution of serfdom precluded the former possibility since an increase in productivity required, above all else, legally free labour and a larger supply of circulating capital — requirements which could be realised only if serfdom were abolished. If labour were legally free the landlord could adjust to market conditions by curtailing or increasing production through the laying off or hiring of workers; but under the obligations of serfdom

> he cannot discontinue production while grain prices on the market become unprofitable; he sells grain 'come what may', particularly in view of the feudal organisation of market supply. In general . . . he could not even exploit a favourable market situation (Lyashchenko, 1949 [1927]: 364).

Similarly, if more capital had been available for investment, agricultural technique could have been greatly improved. But under serfdom insufficient capital was accumulated for such purposes. In order to increase his money income the landowner expanded production by simply 'tightening the screws' of feudal exploitation. This could only lead to the peasant unrest reflected, albeit with questionable accuracy, in the following official statistics: peasant uprisings increased from 148 in the years 1826 – 34 to 216 (1835 – 44) to 474 (1855 – 61) (ibid.: 370). Outbreaks were, moreover, more numerous and violent in the central districts and the Ural region — areas which Peter Lyashchenko calls 'bulwarks of serfdom' — and fewer and milder in the south. No exceptional intelligence was required on the part of Tsar Alexander II to come to the conclusion on the eve of the 1861 emancipation that 'it is better to abolish serfdom from above than to wait until the serfs begin to liberate themselves from below'.

Contradictions in the serf system became increasingly apparent by the nineteenth century not just in agriculture, but in manufacturing as well. The large-scale industry which had first sprung up during the reign of Peter the Great was first supplied with imported labour, the wives of military men on duty, vagrants, beggars, prostitutes, criminals and the like. There was, nevertheless, a dearth of workers throughout the eighteenth century. It thus came about that, through the extension of serfdom, many peasants were legally bound to factories.

Not that this permitted large industry to flourish. On the contrary, peasant cottage (*kustar*) production actually grew at the expense of large factories well into the nineteenth century. This phenomenon is readily explicable in terms of the economic advantages which *kustar* manufacturing had over large-scale production. The gains achieved by concentrating many workers together in one industrial establishment were outweighed by the ready supply of labour, raw materials and markets available to the gentry. The gentry, after all, owned the serfs; their estates were located close to sources of raw materials; and the peasants were obliged to transport finished products to market without charge. Moreover, the level of technological development was so low that the bound factory workers were little more productive than the peasants working in their cottages. Thus, as late as the 1850s, small-scale production flourished as the *kustar*s actually drove many large factories out of business (Tugan-Baranovsky, 1970 [1898]: 171–214). The average number of workers per industrial establishment — a good index of industrial development — consequently stood at 41 in 1815, rose to a high point of 68 in 1843, and then plummetted by 1861 to only 37 (ibid.: 61). Clearly, under serfdom industrial progress was largely blocked (Blackwell, 1968: 57–8).

Several factors which were to render the situation of Russian industry even more problematic began to make their influence felt with the onset of the nineteenth century. The Napoleonic wars brought about an increased demand for military wares; the continental blockade closed the Russian market to English manufactured goods, thus stimulating local industry; the annexation of Poland, Finland and other territories increased the size of the Russian market; and after Napoleon's defeat Russia became inextricably tied to the world market. But although the forces pushing Russia toward capitalism burgeoned, no advance could be registered in those factories where serf labour prevailed. Russian iron production, controlled by the gentry and the state, and employing serf labour, was actually lower in 1850 than in 1800; but in the cotton industry, controlled by the middle class and employing hired labour and English technology, the amount of fibre processed increased by 2,620 per cent from 1812 to 1860 (Tugan-Baranovsky, 1970 [1898]: 61, 49).

The picture of Russian industry in the middle of the nineteenth century that emerges from the above discussion brings into relief the stifling effects of forced labour. Where serfdom persevered large industry stagnated and 'petty production' flourished; where capitalist methods were introduced large industry prospered. By the 1850s it became clear that it was only a matter of time before capitalism would break the constraints on its growth imposed by serfdom.

The inefficiencies in the serf system which led to the Emancipation decree of 1861 represented, in a sense, the 'internal preconditions' for capitalist development in Russia. But, given the fact that these preconditions were met only in the second half of the nineteenth century, one may also speak of an 'external source' of capitalist development, a source located in western Europe.

By the third quarter of the nineteenth century capital had accumulated in the west to such an extent that the search for new investment outlets became the chief desiderata of merchant bankers. Savings in France amounted to between two and three billion francs per year in the final decades of the nineteenth century; about half of England's larger capital surplus was being invested abroad by 1900; and roughly one-tenth of smaller German savings found their way abroad in that year (Feis, 1930: 5, 35, 61). The growing profitability of foreign investment, combined with the inability of individual merchant bankers to mobilise large reserves of capital for extended time periods, led to the formation of banking structures designed specifically for this purpose. By the 1870s the opening up of further investment opportunities required the organisation of consortia of investment bankers amalgamated for the flotation of single security issues (Anderson, 1974). These were the basic organisational steps which progressed by the end of the century to the stage of capitalist development which came to be known as imperialism. Russia was by no means unaffected.

Already in the 1850s, but especially by the 1890s, the enticing capaciousness of the internal market, combined with the swelling coffers of western financiers, created an imbalance that was rectified by a massive inflow of foreign capital. Through government deficits, a highly protective tariff and the farming out of government contracts, the state played a major role in facilitating this inflow. Together with smaller internal sources, examined in greater detail below, western bankers first established local credit institutions and then financed railroad construction. This provided the groundwork for the redirection of foreign investment into industry itself, which was able to register a 113 per cent increase in production between 1887 and 1897 (Lyashchenko, 1949 [1927]: 526). Given the fact that foreign capital constituted more than one-third of all corporation capital in 1890 and nearly one-half in 1900, and that 30 per cent of the total state debt in 1895, and 48 per cent in 1914, was held abroad (ibid.: 535; Falkus, 1970: 25–7), one Russian citizen could credibly argue that

> Thomas and Knopp taught us the textile trade. The Englishman, Hughes, implanted a metallurgical industry in the southern part of Russia; Nobel and Rothschild transformed Caucasia into a fountain of oil gushers. And at the same time the viking of all vikings, the great, the international Mendelsohn brought Russia into the domain of the stock exchange (Trotsky, 1971 [1909]: 35).

Beside the strength of foreign capital, the Russian bourgeoisie paled. Historically, the stunted growth of what one scholar has called 'the forgotten class' (Bill, 1959) is usually viewed partly as a result of 250 years of Tatar domination, which stopped all progress in Russia at a time when western Europe experienced a commercial revolution and a Renaissance. The entrenchment of Tatar methods of rule, together with the demands imposed by the vastness of the Moscow state, led to the rise of a 'semi-Oriental despotism' (Wittfogel, 1957; Ulmen, 1975; Baron, 1958; Sawer, 1975) which, in turn, ensured the perpetuation of serfdom for centuries. Geographical factors, such as poor climatic conditions, deficiencies in the location of natural resources and so forth, were also unfavourable to economic growth (Baykov, 1954). But probably more important was the fact that, beginning in the middle of the seventeenth century, the all-powerful state imposed on Russian merchants what one historian has called 'a form of bondage, which may well be described as commercial serfdom' (Bill, 1959: 69). Burdensome taxes and service obligations stifled the growth of the merchant stratum — or at least most of it[9] — so that in the nineteenth century foreign capital formed the spearhead of industrial advance.

These then were the general conditions which circumscribed the life of worker and peasant in the second half of the nineteenth century: the collapse of serfdom and the subsequent rapid growth of industry under the stimulus primarily of foreign investment. Because of the manner in which these processes worked themselves out, peasant and worker were both driven to rebellion.

C. Peasant and Working Class Unrest

In neither case did rebellion simply 'result from' the rapid pace of social change or from the multiple hardships which change generated (Olson, 1963). Suffering on the part of peasants and workers was translated into political unrest only because the structural transformation of Russian society increased their solidarity and thus enabled them to organise an effective assault on the regime.

Of course, rebellion was nothing new to Russia. The Russian peasantry had for centuries 'been schooled in collective action by the internal organisation of village society' (Robinson, 1969 [1932]: 10). From earliest times the village was not merely a village but, simultaneously, a complex, extended kin network. Because family and village were one, members of peasant settlements 'held their lands and performed their labors collectively, and it is also possible that they regarded the product of their work as common property' (ibid.). Peasant communalism not only persisted, but advanced in the centuries to come, especially when in the sixteenth century landholdings came to be periodically redistributed among members of the commune in order to preserve equality.

Nor was communalism the only aspect of peasant life which was to have far-reaching political consequences in the future. Valuable instruction in collective action was also gained through the well-developed tradition of peasant rebellion. Reacting against the encroachments of serfdom, peasants began to flee from noble-owned estates to the open *step*. There, where they joined and were led by cossacks resentful of the growth of the Moscow state, began the first of a long series of peasant rebellions (Yaresh, 1957). Stenka Razin and Emelian Pugachev are but two of the most famous names associated with the attempt to resist the demands of centralism and the yoke of serfdom.

When in 1861 the yoke was finally lifted it was, as Alexander Herzen bitterly remarked in that year, 'replaced by a new form. Serfdom was not abolished at all, and the nation has been deceived'. The principle, expressed in preparing the Emancipation decree, that land allotments should be sufficiently large to ensure the sustenance of the peasant and the payment of his new obligations, and no smaller than his pre-Reform allotment, was largely ignored. On the average, the peasant had 4 per cent less land after Emancipation than before (Gerschenkron in Habbakuk and Postan, 1941–67: 729). And he was now faced with the new obligation of paying labour and money dues to the landowner in exchange for the 'indefinite use' of the allotted land—an obligation which in many cases actually exceeded that required of the peasant before 1861. Such a 'temporarily obligated' peasant (as he was euphemistically designated) was able to become proprietor of his land by giving a certain sum of money to the landowner, 80 per cent of which was underwritten by the state in the form of a 49 year, 6 per cent loan.[10] In practice the scheme was a dismal failure. Not only were allotments valuated far above their market value; not only did peasants have great difficulty in raising the 20 per cent of the valuation which they were required to pay directly to the landlord; but, in addition, they were largely incapable of keeping up payments on their government loans.

Although Emancipation hardly improved the peasant's lot, it did aid him indirectly; peasant social organisation was strengthened, partly because the government sought to develop its traditional forms as institutional mechanisms for extracting loan payments, partly because these forms were viewed (incorrectly as things turned out) as the very foundations of Russia's political stability. The creation of peasant assemblies, with the responsibility of apportioning the tax burden and conducting the general affairs of the community; of peasant *volost*s, with judicial responsibilities; and of district *zemstvo*s, organs of local self-government with peasant representation, further strengthened the ties among peasants. The 'school for collective action' increased the quality of its instruction concomitantly. Emancipation also preserved both traditional forms of land tenure: repartitional (which involved the periodic communal redistribution of land among the members of the commune) and hereditary (in which land was herdetarily attached to an individual household) (Robinson, 1969 [1932]: 71). However, the complex legislation regarding tenure ensured that social organisation would be most strongly reinforced where repartitional tenure obtained, for under hereditary tenure 'the land-relations of the households were by no means so intimate as under the repartitional communal tenure' (ibid.: 74). This turned out to be an important factor in determining which peasants would participate most militantly in the increasingly numerous disturbances which swept the countryside.

The decades after Emancipation witnessed a rapid increase in peasant population—from 50 to 79 million between 1860 and 1897—and a concurrent shrinkage in the average size of peasant allotments from 13.2 *desyatinas* in 1877 to 10.4 in 1905. Peasants consequently suffered both from 'land-hunger' and physical malnutrition. It has been estimated that by the turn of the century they produced roughly 11.5 per cent less grain and potatoes than was required for their physical well-being. And then, around 1901, agricultural day wages proceeded to decline as the price of rye (which millions had to purchase for their own consumption) rose (ibid.: 94, 98, 102, 103, 106).

It is little wonder that under such conditions 'the communes began to function as veritable pressure cookers of discontent' (Wolf, 1969: 65). Significantly, the 'miniature revolution' of 1902 took its most widespread form in the provinces of Kharkov and Poltava, where repartitional tenure predominated, while 'among the twenty *guberniia*s [provinces] in which the landlords suffered the heaviest losses during the autumn of 1905, sixteen show a predominance of repartitional tenure over hereditary holding by individual peasant households' (Robinson, 1969 [1932]: 138, 145, 153). In short, rebellion was most widespread and violent where the peasants were most solidary.

But which peasants? Rebellion was hardly engaged in by an undifferentiated mass. Classes parallel to those in the city were already developing in the countryside. Landlords and poor peasant sharecroppers existed as remnants of the pre-capitalist era; a large middle peasantry with meagre allotments and considerable obligations emerged from the 1861 reform; finally, a rural middle class employing hired farm-hands had made its appearance. Because poor peasants were too dependent on landlords to rebel without reliance on some external power and because wealthy peasants had become landlords in their own right, it was the middle peasantry which led the agrarian disturbances of 1905 (Alavi, 1965; Perrie, 1972; Shanin, 1971–2; Wolf, 1969; Wolf in Shanin, 1971). An official questionnaire circulated in 1907 accurately isolated the principal cause of rural unrest: land shortage. That the 'widest and deepest interest of the peasants was in the land' (Robinson, 1969 [1932]: 204) is amply demonstrated by the geographical distribution of uprisings, which were most violent and numerous in the fertile, black soil region where reductions in the size of peasant allotments were greatest (Lyashchenko, 1949 [1927]: 742; Maynard, 1962 [1942]: 59). Robinson adequately sums up the situation when he writes that

> Such revolutionary leaning as existed in rural Russia had come chiefly out of the relations of small, land-short farmers with large landholders, rather than the relations of proletarian and 'half-proletarian' laborers with capitalistic cultivators; and such limited capacity as the villagers possessed for collective thought and action was connected primarily with the old communal land system, and only in a much less degree with proletarian experience under a capitalistic discipline (1969 [1932]: 206).

The middle peasants wanted land reform. In this sense their unrest manifested a distinct 'populist' colouring which is typical of independent commodity producers (cf. Ionescu and Gellner, 1969; Macpherson, 1962 [1953]). Very different was the situation in industry.

The existence of a pool of cheap labour was a condition of vital necessity for the emergence of capitalism in Russia. Many impoverished peasants, driven by the terms of Emancipation to seek part- or full-time work in industry, were transformed into an industrial proletariat. Emancipation, therefore,

> was not only a 'Peasant' Reform, but, having freed ten million serfs from personal bondage and from a substantial part of the land belonging to them, thereby also resolved the major problem of capitalism — its demand for 'free' manpower (Lyashchenko, 1949 [1927]: 418).

One must be careful not to over-emphasise the 'proletarian character' of this new class — an important point to which we shall return below. Nor should one infer that all emancipated peasants joined the ranks of industrial workers. Many became agricultural wage-labourers; some became landlords or merchants; and a growing number resettled in Siberia and the eastern reaches of the Empire. Such outlets were, nevertheless, insufficient. In all of Russia the supply of industrial and agricultural wage-labourers at the end of the century was a full three times the size of the demand (ibid.: 420). The expansion of opportunities in industry — which employed about 1.6 million workers in 1860, 3 million in 1897 and 5.9 million in 1913 (Rashin, 1954: 162; Rimlinger, 1961: 209; Tugan-Baranovsky, 1970 [1898]: 299) — simply could not keep pace with the swelling ranks of employment-seeking peasants. The sheer size of this 'industrial reserve army' drove wages down and was therefore an important factor encouraging industrial expansion.

In absolute terms the Russian working class was small: scarcely larger than the working class in the United States, whose population was only about 60 per cent of Russia's at the turn of the century. But in gauging the Russian worker's potential for collective action one would do better to focus not on size but on the degree of concentration of industrial workers in particular. This was striking. Factories employing more than 1,000 workers represented the fastest growing category of industrial establishments in Russia. They employed a much larger percentage of the industrial labour force than the same size factories in the U.S.A., Austria, Belgium, Germany and other industrialised countries. And nearly 60 per cent of factory workers in Russia were compressed into only eight regions (ibid.: 531; Gordon, 1941: 354; Lyashchenko, 1949 [1927]: 538–9, 550; Rashin, 1954; Trotsky, 1971 [1909]: 39, 306; Wolf, 1969: 75).

From the point of view of those opposed to the regime this was, in Thorstein Veblen's apt phrase, one of the several advantages of Russia's backwardness. Because Russia was late to industrialise, it could import some of the latest technology and construct some of the largest factories in the world. (The Putilov complex was in fact *the* largest industrial establishment in the world.) Large enterprise was favoured for less obvious reasons as well: it represented a 'much more lucrative source of graft' and compensated for 'the lack of managerial and entrepreneurial personnel . . . by a scale of plant which made it possible to spread the thin layer of available talent over a large part of the industrial economy' (Gerschenkron, 1962: 129). The social concentration of industrial workers which resulted was 'bound to contribute to the development of labor solidarity and consequently increase the possibilities of collective action, in spite of government prohibitions'. Thus, the 'metal and textile factories, which were the most highly concentrated, also had the highest percentages of workers involved in strikes and the largest strikes in terms of participating workers' (Rimlinger, 1960: 227–8, 230).

It is less certain that the 'instability of the work force', which also resulted from Russia's backwardness, was a factor 'counteracting this facilitation of collective action' (ibid.: 228). For what Rimlinger has in mind when he refers to 'instability' is the tendency of many Russian workers to move frequently from the factory to the village and back again.

And this, I suggest, actually *increased* the solidarity of many workers and consequently their radicalism.

We have already seen why the peasant was driven out of the countryside after 1861. Here it must be added that powerful forces also prevented his complete integration in the city. First there were the problems of insufficient industrial jobs, low wages and seasonal work — factors which led the factory worker to spend a good deal of time back in the village working his plot and / or visiting the family he could not afford to bring to the city with him. Second, the government proved largely unwilling to create institutions and introduce legislation which would sever once and for all the connection of the worker with his peasant origins, seeking instead to preserve the worker's links with his village in the hope that this would prevent the creation of a radical western-style proletariat. Thus, before the peasant could obtain permanent release from his village he had to pay large sums of money, relinquish all rights to the land and procure the consent of the head of his household (who was not favourably disposed to such a move in cases where periodic repartitions of land were conducted on the basis of manpower available to the household). In short, general socio-economic conditions combined with government policy to create the hybrid 'peasant / worker' or, to borrow one anthropologist's term, the 'protoproletarian' (McGee, 1973; see Gerschenkron, 1962: 120–1; Glicksman in Black, 1960: 311–23; Johnson, 1975; Von Laue, 1961; 1964; Zelnik, 1968; 1971; 1972–3.) The protoproletarian type was not evenly distributed across the Empire, for in some regions an urbanised working class predominated. But the existence of the type was fairly widespread, as is evidenced by the fact that in the early 1900s nearly 30 per cent of industrial workers still held allotments of land in rural Russia.

The whole network of rural institutions which created such a high degree of solidarity among the peasants functioned in roughly the same manner for the protoproletarians. Moreover, protoproletarians brought to town several forms of rural social organisation. One such form was the *artel'*, the 'traditional association of peasants, usually from the same rural commune, who worked or sought work together away from the village' (Zelnik, 1971: 21). Less visible perhaps were the regional brotherhoods (*zemliaks*; *Landsmannschaften* in German). As one study of workers in the Moscow industrial region has shown, peasants looking for work immediately formed very strong ties with countrymen already in town. The latter helped newcomers find work, get settled and link up with vigorous *zemliaks*. This helps explain the fact that workers recently arrived from particular regions in the countryside clustered together in certain branches of production, in individual factories, in specific occupations within these factories, in particular residential districts, in legal mutual aid associations and in illegal economic and political organisations (Johnson, 1975: 124–52; cf. MacDonald and MacDonald, 1964). Protoproletarians thus formed extremely dense networks of association at work, at home and in leisure time activities. As in scores of other such cases (Smith and Freedman, 1972: 86–114; Spinrad, 1960), this facilitated communication among them as well as mutual assistance and, eventually, joint action of a political and economic nature. Peasant communalism and its derivatives did not, as the conservatives believed, ensure social stability (Von Haxthausen, 1972 [1843]: 292–3). Level of working class radicalism did not, as the Russian Marxists suggested, vary proportionately with workers' degree of urbanity (Lyashchenko, 1949 [1927]: 540). Nor was *extreme* radicalism, as some contemporary western historians claim, a function of the protoproletarian's 'rootlessness' in his view urban environment (Haimson, 1964). Rather, level of radicalism appears to have been a function of density of social ties among workers. The protoproletarian brought transmogrified communal institutions to the city and were therefore more radical than more urbanised workers for whom village ties and associations were probably already meaningless.[11] Not by accident, the great waves of industrial unrest occasioned by the industrial expansions of the 1890s and the year 1912–14 were associated with the influx of whole armies of fresh industrial recruits from the countryside (Zelnik, 1972–3); and, as we shall see, the most violent event of 1905 — the Moscow uprising — was led by the protoproletarian.

The motives which prompted the worker and protoproletarian to rebel were rather different from those which activated the peasant. Above all else the peasant wanted land reform. But once he entered the factory gates he translated his sufferings — caused by sixteen-hour work days, subsistence wages, frequent physical disablement by the age of thirty-five or forty, and so forth — into something more radical. By 1905 the reticence of the government to pass labour legislation capable of easing somewhat the effects of exploitation, the onset of an industrial crisis leading to widespread unemployment, the disgrace of the Russo-Japanese war and contact between workers and *intelligenty* encouraged the working class movement to assume an increasingly militant and political form. Both official and revolutionary sources confirm the view that the hundreds of thousands of workers involved in the general strike of October 1905 had overwhelmingly political aims in mind (Robinson, 1969 [1932]: 165–6). The social organisation of the workers eventually produced a widespread demand not just for reform, but for revolution.

D. The Jews Between Feudalism and Capitalism

In one of Russia's principal industrial regions, the area that had formerly been independent Poland, one could in the nineteenth century observe many of the same problems that characterised the larger Russian society. However, as the Crown was from the sixteenth century unable to exercise centralised control, Poland had earlier been faced with the additional problem of political disintegration. Thus weakened, uprisings in the Ukraine and wars with Sweden and Russia devastated the country in the second half of the seventeenth century. By the beginning of the nineteenth century Poland disappeared as an autonomous state, most of it being incorporated into the Russian Empire.[12]

Some 750,000 to 800,000 Jews thus entered the orbit of Russian domination. Since the economic functions of the Jews were intimately linked to the feudal system, the development of capitalism was bound to send resounding shock waves through the community. These waves did not, however, break evenly on its shoals: capitalist development had different repercussions on its various segments. But this should not blind us to the fact that these repercussions were all in one way or another associated with the rise of an industrial and financial bourgeoisie and a modern state apparatus.

The over 85 per cent of Jews who depended on commercial pursuits in 1800 were driven in four discernible directions. First, a tiny group of very wealthy rentiers, purveyors of military supplies, traders and money-lenders — those men of means who had been highly successful in accumulating merchant's capital — linked up with western financiers to form modern banking institutions, invest in railroads and organise industry. Although one need not endorse the historically inaccurate and theoretically questionable views of Werner Sombart (1951 [1911]; cf. Litman, 1968: 63 ff.; Rivkin, 1971: xxvi and *passim*), there is no doubt that one can here detect the origins of a Jewish *haute bourgeoisie*.[13]

Large Jewish merchant bankers were already present in Poland at the end of the eighteenth century, at which time Warsaw was the home of nineteen such men. Even at this early stage foreigners had entered the eastern money market: a majority of the nineteen had come from Germany during the Prussian regime (Weinryb, 1972 [1934]: 55). By the 1860s, with the growth of investment opportunities, some merchant bankers had amalgamated to form large Jewish banking houses in such centres as St Petersburg, Warsaw, Kiev and Vilna.

Most of the capital being organised for investment was first directed toward railroad construction. In 1856 the Franco-Jewish Pereire brothers established the *Crédit Mobilier* as a challenge to the Rothschilds. Together with other Jewish-owned western banks (Mendelsohn in Berlin, Oppenheim in Cologne), Christian-owned western institutions (Baring in London, Hope in Amsterdam) and Jewish-owned eastern banks (Steiglitz in St Petersburg, Fraenkel in Warsaw) they founded the 'Main Company' with 275,000,000 rubles initial capital (Westwood, 1964: 40 ff.). The purpose of the company was to finance the construction of railways from Moscow to the Crimea, from either Orel or Kursk to the Baltic, from Moscow to Nizhnii-Novgorod and from St Petersburg to Warsaw. Complexities concerning the connections among these and other banks responsible for the funding of the Main Company need not detain us here.

The important point for our present purposes is this: Capital was being organised on an international basis and this involved not just the import of foreign capital, but the mobilisation of domestic sources as well (cf. McKay, 1970: 212 ff.). To cite but a few of the many examples of local Jewish involvement in succeeding decades: The Poliakovs financed lines in central Russia; Schöpsler combined with Sulzbach in Germany to finance the Moscow-Smolensk railroad; Bliokh, together with Bleichröder in Germany, undertook the financing of the line from Kiev to Brest (Grunwald, 1967: 191). In all, 'it was the initiative of Jewish contractors that accounted for the construction of fully three-fourths of the Russian railroad system (Sachar, 1959: 190).

Under such conditions local Jewish banking could not but flourish. Ginzburg, backed by Rothschild and Mendelsohn, created one of the most important banks in St Petersburg; the Poliakov brothers founded a series of banking houses in Moscow, Rostov, Kiev and Orel; the Azov-Don Bank was headed by Kaminka; Steiglitz, in his time the wealthiest banker in Russia and state banker to two Tsars, raised a son who became head of the State Bank; Soloveychik founded the Siberian Commercial Bank; Zak was chairman of the board of the Petersburg Discount and Loan Bank; Bliokh founded the Warsaw Commercial Bank; and a host of smaller provincial houses were created by such men as Wawelberg, Landau, the Epsteins and Krongold (Aronsfeld, 1973; Blackwell, 1968: 255–61; Dijur in Frumkin *et al.*, 1966: vol. 1, 136–7). One far from perfect index of the extent of Jewish participation in banking is provided by the fact that by 1916 the fourteen St Petersburg banking houses operating with joint-stock capital had 70 managers, 28 of whom (or 40 per cent) were Jews (Dinur, 1957: 100). One liberal Jewish commentator of the period was prompted to remark that there 'is hardly a loan the Russian Government seeks to negotiate but some Russo-Jewish agents are, directly or indirectly, connected therewith' (Raisin, 1919: 874).

Investment was not, of course, restricted to railroads. Thus, the Polyak brothers began with the aid of Rothschild money to exploit the vast oil reserves of Transcaucasia in the 1870s through the Mazut Company. Similarly, the Batum Oil Association, again backed by Rothschild, was owned almost entirely by Jews. Both of these companies were later absorbed into a larger corporation formed by Rothschild — a corporation with the rather unassuming name of Shell (Landau, 1939).

Beginning as purveyors of military supplies (Zeitlin), court Jews (Steiglitz), large exporters (Strousberg), liquor monopolists (Benardaki), lessors of estates (Ginzburg), or even as poor Jews who, through kin or other connections, probably acted as agents for western or local sources of capital (Poliakov, Zak; see Bill, 1959: 123–4; Von Laue, 1974 [1963]: 45), eastern European Jewish merchant bankers were thus transformed into finance capitalists who eventually began to invest to some extent in industry. By connecting up with western banking houses or independently getting involved in financial and industrial ventures[14] these men made the transition from feudalism to capitalism. But in order to do so it was necessary to break an old social tie: that which they had formerly had with the rest of the Jewish community.

Up to the end of the eighteenth century the merchant banker in his various guises had propped up the Jewish community in a number of ways, some of which were discussed above, and all of which involved the extension of credit, the investment of capital and the purchase of goods which directly or indirectly employed other Jews. But old modes of investment now became unattractive or ceased to exist. New investment opportunities arose. And the redirection of capital flow was partly responsible for the demise of the Jewish community.

The ways in which old patterns of capital flow became unprofitable were several. Consider first the 40 per cent or so of the Jewish work force involved mainly in Polish trade at the end of the eighteenth century—a stratum which controlled 75 per cent of all exports, 10 per cent of all imports and 100 per cent of internal (Polish) trade (Weinryb, 1972 [1934]: 25–7). Before the nineteenth century, importers profited from the absence of local industry since their livelihood was contingent upon a scarcity of locally-produced goods. They thus sought to discourage industrial growth. The burgesses had been suppressed since 1565 when 'in the interests of the landed proprietors and their mostly foreign commercial agents the privileges so long enjoyed by the townsmen were rudely cut off' (Rose in Reddaway *et al.*, 1950: vol. 2, 157). In contrast, the desire of the rising middle class in the course of the nineteenth century to develop local industry and their ability, under the aegis of the state, to implement this desire, meant that such importation as took place did so only at the convenience of industry (cf. Marx, 1971 [1867–94]: vol. 3, 323–7). Needless to say, the entry of foreign manufactured goods into the Polish-Russian market was not at all convenient to local industry so that tariffs were established. Thus, for the wealthy trader, keeping one's money tied up in the import business (and thereby employing scores of Jewish peddlers as purchasing agents) became much less attractive than other and newer investment opportunities in industry itself. The less well-to-do, in contrast, were likely to become petty merchants whose well-being suffered from the growth of local industry.

This growth stimulated the internal consumption of raw materials and consequently the initial decline of the export business as well (Luxemburg, 1972:151–2). To be sure, the virtual unification of the Russian and Polish markets eventually compensated for this, as did the growth of the grain trade. But along with such compensatory forces came other more powerful ones. Polish merchants began to take over exports, thereby displacing many Jews (Weinryb, 1972 [1934]: 30). The control of exports by foreigners became increasingly widespread (ibid.: 49). Finally, peasants in many cases no longer required Jews to dispose of their surplus produce since Emancipation allowed them to do this themselves (Greenberg, 1944–51: vol. 1, 165). Wealthier traders were able to overcome this competition. Poorer ones were not.

The vast majority of merchants, unable to redirect their trifling capital into new channels[15] and unable to obtain credit with customary ease, were forced to concentrate on petty internal trade with its limited horizons for profit. For example, small Jewish grain traders in Berdichev increased in number by over 1,200 per cent between 1849 and 1897, thus leading to deadly competition (Weinryb, 1972 [1934]: 58). Many turned to smuggling as a livelihood but even here their activities were circumscribed. The government hastened the extinction of this profession by expelling all Jews living within 50 *versts* (about 35 miles) of the western border in 1825 (Levitats, 1970 [1943]: 78). The abolition of the eastern toll border removed the very barrier which smuggling was designed to overcome. If, as mentioned above, there were four directions in which the Jewish commercial intermediary was driven with the development of capitalism, then this was the second: impoverishment. By the end of the century the bulk of the Jewish merchant population had been reduced to a mass of peddlers, hawkers, petty money-lenders and small shopkeepers. The era of the 'ol' clo's Jew' and the *Luftmensch* was at hand.

Similar patterns of development were discernible in spheres of commercial activity other than trade. For example, the combined forces of the state, the poorer noblemen and the rising class of Christian merchants produced a situation which was equally disastrous for those employed in the liquor trade (innkeepers, lessees, etc.). Situated predominantly in rural areas, such persons constituted over 40 per cent of the Jewish work force at the beginning of the nineteenth century (Dubnow, 1916–20: vol. 2, 72; Mahler, 1971 [1952–6]: 392). Under the Polish regime landowners were given the right to manufacture and sell spirits upon payment of a small tax. This privilege was in turn rented out to thousands of Jews, some of whom became wealthy and sub-contracted other Jews to sell their liquor. In Russia, on the other hand, the production and sale of spirits was a government monopoly that was given over to a handful of large rentiers. The conflict between the Polish and the more centralised Russian systems became evident immediately after the partitions. Since in Poland prices were lower than in Russia there developed a considerable smuggling trade. The large Russian rentiers were naturally opposed to this competition while, in Poland, Christian merchants and poor noblemen were anxious to take over the enterprises themselves. These interests encouraged the state to drive the Jews out of the liquor business. Thus in the first decades of the nineteenth century there began an expulsion of Jews from rural areas. Not that the state had to be forced to do this. Revenue from the sale of spirits constituted a full 16 per cent of Russian state income in 1819. In desperate need of money, why could the state not monopolise liquor sales and increase its revenues even more? This policy of consolidation and monopolisation was reflected in the increase of liquor revenues from 28 per cent of total state income in 1846 to an amazing 40–50 per cent in the 1890s. After Sergei Witte, the Russian finance minister, placed the liquor trade completely under government control at the end of the century there were only about 12,000 Jews left in this line of endeavour. Four-tenths of the Jewish work force was thus robbed of its livelihood (Dubnow, 1916–20: vol. 3, 222–3; Mahler, 1971 [1952–6]: 377 ff., 406 ff.; Rubinow, 1907: 556; Von Laue, 1974 [1963]: 102–4). One could repeat substantially the same story for still other sources of livelihood such as tax collecting (which was taken over by the state) and money lending (which was taken over to a degree by commercial banks). Here, too, the old occupational structure was rendered anachronistic. All this was, of course, no problem for the extremely wealthy Jews who had in one way or another formerly employed scores of thousands of their co-religionists: for the wealthy, banks and railroads beckoned. It was otherwise for the vast majority, who drowned in the morass formed by the disappearance of those jobs which large Jewish capital had once created for them. In other words, the Jewish *haute bourgeoisie* played a double-edged role with respect to the larger community. By hastening the development of capitalism it both rendered the traditional functions of the Jews ever more anachronistic and ceased to invest its capital so as to employ other Jews.[16]

But this exhausts only two of the four, more or less distinct paths open to the former commercial intermediary. The third route—taken primarily by the *middle* merchant who was neither wealthy enough to become a financier or a railroad baron, nor poor enough to suffer the fate of the petty merchant—was to invest in small-scale manufacturing. There were two ways in which a middle merchant might do this. The path 'from above', probably restricted to the wealthier elements of this stratum, entailed the leasing and subsequent purchase of manufacturing establishments directly from needy landowners. The path 'from below' involved the wresting of independence from artisans. The former method was prominent even in the eighteenth century while the latter became increasingly important in the first decades of the nineteenth as artisans found it more and more necessary to borrow money and raw materials from Jewish merchants. From here it was but a short step to the 'putting out system' and then to the direct employment of wage-labourers. In the fifteen provinces of the Russian Pale in 1864, 37 per cent of all industrial establishments were owned by Jews (Weinryb, 1972 [1934]: 90). By *fin de siècle* standards these establishments were small. They were, with growing competition from large factories, driven out of business. And they employed exclusively Jewish labour.

Before discussing the position of the Jewish worker let us examine the ways in which the Russian government sought to resolve the problem of what might be done with (or to) the bulk of the Jewish population now that the period of its economic usefulness had expired. Constantine Pobedonostsev, Procurator of the Holy Synod (and a man once referred to by Turgenev as the 'Russian Torquemada'), summed up a century of attempts to deal with the Jewish problem when he declared that the government could best solve it by forcing the assimilation of a third of the Jews, encouraging the emigration of another third and killing the remainder (but see Aronson, 1975).

In 1794 a *ukase* was promulgated which restricted Jewish residence to a Pale of Settlement. The impetus behind this piece of legislation came 'from the influential Christian middle class, which, fearing free competition, began to shout for protection' (Dubnow, 1916–20: vol. 1, 315). Enlarged by the partition of 1795 and defined more precisely by legislation enacted in 1835, the Pale consisted of the 362,000 square miles of the western Russian provinces, including Russian Poland. Beyond the Pale Jews were forbidden to reside. Initial attempts to syphon off into agriculture those persons displaced by expulsions from the liquor trade met by and large with failure, mainly because of the government's inability to underwrite the costs of agricultural settlement. As a consequence, Jews became more highly concentrated in urban areas than they already were.

The four decades from the establishment of Congress Poland to the death of Nicholas I reflected three successive tendencies with respect to the Jewish problem that are conveniently summarised by Shimon Dubnow as follows:

[F]irst, in the last years of Alexander I's reign (1815–1825), a mixed tendency of 'benevolent paternalism' and severe restrictions; second, during the first half of Nicholas I's reign (1826–1840), a military tendency, that of 'correcting' the Jews by subjecting their youth, from the age of childhood, to the austere discipline of conscription and barrack training, accompanied by compulsory religious assimilation and by an unprecedented recrudescence of rightlessness and oppression; and third, during the latter part of Nicholas's reign (1840–1855), the 'enlightened' tendency of improving the Jews by establishing 'crown schools' and demolishing the autonomous structure of Jewish life, while keeping in force the former cruel disabilities (1916–20: vol. 1, 391).

A more liberal policy, which gained in popularity during the early years of Alexander II's reign, involved the attempt to 'turn the Jews to productive labor' (Greenberg, 1944–51: vol. 1, 39, 91; Leshchinsky, 1928: 30 ff.). Beginning in 1855 residence restrictions were eased somewhat in the hope of integrating the more 'useful' elements of the Jewish population into the Russian economy. Similarly, educational reform which permitted the entry of some Jews into the Russian university system was viewed by Alexander and his ministers as a means of encouraging 'productivisation'.

But such liberalism was merely a respite. Rebellion in Poland in 1863 sparked a reaction to old ways and means of dealing with the Jews. From there it was but a short downhill road to the infamous pogroms of 1881. The government decided at that time to canalise increasingly dangerous peasant unrest—occasioned by the depression then affecting all of Europe—against the increasingly intractable Jewish problem. The southern Russian press spread the news that attacks were being prepared against the Jews; government emissaries warned the local police against interference with 'demonstrations of the public will'; and Russian businessmen assured the peasants that a *ukase* had been issued calling on them to attack the Jews during the coming Easter holiday. The results were, from the governmental and Christian middle-class standpoint, remarkably successful. By 1882 pogroms had 'erupted' in 225 communities, leaving 20,000 Jews homeless and a trail of extensive property damage (Dawidowicz, 1967: 47).

Although the official explanation for the pogroms first pointed the accusing finger at 'terrorists', the putative cause was soon changed to 'Jewish exploitation'. Ignatyev, Minister of the Interior, was now instructed to formulate legislation capable of eliminating the problem. The Ignatyev Report of 1882 dropped 'a paralysing grill-work of legal disabilities . . . on the Jews which was not lifted until March 1917' (Sachar, 1959: 243). The remaining rural elements of the Jewish population were now forced into the already overcrowded cities, while a *numerus clausus* for Jewish students was established. The Jews were further subjected to a whole series of oppressive laws and additional pogroms in the following years. During the reign of Alexander III (1881–94) alone, some 65 anti-Jewish *ukases* were promulgated (Dinur, 1957: 113); between 18 and 29 October 1905, pogroms broke out in nearly 700 communities, leaving 800 Jews dead, 700 wounded and damages estimated at over 60 million rubles (Ginzburg, 1937: 153); and so forth.

E. Jewish Workers

The undermining of the Jewish middleman's position in Russian society and the resultant government policies were bound to alter the physiognomy of the Jewish community. Some statistics which will help us gain an understanding of its structure at the end of the century are collected in Figs. 4 and 5.

The tables reveal several interesting facts. While in 1897 Jews constituted about 4 per cent of the total Russian population, over 92 per cent of them lived in the Pale, where they formed over 11 per cent of the population. They were, moreover, highly concentrated in urban areas: almost 49 per cent of the Pale's Jewish population lived in incorporated cities and almost 82 per cent in incorporated cities and towns. Nearly 37 per cent of the city population in the Pale was Jewish.

The Jewish work force was remarkably different from that of the non-

Fig. 4. Occupational Distribution of Jews and non-Jews in Russia (figures for Pale only in Brackets)

occupation	% non-Jewish work force, 1897	% Jewish work force, 1897	% Jewish work force, 1818
agriculture	60.5 (63.2)	2.9 (2.9)	(1.9)
professions	3.0 (2.6)	5.0 (5.1)	——
personal service	⎤	⎤ (17.9)	——
liquor trade and	16.2 (19.8)	19.4	
related fields	⎦	⎦ (0.9)	⎤ (86.5) ⎡ (>43.3)
commerce	2.7 (1.4)	31.6 (32.0)	⎦ ⎣ (<43.3)
transportation	2.2 (1.8)	3.2 (3.3)	——
manufacturing and mechanical pursuits	15.4 (11.2)	37.9 (37.9)	(11.6)
	100.0 100.0	100.0 100.0	100.0

Sources: Compiled from data in (Dubnow, 1916–20: vol. 2, 72; Leshchinsky, 1928: 30; Rubinow, 1907: 500–1).
Note: See Technical Appendix.

Fig. 5. Jewish Population in Russia, 1897

	Russian Empire	Pale only
Jews	5.2 mil.	4.8 mil.
Jews as % of total pop.	4.2	11.6
Jews as % of total pop. in incorporated cities		36.9
% of Jews in incorporated cities		48.8
% of Jews in incorporated cities and towns		81.9

Sources: Compiled from data in (Leshchinsky, 1922: 43, 47; Rubinow, 1907: 490–1, 494).
Note: See Technical Appendix.

Jewish population. In the Pale, where more than 63 per cent of the non-Jewish work force was involved in agriculture, less than 3 per cent of the Jewish work force were so employed. Less than 2 per cent of non-Jews and 32 per cent of Jews were engaged in commercial activities. In other fields of employment —including the free professions, personal service (domestics, janitors, night watchmen and the like), transportation (in the case of Jews, mainly draymen; in the case of non-Jews, mainly railwaymen), artisanry and factory labour—we find less than 35 per cent of non-Jews and over 64 per cent of Jews. By comparing this last figure with the very rough figures for the year 1818, we see that entry into 'other' fields of employment was the fourth path taken by the former commercial intermediary in the course of the nineteenth century.

It would of course be mistaken to consider all those in the 'other' category as having the same organisational potential for becoming active in radical movements. Probably half of the non-agricultural day-labourers and nearly all of those in transportation were in fact self-employed; and the many socially-dissociated Jews engaged in personal service did not work in conditions which promoted solidarity among them (Menes, 1939: 2). From the point of view of radical activity, the important occupations were artisanry and factory labour. In the fifteen provinces of the Russian Pale there were in 1897 over 500,000 Jewish artisans[17] and about 50,000 factory workers (Evreyskago . . ., 1904: vol. 2, table 41; Leshchinsky, 1906: 19). Most of the Bundist and Poalei-Zionist mass base was drawn from these two groups.

The 500,000 Jewish artisans had much in common with Russian labourers in giant industrialised factories. They were certainly advancing along the road of proletarianisation. The vast majority of master artisans had begun to accrue burdensome debts to money-lenders and work under the putting-out system (Evreyskago . . ., 1904: vol. 1, 214–19), while of the dependent position of journeymen and apprentices there can be no doubt. True, in terms of social solidarity, the Jewish artisans had no peasant-based communal associations to bind them together. But they, unlike Russian workers, had a long history of organisation in guilds and self-help funds (Kremer, 1956–7; Rabinowitsch, 1903; Zelnik, 1971–2: 11–12); and the high degree of concentration of artisans in an urban setting permitted a frequency of contact and a similarity of work conditions which were conducive to organisation.

But, in spite of all this, several factors constrained the consciousness and action of the artisans. In the Pale, the average Jewish workshop employed, on the average, one master and one journeyman or apprentice (Evreyskago . . ., 1904: vol. 1, 255). Consequently, the artisan was in his place of work brought into contact with only a handful of other workers, all of whom were Jews. The homogenising influence of the large factory, capable in some instances of wiping out particularism, was missing. In addition, the fact that adverse conditions affected master and journeyman with equal force meant that class antagonisms were muted: it makes sense to an industrial worker living in misery to rebel against his well-to-do employer, but when the employer suffers as much as the worker, against whom is the worker to rebel (cf. Thompson, 1968: 815)? In fact the differences between master and journeyman were so slight as to allow for a considerable degree of anticipated social mobility on the part of the journeyman, so that 'the Jewish journeyman by no means considered himself permanently a wage-earner' but looked forward to the day when he would own his own workshop (Mendelsohn, 1970: 9). Again, this had the effect of restraining class conflict.

The artisan lived in conditions even more abhorrent than those of the average industrial worker. In one respect his plight was, however, short-lived, for with the advance of highly competitive industry he was inevitably driven out of work altogether. The tiny workshop, heritage of the pre-capitalist era, was doomed. To the extent that he was forced into the factory the artisan was, by entering an expanding niche in society, transformed into a member of an ascending class. But this route was rarely taken. Due largely to competition from millions of starving peasants for scarce industrial jobs, and restrictions on labour mobility,[18] the Jewish artisan was more often than not driven either out of the country or out of existence.

Fig. 6. Selected Statistics on Russian Industry, 1897

	average annual production per factory (in '000s of rubles)	average number of workers per factory	% of Jewish factory proletariat	growth in average annual production since 1889 (%)
Northern Pale	18	17	66	5
Southern Pale	60	36	34	24
Fifteen provinces of Russian Pale	47	30	100	22
European Russia (excl. Pale)	82	74	0	80

Source: Compiled from data in (Leshchinsky, 1906: tables 1–3, 5, 23).
Note: See Technical Appendix.

Jews employed in factories were victims of the same process. Fig. 6 contains data which are in this respect extremely revealing. The largest, most productive and fastest growing factories in Russia were located outside the Pale, where only 8 per cent of the Jewish population resided. Moreover, within the Pale itself, factories became smaller, less productive and slower growing as one travelled north. But it was precisely in the north that most of the Jews lived; and over 66 per cent of the Jewish factory proletariat worked in that region. The inescapable conclusion is that Jews in industry were employed in those small and backward establishments which were forced out of production as competition from larger and more efficient factories mounted (Leshchinsky, 1906: 31; Margolin, 1908: 261).

The Jewish labourer, whether working in an artisan's workshop or a small factory, was thus in an ambiguous position. On the one hand, he was a dependent wage-labourer and solidary with his fellow workers. In fact, until 1905 the Jewish proletariat was far and away the best organised segment of the working class movement — the 'vanguard', as Georgi Plekhanov put it in 1896. On the other hand, the Jewish labourer was, like the bulk of the Jewish community, in a declining position, a position that, with the advance of industry, was being eliminated altogether. This helps explain the fact that his pre-eminence in the working class movement was brief. After 1905 the gains made by the Jewish worker in terms of wage increases and a shorter working day were reversed (Mendelsohn, 1969; 1970), for he did not occupy the structural position which produced the type and intensity of class conflict necessary for the success of the labour movement.

The Jewish worker was still bound by employment and/or credit ties to the Jewish community and therefore suffered its fate: Jews were 'strangers' in pre-capitalist Poland because they stood between lord and serf. By and large, they continued to be strangers in early twentieth-century Russia because they now stood between two social epochs. Polish feudalism was gone; Russian capitalism could find no place for them. This was the historical legacy bequeathed to the Jewish community.

3 The Embedding Process

> In the last few years I have often asked myself if it would have been possible for my life to have taken another ideological direction. And I must answer decisively: no. Everything had to be as it was.
>
> *Avraham Mutnikovich*

Avraham Mutnikovich, a founder of the Bund, no doubt underemphasises his creative role in the formation of an organisation which stood for a full decade at the forefront of Russian Social Democracy. Yet he places before us the central problem of this chapter: analysing the social conditions underlying the 'ideological directions' taken by Russian-Jewish *intelligenty*. When the contribution of these men and women to the revolutionary movement is examined in Chapter 4 it will be possible to recognise them as both products and agents of the historical process. Here I am concerned only with the context of their creativity, with the social forces which produced the opportunities allowing them to become radicalised and support conflicting ideologies. We begin a century or so before the emergence of the Social Democratic movement.

A. Classification

It has become something of an historical commonplace that the insulation of the medieval Jewish community from the surrounding society was a result of two parallel desires which are summarised by Katz as follows:

> [T]he demand of the non-Jewish authorities for the creation of Jewish communities was by no means complied with only as a necessity. On the contrary, it corresponded fully with the Jewish aspiration to retain as great a measure as possible of self-government (1973: 19; also Wirth, 1956 [1928]).

What is sometimes forgotten, however, is that underlying these desires were the very real foundations discussed in Chapter 2: the community remained an integral unit to the extent that the functions of the Jews and their internal ties of socio-economic dependence combined with the lords' desire for a group capable of providing mercantile and related services:

On the one hand, the Jewish community could exist as a discrete corporate entity only to the extent that it performed those specialised tasks demanded by the authorities. This was recognised by Weber, who noted that the Jews 'are tolerated, indeed, frequently privileged, and they live in interspersed political communities . . . by virtue of their economic indispensability' (1946: 189). Moreover, profound religious differences reinforced the separateness of the community so that, in the eyes of Gentiles, Jewishness as a cultural system came to be associated with the social functions performed by Jews. As is well known, in many areas of Europe the terms 'Jew' and 'merchant' became synonymous. Allowing Jews to assimilate into the larger society was consequently out of the question, for assimilation in the cultural sense appeared to the authorities to pose a threat to the performance of these socially important tasks.

On the other hand, from the Jews' point of view, the maintenance of a separate community and identity was literally profitable. The connections of the merchant capitalist with his co-religionists extended all through Europe and beyond. Much like Protestant sectarianism in the United States during the early years of this century (ibid.: 302–22), Jewish ethnicity combined with kinship ties to solidify credit connections, help secure ancillary trade agents and exclude would-be competitors: even in the nineteenth century a wealthy Jew's last will and testament might transfer accumulated wealth to an eldest son only on condition that the son agree to remain Jewish (Ginzburg, 1937; cf. Cohen, 1969; Ianni and Reuss-Ianni, 1972; Leyton, 1965; Parkin, 1971: 14 ff.; Schumpeter, 1951 [1919–27]: 108, 113; Wolf, 1966). It is undoubtedly the case that 'parallel to the Jews' cultural connections were the business activities of the capitalist' and that, partly as a consequence of these international activities, 'there emerged a consciousness of a broader society and, beyond this, a commitment to the idea of a Jewish nation that included every Jew in the world' (Katz, 1973: 23).

As was the case with other marginal trading peoples in other times and places (Bonacich, 1973; Stryker, 1959), the Jews' group commitments, internally generated and externally imposed, necessitated proscriptions against inter-marriage and conversion, a more (Scholem, 1973 [1957]) or less (Weinryb, 1972) deeply-implanted yearning for return to the ancestral fatherland, a sense of 'chosen-ness', and the erection of a whole complex of autonomous communal institutions which were controlled by the wealthy and learned (generally the same people; see Abramsky, 1974: 22; Katz, 1973: 21; Levitats, 1970 [1943]: 134) and which reinforced the separateness of the Jewish community. In a word, an ideological and institutional system of what Katz (1961) has called 'exclusiveness' was erected by and for Jews in the medieval world.

By the second half or the final third of the eighteenth century a perceptive observer could no doubt have detected the first fissures in the community structure. The community tended to be pulled apart to the extent that it became both possible and desirable for persons to form new ties with classes in the larger society and break old ones with the Jewish community. It is therefore of paramount importance to note that in late eighteenth-century eastern Europe, and even more so in the nineteenth century,

> there was increased and varied contact between Jews and Gentiles. The earlier type of relationship, as between merchant and customer, or lender and borrower, was superseded by more complex associations. The scope of economic life, being now based on the investment of capital, was broadened. This afforded Jews an opportunity of employing their money in various undertakings and proffering their services in many new ways (ibid.: 156).

Contact with non-Jews was at first most frequent and intimate among the well-to-do. Thus, a wealthy purveyor of military supplies, who was ideally situated for using Jewish peddlers throughout Europe as purchasing agents, found it both necessary and profitable to counsel his patrons. He thereby became attached to higher circles in the larger society, thus removing himself from the strict supervision of the Jewish community and partaking of the forbidden fruits of aristocratic life. Such persons — in Germany their functional equivalents were known as 'court Jews' (Balaban, 1930: 59–66; Carsten, 1958; Coser, 1972; Stern, 1950) — remained committed to their religion; but throughout Europe, those who acted as purveyors, finance ministers and the like found their offspring eager to convert to Christianity (Carsten, 1958: 153; Katz, 1961: 250).

Many such merchant bankers, as they transformed themselves into modern finance capitalists, furthered this process of community dissolution. Whether through outright conversion — Steiglitz, Bliokh and Strousberg, mentioned above in connection with railroad investment, are the examples which come immediately to mind here — or through involvement in the liberal and somewhat assimilationist *haskala* movement, Jews began to integrate structurally, and therefore ideologically, into the non-Jewish environment (cf. Gordon, 1964: 81; Sharot, 1974).[1]

In backward Russia the conversion movement was naturally less widespread than in Germany. However, one contemporary recorded that in 1848 nearly 2,500 conversions took place. Six years later the number grew to 4,500 (Raisin, 1914: 328). And one traveller to Russia in 1839 observed that 'there are about forty thousand [converted Jews] in Petersburg and Moscow' alone (Lilienthal, 1915: 162). Even in Russia Jews purchased in large numbers what Heinrich Heine once referred to as the 'entrance ticket to western civilization'.

i. *Patterns of Withdrawal*
'In progressive Jewish homes', wrote one Jewess of mid-nineteenth century Russia, 'mostly among wealthy families whose fathers and sons were

engaged in commerce with Germany and who frequently travelled across the border, the deviation from Jewish tradition was great' (Wengeroff in Dawidowicz, 1964: 164). Maxim Litvinov's father, a produce merchant in Belostok who had to travel 'through the region buying up the local crops and into Prussia, his chief market' (Pope, 1943: 32) was the head of one such home. Later, he rose to the position of director of the town bank. The elder Litvinov remained an observant Jew but, as his business contacts broadened, so did his ideas. His house in fact became a rendezvous for the intellectuals of Belostok who, in his book-lined sitting room, engaged in 'middle-class talk' on literary and political themes (ibid.). Herzen thus became as important as Rashi in his intellectual outlook. His son broke completely with Judaism, eventually becoming one of Lenin's most trustworthy lieutenants and, after the 1917 revolution, Commissar of Foreign Affairs of the new regime.

Others in similar social positions followed the same pattern of withdrawal from the Jewish community. Adolf Ioffe, one of Trotsky's closest friends and first Soviet ambassador to Germany, came from a wealthy merchant family in the Crimea (Barzilai, 1970; *Deyateli . . .*, n.d. [1927–9?]: pt. 1, 152–6).[2] Alexander Martynov, a leading Menshevik, came from identical social origins in Pinsk (ibid.: pt. 2, 1–20); so did Leo Jogiches, prominent in the early years of Russian Social Democracy in Vilna (Frölich, 1972 [1939]: 12 ff.; Nettl, 1966: vol. 1, 50 ff.). Angelica Balabanov, known not only as a Russian Social Democrat but also as a leader of the Italian socialist movement, was of a particularly rare group of Jews — those who were members of the wealthy landowning class. That she does not mention her Jewish origins even once in her three-hundred-page autobiography is therefore not surprising. There was little contact between her and the surrounding Jewish community of Chernigov in the Ukraine. Russian and French were the languages of discourse in her home, not Yiddish; while other Jewish girls of her age read *Yosephon* or *Bovebukh* — if, that is, they could read at all — Balabanov was absorbing the latest trends in western literature during frequent jaunts to Switzerland with her mother (Balabanoff, 1973 [1938]).

However, far from all Jewish Mensheviks and Bolsheviks came from wealthy families which formed new business ties with Gentiles and in substantial measure cut off old ones with fellow Jews. Withdrawal from the community could also be effected by moving out of traditional 'Jewish occupations' through newly-arisen opportunities, particularly in the school system. Frequently this involved physical isolation from Jewish population centres as well.

During a characteristically brief, relatively liberal period, the government opened the university system to Jewish enrolment. This was a device for breaking down the walls of isolation and, of course, for providing the country with cadres of lawyers, doctors, bureaucrats and so forth, needed for its efforts to modernise. But the very weakness of Russian liberalism prevented large numbers from getting involved in this aspect of the movement towards assimilation.

In the west liberalism proved capable of opening up a common ground where Jewish and Gentile intellectuals could meet and engage in discussions concerning philosophy, literature and politics, or merely in *repartie*. Jews were not often required to pay the entrance fee of conversion, which was consequently effected gradually, almost seductively and therefore more effectively over a period of a generation or two (Meyer, 1967; Stern-Taubler, 1940). But the salon of Henriette Herz in Berlin had few counterparts in Russia. For in Russia liberalism was virtually non-existent in midcentury. Until the 1890s it was capable only of stirring some capitalistically-inclined gentry (Venturi, 1960 [1952]: 172) to engage in mild-mannered talk of what was at the time known as 'small deeds'.

The critical difference between Russia and the west appears to have been that liberal elements in Russia were, as Fischer (1958) has shown, happy to accommodate themselves to their employer or overseer, the autocratic state; while their counterparts in the west, working in a social order with a stronger middle class, absorbed the *élan* of the developing bourgeoisie. Russia, like all underdeveloped countries, possessed no self-confident bourgeoisie. Liberalism of the western variety was consequently a delayed and emasculated ideology there (Chamberlin, 1967). There was thus little chance for a tolerant liberal path to Jewish emancipation to emerge in Russia (Greenberg, 1944–51: vol. 1, 187): the western model of economic integration leading to legal emancipation leading to cultural assimilation (Ruppin, 1973 [1934]: 271) was followed, but at a retarded pace. A faster pace would have required a capitalist economy sufficiently well developed to allow a strong middle class to feel that the integration of the Jews did not threaten its own well-being. And it would have required that more intellectuals be better integrated in the middle class so as to be able to act as its ideological supporters. But capitalism was immature in Russia and tolerance quite foreign (Hamm, 1972; Harcave, 1944; Slutzky, 1960: 232 ff.). The number of Jews who did enter the professions was therefore comparatively small. Needless to say, the 'great majority' of these persons 'were able to obtain recognition only through conversion' (Greenberg, 1944–51: vol. 1, 185).

The father of Lev Kamenev was one of the few Jews who did manage to become a professional. An engineer on the Moscow-Kursk railway and a graduate of the St Petersburg Technological Institute, he apparently had no desire to give his son a Jewish education. Indeed, Kamenev, like most of his ideological comrades, never saw the inside of a traditional Jewish school (*Deyateli* . . ., n.d. [1927–9?]: pt. 1, 161–8). The Bolshevik, Grigory Sokolnikov, was in a similar position. Although born in the Pale, his father, a doctor on the Libau-Romny railway, moved with his family to Moscow when Grigory was still a child (ibid.: pt. 3, 73–90). As in the case of Y. Sverdlov's father, who was a skilled craftsman and therefore allowed to live in the Russian interior, such 'occupational isolation', or relative independence in the search for a livelihood from other Jews, forced him to assimilate into non-Jewish society (ibid.: pt. 3, 13–25; Barzilai, 1968b; Uron, 1968).

It must be emphasised that mere geographical isolation did not produce assimilation; and that residence in centres densely populated with Jews did not ensure the persistence of one's Jewish identity. Even in the heart of the Pale it was possible, as indicated by the cases of Balabanov, Jogiches, Litvinov and Martynov, to assimilate.[3] And in remote communities such as Bodiboy, Siberia, the local Jews had 'little interest in Jewish culture and education' and 'married Christian women and raised their children as Gentiles' mainly because they were 'anxious to get into the good graces of the Russian officials' and consequently 'eager to identify with the majority' (Kushnir, 1967: 94). Assimilation in Bodiboy or in Vilna was a function of occupational isolation from other Jews. Everything hinged on whether or not ties of socio-economic dependence bound persons together and necessitated the continuity of old ethnic identities. Only if one were, or anticipated being[4] decoupled from such networks did one's Jewish identity weaken.

This does not mean that assimilation and conversion took place for purely 'economic motives'. Only the crudest materialist could ignore the complex motivations which prompted Jews to act in this manner. Genuine respect for western and Russian culture, love for a non-Jewish woman, scorn for outmoded Jewish traditions — on the motivational level all these factors and more were as important as the pursuit of economic advantage in leading Jews away from the community. But motivation, a social-psychological problem, must be analytically distinguished from structure, a purely sociological domain. (For a good example of how the two levels of analysis may be confused, see Feuer, 1974.) And it was the structural evolution of Russian society which enabled the diverse motivations mentioned above to emerge: in the seventeenth century inter-marriage was unthinkable but it became a distinct possibility once the walls of isolation began to crumble.

In any event, similar forces caused some intellectuals, too, to break ties with the community. Some were sponsored by wealthy patrons to leave Russia altogether and study in Germany. Others, less fortunate, left by dint of necessity. These poor scholars, far more numerous than their sponsored colleagues (Raisin, 1914: 80), wended their way westward as a consequence of the fact that traditional jobs for Jewish intellectuals, bound up in one way or another with the observance and inculcation of religion, had been growing scarcer ever since the community's fortunes began to decline (Lilienthal, 1915; Maimon, 1947 [1792–3]).

Although many of these persons were lost forever to the west, some, such as Alexander Tzederboim, the father of Julius Martov, were able to enter the thriving intellectual life of the wealthy Odessa and St Petersburg

Jewish communities. There, beginning in the 1850s, Tzederboim founded and edited the first Jewish periodicals in Russia (Tzitron, 1921–2: vol. 3, 96–129). He was a 'great champion of Jewish liberal causes'. But his son, Osip, who became director-general of the Russian Steamship Company, was 'cosmopolitan, polyglot [and] widely-travelled [:] . . . a europeanised and russified Jewish intellectual with liberal-democratic leanings [who] may also have been a conscious assimilationist' (Getzler, 1967: 1–2). Osip's son, Julius, was raised on the standard fare of a person of his social standing: Belinsky, Schiller, Hugo and Stepniak, not the Bible and the Talmud. At the age of twenty-eight Julius Tzederboim adopted the name of Martov on his way to becoming perhaps the most important figure in the Menshevik party.

Two patterns of withdrawal from the Jewish community have been discussed thus far. One followed the establishment on an intimate basis of business ties with Gentiles and a concomitant weakening of ties with Jews. The second followed the opening of educational opportunities which also led persons away from the community and promoted their integration in the class structure of the larger society. In both cases, the socialisation patterns of children were markedly different from those of their parents: the children were secularised and their Jewish identity weakened to the extent that their fathers were directly dependent on non-Jews for their livelihoods. These paths were taken by privileged groups. A third route was traversed by some less fortunate members of the community.

As wealthier elements left to pursue enticing livelihoods, communal responsibilities tended to be transferred to members of the community's middle strata. The latter were now responsible for the maintenance of tradition. This responsibility, in interaction with government attempts to integrate Jews into Russian society, inadvertently created a reservoir of persons from the lower reaches of the community whose children might also enter the ranks of Russian Social Democracy.

For example, brutal conscription laws that were in effect from the 1820s to the 1860s required the Jewish community to take collective responsibility for supplying seven recruits per 1,000 population. Not only was this 40 per cent higher than the corresponding rate for the general population, but it was instituted as a means of converting Jews to Christianity — not an unrealistic hope on the part of the authorities given the fact that military stints ran from twenty-five to thirty-one years. The relatively well-off middle strata were, however, able to grease the palms of those in a position to strike names off the lists of conscriptees (Tzunzer, 1905: 14 ff.). What remained was a pool of indigent and orphaned children.

When Tsar Nicholas implemented this policy he had no inkling that some future Romanov would have to contend with the consequences. But twenty-five years of military service left one Sosnovsky with little more than an untypically stubborn awareness of his Jewish identity. His son,

Lev, grew up not in the Pale but in central Russia since army veterans were given the privilege of residing in the interior. Lev received little if any Jewish education; and when he later became a Bolshevik journalist he helped overthrow the Romanov dynasty, which had helped create the very conditions that enabled him to take that ideological direction (*Deyateli* . . ., n.d. [1927–9?]: pt. 3, 90–107).

Similarly, the government endeavoured in the 1840s to reform the system of Jewish education by supervising the operation of Jewish schools and creating state-sponsored institutions designed to inculcate a sense of loyalty in, and promote the assimilation of Jewish children. But the reform effort 'came to naught in the face of the grim, determined resistance of the Jewish masses' (Levitats, 1970 [1943]: 69). In some communities the subsequent establishment of a minimum quota of students for the schools left community elders in a quandary: they were unwilling to send their own children yet were responsible for seeing to it that the quota was reached. The obvious answer was to entice the children of the poor into the heretical institutions. It was precisely in this manner that the Menshevik, Pavel Axelrod, took his first step outside the sphere of strictly Jewish concerns (Ascher, 1972).

Finally, mention should be made of those persons who escaped penury by getting involved in the government's largely unsuccessful and short-lived scheme to create a string of Jewish agricultural settlements in the southern Pale (and thereby draw some impoverished artisans and petty merchants out of the north). The families of Zinoviev and Trotsky were among those who took advantage of this project (*Deyateli* . . ., n.d. [1927–9?]: pt. 1, 143–9; Trotsky, 1970 [1930]). This was yet another form of the third withdrawal pattern, which permitted some poorer families to join the more privileged in contributing sons and daughters to the Menshevik and Bolshevik parties.

ii. Degree of Embeddedness

The Jewish community of medieval times was in the nineteenth century not only in the process of 'class distintegration' (Katz, 1961: 178), but also in the process of integration in the class system of the larger Russian society. More precisely, and in terms of the argument made in the preceding chapter, relatively small segments of the community were no longer located 'between', but 'within' the classes of the larger society. Diverse categories of persons (bankers, professionals, army veterans and so forth) were consequently to be found in the ranks of the assimilating, the assimilated and the converted. This diversity should not prevent us from seeing what these categories have in common: they were all comprised of persons who, in terms of their occupational ties, stood on the periphery of Jewish society.

It would be altogether too simplistic to refer to these persons as 'marginal men'. The term as it is commonly used by sociologists refers to a relatively *constant* state of having one's feet *in zwei Welt* simultaneously. But in actuality different segments of Russian Jewry were tied to the Jewish community or to the class system of the larger society to *varying* degrees (cf. Antonovsky, 1956). This observation permits us to say that the degree to which a person (or, more accurately, his family of orientation) was *embedded* in one or another group depended upon the strength, number and direction of his occupational ties. The implications of this statement are exceedingly important in the present context, for the type of education—both formal and informal—received by an *intelligent* in his early years was a function of the degree to which his family was embedded in the Jewish community. Strong, dense ties ensured that the child would absorb traditional *mores*; few, weak ties permitted exposure to Russian and western culture. The type of education an *intelligent* received in turn shaped his identity and his propensity in later years to accept one political ideology rather than other. Jewish *intelligenty* in the Bolshevik, Menshevik, Bundist and Poalei-Zionist parties were ranged along a continuum of embeddedness, and their clustering at certain points on this continuum is thus a regularity of more than passing interest. In order to introduce some of the concerns which will later occupy our attention, the following discussion illustrates the ramifications of degree of embeddedness on the type of education received by *intelligenty* located at various points on the continuum; the repercussions of type of education on identity; and the impact of identity on later affinities to Jewish nationalism.

At one extreme on the continuum were such half-Jews as the Bolshevik, Ivan Maisky, the first Soviet ambassador to England. Maisky in his youth was able to develop a genuine and deep-seated love for an identification with the Russian people. What other group could he identify with in the remote city of Omsk, Siberia, where his father practised medicine? The full-blown assimilationist attitude had already gripped his father and Ivan, educated in the Russian school system, was oblivious to his origins (Maisky, 1944).

Leon Trotsky remained a left-wing Menshevik until the events of 1917 won him over to the Bolsheviks. Trotsky's parents were both Jewish and his mother clung rather tenaciously, at least while Trotsky was a child, to certain elements of orthodoxy. He attended Jewish elementary school (*kheder*) for a few months; at the age of eleven he studied Hebrew for a short time; and he had some knowledge of the Yiddish language. These early experiences were, however, far outweighed by the educational consequences of being born into a family which farmed for a living and therefore had little contact with other Jews. Trotsky was probably more Jewish than he would have us believe. But his exposure to Jewish culture was both brief and unimpressive so that he exaggerates only slightly. His education on the farm was decidedly Russian. Later, in *Realschule*, it was strongly western European.[5]

The same cannot be said for either many of the Mensheviks who stood to the political right of Trotsky or for most Bundist *intelligenty*. Consider the case of Yalkutiel Portnoy, one of the founders of the Bund (Hertz, 1956–8: vol. 1, 68–122). His family was not from a remote Siberian community (as was Maisky's) or an isolated agricultural settlement in the Ukraine (as was Trotsky's), but from the heart of the northern Pale: the area around Vilna. His mother was engaged in a typical Jewish occupation, that of small shopkeeper; his father, in contrast, was something of a modernist and contributed articles to a Russian-language businessman's newspaper. Yalkutiel's education reflected these two-directional occupational ties: he attended *kheder* but, upon completion, was enrolled in a state school.

Still closer to the Jewish community both occupationally and culturally was the father of Zalman Shazar, a leading Poalei-Zionist who was to become the first president of the state of Israel. Shazar's father was an agent for a Jewish lumber merchant. But although he found it necessary to take many trips away from home, he did not venture into the Gentile world alone: the presence of Jewish clerks and 'markers' in the woodlots reinforced the occupational and ethnic ties he had with his employer. The Shazar family was therefore very much a part of the Jewish community. Zalman attended *kheder* and then *yeshiva* (Jewish secondary school) for twelve hours per day and viewed the little synagogue which he and his father frequented as 'a second home' (Shazar, 1967 [1950]: 11).

The data collected in Fig. 7 follow the pattern illustrated by these four

Fig. 7. Classification: Intelligenty by Party and Degree of Embeddedness in Russian Class Structure (%*)*

degree of embededness	party				
	a. Bolshevik (n = 17)	b. Menshevik (n = 24)	c. Bund (pioneers only) (n = 12)	d. Bund (n = 95)	e. Poalei-Zion (n = 50)
1	5.9	12.5	0	35.8	66.0
2	11.8	25.0	33.3	36.8	30.0
3	11.8	16.7	41.7	17.9	2.0
4	70.6	45.8	25.0	9.5	2.0
total	100.1	100.0	100.0	100.0	100.0
x̄	3.5	3.0	2.9	2.0	1.4

Notes: (a) For sources and method of construction, see Technical Appendix.
(b) x^2 for columns a, b, d and e = 77.2, sig. at < .001, d.f. = 9.

cases. The table compares two variables: degree of embeddedness of *intelligenty*'s families of orientation in the Jewish community and affiliation of *intelligenty* with the Bolshevik, Menshevik, Bundist and Poalei-Zionist parties. Details concerning the manner in which the table was constructed will be found in the Technical Appendix, but it should be mentioned here that the four degrees of embeddedness correspond to the four cases discussed above. That is to say, some *intelligenty* were born into families closely tied to the Jewish community and received a traditional Jewish education (e.g., Shazar). Others grew up in families which were just beginning to break out of the traditional milieu because some of their occupational ties extended to the non-Jewish world (e.g., Portnoy). A third group consisted of persons who were brought up in more or less secularised families and received only a minimal Jewish education in their early years because of relative occupational isolation from the Jewish community (e.g., Trotsky). Finally, there were those whose break with the community was complete and whose education included virtually no elements of Jewish culture (e.g., Maisky). Individuals falling into these groups were assigned the scores of one, two, three and four, respectively.

The results are of considerable substantive and statistical significance (Taylor and Frideres, 1972). The table indicates that Bolshevik *intelligenty* were most securely embedded in the class structure of the larger Russian society and least securely embedded in the Jewish community. The mean degree of embeddedness ($\bar{x}$) of the Bolsheviks was 3.5. At the opposite end of the continuum were the Poalei-Zionists ($\bar{x} = 1.4$). The Mensheviks and Bundists had mean scores of 3.0 and 2.0, respectively. The chi-square test confirms what should already be apparent: the strong relationship between degree of embeddedness and party affiliation was almost certainly not due to chance.

This leaves us with a credible (although, as we shall see, partial) explanation for at least one aspect of ideological divergence among the *intelligenty*: The Bolsheviks were vehemently opposed to Jewish national-ism. So for the most part were the Mensheviks, although some members of this party, such as Pavel Axelrod (Ascher, 1965; Axelrod, 1924) and David Shub (Shub, 1970: vol. 1, 56 and *passim*) had serious misgivings about their stance. Bundists, in contrast, sought to encourage the development of Jewish culture and have the Jewish workers movement remain organi-sationally apart from the Russian. And Poalei-Zionists were the most Jewish-nationalistic of all, working as they did for the creation of a Jewish state in what was then Ottoman Palestine. In short, degree of affinity to Jewish nationalism varied proportionately with degree of embeddedness of one's family of orientation in the Jewish community (and therefore inversely with degree of embeddedness in the larger Russian class structure).

It should hardly be necessary to add that there were individual exceptions. What needs emphasising, though, is that many of the exceptions are only apparent. For example, Fig. 7 indicates that the so-called 'pioneer' Bundists — the thirteen men and women who formed the 'Vilna Group' which eventually gave birth to the Bund[6] — displayed almost the same degree of embeddedness in the fabric of Russian society as the Mensheviks (Hertz, 1956–8: vol. 1, 1–192, 241–3; Kremer in *Arkady* . . ., 1942: 22–72; Mill, 1946: vol. 1, 13–38; Niger and Shatzky, 1956–8: vol. 2, 7–8; Raizen, 1928–30: vol. 3, 518–20). Given the fact that they were as un-Jewish as the Mensheviks, how could they have not just joined, but actually helped create the Bund? Can these cases be dismissed as mere exceptions to the general rule? I think not. What these cases suggest is that embeddedness in the Jewish community was not the only determinant of one's ideological proclivities.

The embedding process was comprised not of one, but of three stages. The *intelligent* was first embedded to varying degrees in the Jewish community. This social fact (his 'classification' as I would prefer to call it) left a distinct residue on his ideological outlook. At the next stage of the embedding process he sought — unsuccessfully — to become integrated in the Russian middle class: he was, to use the sub-title of this chapter's next section, 'declassified'. Finally, he was more or less securely re-embedded in the working class, or 'reclassified'. This third stage of the embedding process, which could under certain specifiable conditions partially, and even substantially erase the ideological imprint of his early years, is discussed in the final section of this chapter. Let us now turn to a consideration of these latter two stages.

B. Declassification

Governor-General Patapov: In addition to all the other good qualities which you Jews possess, about the only thing you need is to become nihilists, too!

Yankele Kovner: Pardon me, General, this is not quite right. As long as *we* educated our children there were no nihilists among us; but as soon as you took the education of our children into your hands, behold the results!

a confrontation in Vilna, 1872, following the arrest of forty Jews suspected of 'nihilist tendencies'

From the above discussion we may conclude that the *intelligenty* of the four parties differed from one another in terms of the degree to which they were tied to the Jewish community in their youth. Here we will be concerned with something they had in common — the fact that they all entered the Jewish or Russian school systems. Most of the *intelligenty* were, in other words, socially mobile. They were on their way to becoming members of what contemporary sociologists like to call the 'new middle class' of 'white collar workers'. Yet instead of becoming solid, middle-class citizens they used the educational system as a platform for launching their revolutionary careers. Why did they become radicalised rather than develop middle-class ideological orientations? In order to answer this question it is necessary to specify just where the intelligentsia as a whole was located in Russian society. For, as I seek to demonstrate below, radicalism became so widespread in Russia mainly because intellectuals were unable to become securely attached to that country's bourgeoisie.

i. The Social Location of the Russian Intelligentsia

Intellectuals in Russia and elsewhere did not participate directly in the social process of production but were employed in cultural, political, educational and 'service' institutions which supported middle-class society to varying degrees. From the discussion of marginality theory in Chapter 1 it seems that, generally speaking, the growth of intellectual radicalism depends on the extent to which opportunities exist which enable intellectuals to become firmly attached to such institutions. If such institutions and opportunities are abundant, intellectuals tend to remain liberals; if not, they are in a position which facilitates the emergence and spread of radical ideologies. It is at this point that the distinction made in Chapter 1 between intellectuals and *intelligenty* becomes important. As Alvin Gouldner (1975-6: 6) writes,

> intellectuals are the educated counterpart of the propertied middle class. They usually are the studious brothers and sisters of those who make their careers through mercantile, industrial or landed property. The intellectuals . . . are a *cultural* bourgeoisie whose capital is knowledge and language acquired during their education.

Intelligenty, in contrast, are generally divorced from the means of middle-class intellectual production and therefore display a marked propensity to adopt leftist ideologies.

It follows that the degree of intellectual radicalism within a given society and among different societies should vary inversely with the number of employment opportunities available to the intellectuals. Such evidence as we possess on the subject confirms our suspicion. For example, nineteenth-century British intellectuals were provided with a host of opportunities — ranging from Colonial Service to the staff of *The Times* — for employment in middle class institutions (Annan, 1955: 244). As Lenore O'Boyle has shown in great detail, there may have been slightly more educated men than employment opportunities during the first half of the nineteenth century, but the British situation could not compare to the French and German. Indeed, the aborted revolutions in France and

Germany in 1830 and 1848 were phenomena closely associated with the large over-supplies of intellectuals in those countries (O'Boyle, 1970; also Heberle, 1951: 127; Namier, 1944). The traditional ability of British society to provide employment for its intellectuals is in fact the chief reason why a large intelligentsia has, as one student of the subject remarks, 'never existed in Great Britain. For the most part intellectuals have been solidly middle class, forming a staunch pillar of the status quo' (Wood, 1959: 28). Similar correlations between surfeits of opportunities and low degrees of radicalism or dearths of opportunities and high degrees of radicalism could easily be multiplied (e. g., Guindon, 1964; Mills, 1951: 142–60).

This should not, however, be taken to imply that only when intellectuals are unemployed and therefore poorly embedded in the middle class do they become radicalised. For class embeddedness is not a dichotomous, but a continuous variable: it depends on the *degree* to which jobs allow intellectuals to attain the levels of income, power, prestige and the kinds of ideological commitments typically associated with the middle class. It is interesting in this connection to cite the results of a survey conducted by Frank Parkin on contemporary English intellectuals. Parkin found that intellectuals 'firmly entrenched' in elite middle-class institutions were 'less susceptible to the appeal of extremist politics' than freelance writers, journalists and dramatists. Employment in elite institutions not only provided intellectuals with job security, but also forced them to conform to 'orthodox standards of behaviour' (1968: 97–9). Not just jobs, but secure jobs which promote orthodox liberal commitments must be available if intellectuals are to be prevented from engaging in left-wing politics. Not just unemployment, but underemployment creates radicals. That is to say, if the job market cannot cope with the products of an academic system — if, for example, intellectuals are prevented from becoming liberals — the resultant contradiction between structure and consciousness will promote radicalisation (cf. Marx, 1972: 123; Stateri, 1975: 215).

These conditions were present in Russia, at least until the beginning of the twentieth century, to a quite extraordinary degree. This was not merely because there was a chronic over-supply of educated men and women in Russia — this aspect of the problem will be discussed below — but because there were few arenas of employment in which intellectuals could freely develop and propound liberal ideas. To be sure, those who were integrated in the government bureaucracy, the free professions and the state school system tended to remain cautious liberals (Fischer in Black, 1960: 253–74). But one cannot speak of anything like a well-developed middle-class press at the time. Journalism and publishing were subject to such rigid censorship and control that the growth of these fields of employment was painfully blocked (Tompkins, 1953; 1957); as late as 1901 the liberal journal *Liberation*, which called for no more than the convocation of a constituent assembly, had to be published in Germany and smuggled into Russia illegally (Harcave, 1970 [1964]: 33; cf. Coser,

1970 [1965]: 7, 88–9, 96). Nor could intellectuals become attached to legal, middle-class, political parties due to the fact that there were none in Russia until early in this century (cf. Lipset, 1968: 14; Weinberg and Walker, 1970). Finally, teachers and professors were under the careful supervision of the autocracy so that those interested in relatively free intellectual enquiry often had to look elsewhere (Eymontova, 1971: 152–4).

If the ability of the intellectuals to become well-integrated supporters of the middle class depended on the growth of truly middle-class arenas of employment, then this depended in turn on the ability of the Russian bourgeoisie to wrest such 'concessions' from the autocracy. Peter Struve realised this when he predicted in 1909 that

> in the course of economic development the intelligentsia will be 'bourgeoisified'; that is, through a process of social adjustment it will become reconciled with the state, and it will organically and spontaneously be drawn into the existing class structure . . . The rapidity of this process will depend on the pace of Russia's economic development and the pace at which the entire state structure is reorganised in a constitutional spirit (1970 [1909]: 197).

But the pace proved too slow because the bourgeoisie was too weak: Russia simply failed to develop a strong 'capitalist bourgeoisie as distinct from a professional and intellectual one' (Kochan, 1962: 175; also Berlin, 1948: 342). The weakness of the Russian capitalist bourgeoisie was, in the final analysis, the main cause of such widespread radicalism in Russia. In fact, if one examines the British, French, German and Russian cases, one is tempted to make the general theoretical statement that the weaker the bourgeois class of a society at any given point in time, the higher the degree of intellectual radicalism.

Nineteenth-century Russia possessed intellectuals but instead of employing them in institutions where liberal viewpoints could thrive it often provoked them. This was apparent from the first sproutings of the revolutionary intelligentsia in the 1840s. During the early years of that decade Alexander Herzen, Mikhail Bakunin and Vissarion Belinsky became the first utopian socialists in Russia. In the 1830s all had been followers of the right-wing, German, romantic philosophies which were fashionable at the time (Berlin, 1955). The key to happiness was, they believed, enlightenment or inner reform rather than social or external reform; men should rest secure in the knowledge that — as one of the foremost Russian idealists of the period was fond of writing in his letters — '*Es herrscht eine allweise Güte über die Welt*' (N. Stankevich, quoted in Kostka, 1961: 160). But such ideological orientations could not persist for long. Herzen was twice arrested for perfectly trivial reasons — once because the censor intercepted a letter to his father in which Herzen mentioned a harmless rumour concerning the Moscow police department! — and spent over seven years in internal exile. His passage from Schelling to Saint-Simon to left-Hegelianism occurred concomitantly. Because the regime often treated even liberals in such a heavy-handed manner this development was not unique to Herzen. By the early 1840s a small group of men in similar social circumstances[7] came to believe that 'socialism is the alpha and omega of belief and knowledge' (Belinsky, 1956: 170).

Two decades passed before an over-supply of intellectuals became evident in Russia. In the 1860s, although the

> nature and distribution of occupational opportunities was undergoing a significant change . . . there was no numerical expansion sufficient to absorb the less opulent and more ambitious intellectuals now coming from the universities (Fischer in Black, 1960: 259).

In the 1870s graduates were still having problems finding work (Brower, 1975: 141). The causes of radicalism thus assumed a new dimension. If before the 1860s *intelligenty* were *déclassé* only in the sense of being unable to find employment in institutions which encouraged them to think along middle-class lines then, beginning in that decade, and for some time thereafter, many were *déclassé* in the additional sense of facing a shortage of jobs, at least in some areas of employment (the government bureaucracy, but not teaching or medicine). This was only one of the many factors which led to a turning point in the evolution of the Russian intelligentsia (Brym, 1977d). In the 1860s the intelligentsia became much more radical. In the 1870s dissent became an *institutionalised* feature of Russian society which operated somewhat *independently* of expansions and contractions in the structure, and changes in the quality of employment opportunities.

Before considering in some detail how this came about it is necessary to emphasise that students formed the 'quintessence of the Russian intelligentsia' (Izgoev, 1969 [1909]: 500). As Fig. 1 indicates (and as at least two independent samples confirm; see Brower, 1968–9: 339; Strauss, 1973: 305, 307) the proportion of student *intelligenty* to the total number of radicals fell over time, but always remained large. Why this was the case is not difficult to explain. In comparing Russian *intelligenty* with those in western Europe it was argued that the rate of radicalism among the former was higher because they were less securely integrated in the middle class. It follows that, *within* Russia, groups of intellectuals which were more tenuously embedded in the bourgeoisie than the average should have manifested higher than average rates of radicalism. Students formed one such group because they were free of *any* occupational ties which might constrain their thoughts and actions (cf. Berger, 1960: 13; Flacks, 1970–1: 151); and, as we shall see, the rate of radicalism was highest among those students whose actual and anticipated degree of middle-class integration was lowest: the Jews.

As Daniel Brower (1975: esp. 116 ff.) has shown, students first developed a sense of solidarity because of the elitist character of education in Russia. From the time of Peter the Great, children were educated with one aim in mind — to provide the state with administrative, military and technical personnel. Students were viewed as future executors of the Tsar's will and themselves tended to develop a keen sense of purpose and self-importance. 'Russian society', wrote a committee of Moscow University professors in the early 1860s,

> inspired students with a feeling of dignity such as hardly exists in other countries. These young men are filled with the consciousness of their high calling [and] in the eyes of many . . . represent the future hope of Russia (ibid.: 119–20).

The students realised that their position in Russian society was that of *Kulturträger*: those responsible for learning, disseminating and implementing western ideas. Many developed a deep respect for learning, even a passion. But, as they assimilated more and more of western thought they moved further and further away from the culture of the Russian people. Students compensated for this isolation by forming intellectual discussion circles through which they were able to develop a sense of identity (Raeff, 1966). The students were, in a sense, cast adrift and had to find refuge. 'Where then is our refuge?' asked Belinsky. 'On a desert island which was our *kruzhok* [circle]' (quoted in Malia, 1966: 65).

Friendship ties are always more important for young persons than adults since in the former case 'the social roles and relationships of maturity are being added to or substituted for those appropriate to the family of orientation' (Du Bois, 1974: 23). But friendship ties in the form of the *kruzhok* assumed special importance in organising the activities of Russian students because formal, legal institutions which could have performed the same functions were by and large outlawed by the government (cf. Boissevain, 1974: 170). Just how great the need for association was among Russian students can be appreciated from a review of their frenzied organising activities during the brief liberal interlude which began Alexander II's reign.

Nicholas had treated the students like 'raw army recruits' (Mathes, 1968: 29) but Alexander, faced with humiliating defeat in the Crimean War, acknowledged that reform was a dire necessity if Russia wished to be a great power. In the early, relatively liberal years of his reign the paralysing system of controls over student life was consequently relaxed. The students responded by associating, by creating various institutions which bound them even closer together than did the circles. Loan banks were formed to help the growing number of needy students; public meetings became regular affairs; in St Petersburg a student court was established; student libraries were organised; student journals were published. The students thus welded themselves into a solidary body, and the organisational lessons they learned were not lost to them when, a few years later, the government again outlawed many of these forms of association.

Student discontent first emerged because the students' elevated sense of dignity was insulted. At the Alexandrovsky Lycée — an elite 'high school' and 'junior college' — a collective protest was staged as early as 1838 when a student was confined to a punishment cell after refusing to have his long hair cut; the first university demonstrations occurred in Moscow in the mid-1850s because a party had been arbitrarily raided by the police; the boycott was used shortly afterward to protest against unqualified and incompetent teachers who were awarded chairs for twenty-five years without a probationary period and subsequently received pensioned, five-year reappointments (Brower, 1975: 95; Mathes, 1968: 34). Anything which offended students' honour and sense of intellectual purpose became an issue worthy of protest. Since such attitudes were most widespread among children of the nobility, the institutions first to develop traditions of dissent were, as Brower has shown, those with the highest percentage of children from that class: the first signs of discontent which appeared in the Lycée in the late 1830s spread to the universities in the 1850s and only in the following decade reached the professional schools where commoners formed a majority of the student body. But once the commoners were provided with a model for dissent they became not only the 'cutting edge . . . of the socialist intelligentsia' (Pomper, 1970: 63) but the muscle which swung the scythe (Brym, 1977d).

The students' timidity was in the process of disappearing when, in the late 1850s, the government decided to put an end to the first signs of discontent by reimposing restraints on university life. Some students were expelled, many were placed under police supervision while outside the university walls, restrictions were placed on admissions and, by 1861, all student organisations were abolished. All this served only to inflame student opinion, which was further aggravated when the sorry terms of serf emancipation were announced. Militancy and politicisation of the student body followed, soon erupting into the widespread street rallies and demonstrations of 1861. This was the first major outbreak of student discontent in Russia. And it established an important cyclical pattern which was to persist for the next half century.

Control over educational institutions was in the hands of government ministries which shifted back and forth from mildly liberal to conservative policies, with the latter eventually winning out (Morison, 1968). But the conservative policies of the government involved the use of moderately repressive anti-student measures. And since, as the Tillys (1975: 244) have suggested, there is a curvilinear relationship between government repression and the mobilisation of already solidary groups for collective action and collective violence, a cycle of student unrest was established.[8]

Militancy and politicisation would in the future grow with government repression, as it had in 1861; and it would blossom as hope for genuine reform dwindled, as disappointment with serf emancipation demonstrated (Johnson, 1950: 151, 176–82; Mathes, 1968: 45). Student radicalism was, then, fuelled by mainly political forces which were quite independent of those which sparked peasant and working class unrest — a fact the ideological significance of which will be appreciated only when we deal with the student disturbances of 1901 in the following chapter.

In an unfree university the various student associations formed what one participant in the Moscow student movement called a 'small island of freedom' (Khersakov, 1952: 230). These associations eventually gave birth to what Brower terms a 'school of dissent' consisting of radical discussion circles, communes and *artels* (workers' co-operatives) which sought to create in miniature form the egalitarian society envisaged for all of Russia. This school of dissent constituted a fully formed social institution by the early 1870s. In preceding decades student radicals very often stopped being radicals once they stopped being students (Brower, 1975: 142–3). But the subsequent formation of a social institution aimed specifically at producing radicals permitted many students to refuse such job opportunities as existed. Because they had formed strong ties with one institution (the school of dissent), the 'pull' of other institutions (in the form of employment opportunities following graduation) was often no longer able to deradicalise them. If in the 1840s intellectual radicalism was a reflection only of the paucity of employment opportunities allowing the unfettered espousal of middle-class view points; and if in the 1860s and 1870s an over-supply of educated men and women exacerbated the situation; then, beginning in the 1870s, the school of dissent actually began to employ *déclassé* radicals. I use the term 'employ' advisedly and literally. For Russian *intelligenty* were able to articulate an occupational role specially suited to the structure of constraints within which they were forced to live. They became 'professional revolutionaries' — a role developed only in the 1870s and destined to have a short fifty-year life span.

ii. Jewish Revolutionaries

The pattern sketched above certainly held true for the Jewish youths who began to enter the Russian school system in significant numbers in the 1860s. Virtually all the Jewish radicals of that decade for whom information is available were deradicalised once they found employment following graduation (Cherikover, 1939: 90, 92). By the 1870s, however, the Jewish professional revolutionary had taken his place beside his Gentile comrade. More than this: over the next thirty-five years the Jews became the predominant element in the intelligentsia. This is demonstrated by Fig. 3. In 1875 Jewish participation in the revolutionary movement was lower than the proportion of Jews in the general population of the Empire. By 1905 it was over nine times higher: Jews constituted some 37 per cent of all political arrests in that year and, according to the 1897 census, just over 4 per cent of the population.

To what can the high rate of Jewish participation be attributed? A frequently-entertained argument is that exposure to the Jewish prophetic and messianic tradition was a causal factor of decisive importance: the Jews, it is held, were predisposed to accept radical secular doctrines because they were steeped in radical religious ones. But there are at least two problems with this view. First, as we have seen, many Jewish *intelligenty* were highly assimilated and did not have the kind of background which is often attributed to them: from what we know of the upbringing of, say, Kamenev and Zinoviev, it is implausible to claim (as does Billington, 1966: 74) that their passionate attachment to Marxism was merely a secularised expression of some underlying Jewish prophetic sentiment or messianic expectation. Second, as Billington himself demonstrates at great length, messianism was at least as important an element in Russian as it was in Jewish culture. If messianism exerted much influence on rates of radicalism (which I doubt), it cannot therefore account for a higher rate among Jews (cf. McCagg, 1972–3).

A more plausible, if less colourful explanation is provided by Yankele Kovner, quoted in this section's frontispiece. The fact that Jews entered the Russian educational system in disproportionately large numbers was at least part of the reason for their high rate of radicalism. As early as 1804 Jews were permitted entry into the system, but it was only in the 1860s that enrolment increased significantly. There is very little question in the serious historical literature as to why this turnabout occurred.[9] In 1861 a law was brought into effect which has been called the 'emancipation manifesto of the Russian-Jewish intelligentsia' (Slutzky, 1960: 224). As part of the government's Jewish policy the right to live outside the Pale was bestowed on Jews with a higher education. This provided Jewish youths with the opportunity and the incentive to move out of the Jewish community and into the Russian middle class. At the same time, for reasons outlined in Chapter 4, wealthy and assimilating Jews were anxious to spread 'enlightenment' among their co-religionists so that aspiring students were frequently awarded subsidies for their studies. Thus, by 1877, nearly 200 of the 300 Jewish students in universities and professional schools received cash grants (Cherikover, 1939: 111).

Spurred on by shifts in the structure of educational opportunities young Jews entered the Russian school system in increasing numbers in the following decades. As Fig. 8 indicates, there were in 1864 some 129 Jewish university students (3.1 per cent of the entire university student body), 556 in 1880 (6.8 per cent) and 1,857 by 1886 (14.3 per cent). (In 1886 there were also 380 Jews in professional schools, or 6.2 per cent of the total, and 14,438 in gymnasia, or 9.3 per cent of the total; see *Evreyskaya . . .*, 1969–71 [1930–]: vol. 13, 58; Trotzky in Frumkin *et al.*, 1966: 412.)

Until 1887 the growing ratio of Jewish students to the total number of

Fig. 8. Jews in Russian Universities, 1864–1907

	number	% of total
1864	129	3.1
1880	556	6.8
1886	1,857	14.4
1894		6.2
1902	1,250	7.0
1907	4,266	12.1

Sources: Compiled from data in (Alston, 1969: 280; Slutzky, 1960: 228; Trotzky in Frumkin *et al.*, 1966: 413).
Note: See Technical Appendix.

students appears to have been roughly equal to the ratio of Jewish radicals to the total number of radicals. This suggests that there were so many Jewish radicals simply because large numbers of Jews were located within the hothouse of Russian radicalism — the university system. But in 1887–8, as part of the general anti-Semitic reaction, the infamous quota system was introduced, restricting Jewish enrolment in secondary and advanced schools to 10 per cent of the student body in the Pale, 5 per cent in other provinces and 3 per cent in St Petersburg and Moscow. From 1886 to 1902 the number of Jews as a percentage of all Russian university students consequently decreased from 14.4 per cent to 7.0 per cent. And in the period 1887 to 1905 the rate of radicalism among Jews increased by nearly 24 per cent, as can be seen in Fig. 3. This indicates that Yankele Kovner's reasoning is only in part correct, for it was not education *per se* which radicalised the Jews but their actual and anticipated degree of class embeddedness. If before 1887 they were radicalised in disproportionately large numbers because they were over-represented in institutions which, for reasons discussed above, contained persons very poorly integrated in the middle class, then the *numerus clausus* radicalised even more Jews because it effectively threatened to block the entry of many more into that class. (Significantly, the rate of Jewish radicalism appears to have fallen somewhat after 1905 or so — i.e., when enrolment rates rose substantially. Compare Figs. 3 and 8.)

In fact, the quota system was only one aspect of the widespread anti-Semitism which exerted such a painful, cramping effect on mobility patterns. The pogroms of 1881 and 1903 were, as is well known, directly responsible for radicalising many Jews, from a social-psychological point of view, instilling in them bitter hatred of a society capable of such excesses and, from a structural point of view, indicating that the society was unable and unwilling to absorb them. Equally effective was the discrimination so pervasive in every aspect of life. Julius Martov, who witnessed the 1881 pogroms in Odessa as a child, felt that anti-Semitism existed only in 'a more civilised form' in St Petersburg, where his family moved (Martov, 1923: 14). The 'natural contempt' of schoolmates and teachers alike for a member of an 'inferior race' was, as Martov himself realised, of considerable importance in causing him to rebel against school authorities and, later, against society as a whole. Such cases were so numerous that only the one example need be cited. Indeed, they were so numerous that, as Grigori Aronson (1961: 9–10) wrote, it is difficult to imagine how a Jewish student could *not* become a radical.

From the 1860s to the 1890s Jewish radicals coming from Russian and Jewish schools joined the various segments of the revolutionary movement with no *known* relationship between their families' degree of embeddedness in the Jewish community on the one hand and party affiliation on the other.[10] But the turn of the century witnessed the creation of a definite fork on the road to radicalism. Jeremy Boissevain has written that 'in a situation of conflict persons will attempt to define the situation and align themselves in such a way that the least possible damage is done to their basic values and to their important personal relations' (1974: 50). It was largely in accordance with this principle that relatively assimilated students who attended Russian gymnasia and *Realschulen* formed circles which eventually served as a recruitment base for the Bolshevik and Menshevik parties, while relatively unassimilated students who attended Jewish schools (*kheders* and *yeshivas*) formed circles which eventually provided much of the intellectual membership of the Bundist and Poalei-Zionist parties: 'similar souls', as John Mill noted in his memoirs, 'discover each other easily' (1946: vol. 1, 25; cf. Adams, 1967; Chambliss, 1965; Kadushin, 1966; Secord and Backman, 1964).

One path to radicalism began, then, in the Russian gymnasium or *Realschule* and tended to lead to the Bolshevik and Menshevik parties. There is virtual unanimity in the memoir literature concerning the character of these institutions. Staffed by petty, bureaucratic types, who exercised strict and arbitrary disciplinary power within their satraps, secondary schools generally bored and frustrated students rather than offering them a sound education. This appears to have been especially the case in gymnasia where classical languages were emphasised; and especially for the brightest pupils. It is surprising that so many of the brightest pupils — who, as in other cases (Hampden-Turner, 1970: 414 ff.), appear to have contributed a disproportionately large number of recruits to the intelligentsia — actually managed to win gold and silver medals for academic excellence rather than give up their studies. Actually, the latter sometimes did occur. Thus, Mikhail Beltman recalled how 'I did not want to fill my head with university nonsense and decided to go on my way' (*Deyateli* . . ., n.d. [1927–9?]: pt. 2, 103).

Because the schools were unable to offer many students an education relevant to their lives the students had, as Mill put it, to 'rely on our own powers and talents and to discover our own paths' to maturity (1946: vol.

1, 24). Bored students thus formed *kruzhok*s in order to read and discuss foreign literature, social philosophy and political economy. First exposures to radical thought normally came about because a student in the *kruzhok* was connected to a person — a father, uncle, brother or former private tutor — who had at one point been a radical or at least read and appreciated radical literature (cf. Wildman, 1960). These students introduced such literature into the *kruzhok*, where it was eagerly consumed. Acts of rebellion against oppressive school authorities soon followed.

For those who managed to enter universities or professional schools later radical activities often represented a development of tendencies originating earlier. Such students crystallised their ideological outlooks and joined political parties not just in Russia, but also in the student 'colonies' in the west. Due to the *numerus clausus* many Jewish students were forced to leave Russia in order to attend institutions of higher learning in Switzerland, Germany and, to a lesser extent, France. Others left because they, like non-Jewish radicals, were attracted to the relative freedom of the west or because they were in trouble with authorities at home. By 1907 some 2,343 Russians attended Swiss universities alone: 34.2 per cent of the entire student body of that country (Senn, 1971: 6; see also Grinfeld, 1918; Meijer, 1955). It is not known exactly how many of these were Jews, but contemporaries (e.g., Mill, 1946: vol. 1, 163–200) make it clear that their number was very large indeed, perhaps 15 per cent or more of the entire student body (Marmor, 1959: vol. 1, 295). Whether in Zurich or Moscow it was for many but a short step from student politics to membership in radical parties.

The second path to radicalism was followed by those who attended *kheder*s and *yeshiva*s, failed entrance examinations for Russian secondary schools and advanced institutions of study, or who were in the process of preparing for such examinations. Although, as always, there were individual exceptions, these persons were usually less assimilated than those who managed to enter the Russian school system with relative ease. In fact, lack of familiarity with the Russian language was the main barrier, aside from the *numerus clausus*, blocking their admittance.

Conditions in the Jewish schools, and especially the *kheder*s, were far from pleasant. Teaching methods were primitive and discipline enforced with a cat-o'-three-tails. As late as the turn of the century, classrooms were normally located in the teachers' living quarters, although it was not uncommon to house *kheder*s in buildings which served in the night as sleeping quarters for indigent migrants (*hegdeshe*s) or even in huts attached to cemeteries where bodies were prepared for burial. Physical conditions were insufferable even in the *kheder*s of such relatively wealthy Jewish communities as Odessa. And the long hours of study gave the student few skills which might enable him to gain employment upon graduation unless he was able to find one of the decreasing number of jobs in the Jewish educational system (Evreyskago . . ., 1904: vol. 2, 284–312).

An attempt was made by Reb Israel Salanter (1803–83), founder of the Musar *yeshiva*s, to adjust to modern conditions by combining some amount of secular study with the traditional regimen (Menes in Frumkin *et al.*, 1966: 397 ff.). Little wonder that students in these institutions were particularly susceptible to the teachings of the liberal Jewish enlightenment, or *haskala*, which very often served as a bridge to more radical ideas (e.g, Loim, 1919). Similarly, the state-run Jewish Teacher Training Institutes in Vilna and Zhitomir were hotbeds of radicalism since the 1870s since they exposed students to secular ideas (Tzitron, 1921–2: vol. 2, 111 ff.). The same boredom and arbitrary exercise of authority afflicted these students as did those in other educational institutions. One student in the Vilna Institute in the 1870s summed up well a situation which was widespread and enduring when he wrote in a notebook accidentally seized by an instructor: '*Malo nauki, mnogo muki*' ('Little science, much suffering') (Cahan, 1969 [1926–31]: 126).

In Jewish schools, too, the formation of circles (here called *kreizlekh* rather than *kruzhok*s) went hand in hand with rebellion against school authorities. If an attempt was made by those unfamiliar with the Russian language to gain a higher education it was necessary to join the growing pool of *extern*s: those preparing to write entrance examinations for Russian schools. These structurally blocked students—'intellectual"*sansculottes*" and *"déclassés"'* Chaim Weizmann called them in one letter (1968–76: vol. 4, 206; also vol. 2, 298) — formed an excellent breeding ground for radicalism. Preparing for entrance examinations was a long and arduous task often lasting several years and often ending in disappointment. In the interim the *extern* eked out a bare existence by tutoring the children of the well-to-do. He had a great deal of time on his hands for reading — and revolutionary activity, which he accurately perceived as his only real opportunity in life (Zinger, 1944: 38–9). Of course, radical *extern*s did their best to infect others with the revolutionary bacillus.

In common with most other radical students they did not, however, entertain any illusions about their ability to overthrow the old regime unaided. The often trying search for an historical agent, a group of which these relatively unattached *intelligenty* could become a part, was on.

C. Reclassification

Leon Trotsky: It's about time we started.
Grigory Sokolovsky: Yes, it's about time.
Trotsky: But how?
Sokolovsky: That's it, how?
Trotsky: We must find workers, not wait for anybody or ask anybody, but just find workers, and set to it.

a conversation in Nicolaev, 1894

i. Temporal Availability

The Russian intelligentsia first found its attention drawn to the peasantry by the increasingly numerous *jacqueries* which swept the countryside in the years preceding Emancipation, the public controversies regarding the form which Emancipation should take and the sheer misery of the bulk of the Empire's population. Efforts to go 'to the people' failed, however, because 'the people' on whom the *narodnik*s pinned their hopes remained politically quiescent; and because government agents effectively stamped out whatever the radicals kindled. In the 1870s there began a mass exodus from the countryside back to the cities (Wortman, 1967: 27): many *intelligenty*, who 'saw clearly that our work among the people was of no avail' (Figner, 1968 [1927]: 63), decided that it was less realistic to go to the people than to go it alone. The intelligentsia thus turned to terrorism. But here, too, they met with little success, for government repression following the assasination of Alexander II in 1881 dealt a blow to the terrorists from which they were never able fully to recover.

Only on one class of 'the people' had the radicals made an impact: industrial workers. Already by the late 1870s this perplexing fact was beginning to produce considerable inconsistency between the ideological pronouncements and the practical accomplishments of at least some populists. By the early 1880s, in the midst of what Richard Wortman (1967) calls 'the crisis of Russian populism', Georgi Plekhanov, the 'father of Russian Marxism', suggested that the efforts of the intelligentsia might more evenly be divided between peasants and workers since 'we cannot determine beforehand from what classes of the working population the main cadres of the social-revolutionary army will be recruited when the hour of the economic overturn strikes' (quoted in Yarmolinsky, 1962 [1956]: 225). A decade later large numbers of *intelligenty*, including Plekhanov himself, felt certain that the agent of revolution could indeed be determined beforehand. They had become Marxists and therefore upheld the view that the industrial working class, not the peasantry, was the only force capable of creating the new order.[11]

In an area so subject to controversy as the study of pre-revolutionary Russia one cannot help but feel somewhat relieved over the fact that little disagreement appears to exist concerning the principle forces which occasioned the shift from populism to Marxism. On the one hand, populism had failed; on the other, the working class appeared on the historical scene. The famine which began in the 1890s revealed the bankruptcy of the autocracy and the helplessness of the peasantry against the vagaries of the capitalist economy (Haimson, 1955: 51). A depression at the end of the decade demonstrated the cruel regularity of the business cycle. These crises required explanation: the populists' belief that Russia would advance to socialism without passing through a period of capitalist development proved groundless. Peter Garvi captured well the mood of the intelligentsia when he later recalled how he decided at this point to fight against this system of injustice, exploitation and hunger! These feelings, these thoughts, I repeat, floated then in the air. Marxist 'training' could give meaning to the surrounding reality and offer a way out of this dark pit. This way out read: to the workers (1946: 16)!

In preceding decades the intelligentsia had been inspired by the call 'to the people'. But the 1890s, a decade of heavy foreign investment and rapid industrial expansion, witnessed a mounting wave of industrial unrest which demanded that the old slogan be revised. Massive strikes, particularly in Yaroslavl (Haimson, 1955: 51) and St Petersburg (Struve, 1934–5: 71–2), confirmed the hopes and expectations of those who adhered to the new credo. It was above all else 'the appearance of a new exploited class of workers [which] called forth a different orientation' on the part of the intelligentsia (Gordon, 1941: 21). In the 1880s, the intelligentsia had been beaten into submission by the regime. In the 1890s, many *intelligenty*, having given up hope of influencing the peasantry, began to forge concrete social ties with industrial workers. A 'Marxist craze', as Victor Chernov enviously put it, swept the educated youth.

Industrial unrest was not restricted to Yaroslavl, located to the northeast of Moscow, and St Petersburg, in the middle of European Russia. Strikes, the establishment of social ties between workers and *intelligenty*, and ideological reorientations on the part of the latter were also evident in the southwest, as the conversation between Trotsky and Sokolovsky, quoted in the frontispiece, indicates. The same was true in the northwest, where most Jewish workers were located. As I suggested in Chapter 2, the Jewish community was in the process of decomposition in the nineteenth century. By mid-century it had reached a stage of social differentiation where workers' interests no longer coincided with those of other segments of the community. Employment in small factories was beginning; the journeyman's hope that he might one day become a master craftsman began to recede as opportunities for such advancement were closed off; and the ranks of the artisan stratum swelled as former petty merchants became proletarianised. The strike movement which began among Jewish workers in the early 1870s thus reached major proportions in the 1880s and especially the 1890s (Menes, 1939). In consequence, there were few Jewish populists left in the Pale by the early 1890s (Kopelson in Dimanshtein, 1930: 78; Litvak, 1945: 203).

Since most historians agree that the major force underlying the intelligentsia's turn to Marxism was the emergence of a militant working class it may seem somewhat paradoxical from a theoretical point of view that many of these same scholars often argue that some *intelligenty* (especially the Bolsheviks) imposed their ideologies on workers. For in the former case ideology formation in social movements is viewed as a process which occurs 'from the bottom up', while in the latter case ideologies appear to flow 'from the top down'. Sociologists, too, have entertained such apparently paradoxical ideas. Followers of Robert Michels like to argue that even in socialist parties ideological and organisational control tends to rest in the hands of a thin stratum of *intelligenty* due to the operation of an 'iron law of oligarchy'. Others, such as Alvin Gouldner (1955), emphasise the operation of an 'iron law of democracy' according to which organisational demands and ideas flow in the opposite direction. These two views are not, I suggest, quite so contradictory as is often maintained. They simply stress different aspects of a complex interaction process about which we know very little. In this section I want to begin discussing the interaction process by focusing on the upward flow of ideas.

Earlier I outlined some of the major reasons why many nineteenth-century Russian intellectuals were superfluous or redundant in terms of the job opportunities available to them. In a sense, this caused them to hang suspended between classes: they had left their class of origin yet were unable to become embedded in the Russian middle class. Subsequent radicalisation transformed them into a social stratum '*shopping* for an historical agent' (Gouldner, 1975–6: 8). For the intelligentsia, as Trotsky once noted, '[d]eprived of any independent significance in social production, small in numbers, economically dependent, . . . rightly conscious of its own powerlessness, keeps looking for a massive social class upon which it can lean' (1971 [1909]: 58). In other words, *intelligenty*, because they were *déclassé*, sought to form concrete social ties with another class or to 'reclassify' themselves. Having become radicals they endeavoured to find a vehicle capable of giving vent to their discontent. Reclassification brought relief from their sense of isolation and uselessness. Change the word 'village' to 'factory' in the following remark by a populist of the 1870s and it could have been uttered by any Marxist *intelligent* of the 1890s: '[E]very moment we felt that we were needed, that we were not superfluous. It was this consciousness of one's usefulness that was the magnetic force which drew our Russian youth into the village' (Figner, 1968 [1927]: 60).

It stands to reason that the availability of social movements in one's environment structured opportunities for the formation of new class ties (cf. Weiss, 1963). And since the character of these mass movements varied over time and place, the practical problems which the intelligentsia had to confront called forth a wide range of ideological responses which varied accordingly. We have already seen how the temporal availability of the working-class movement helped bring about a significant ideological transformation from populism to Marxism. In the remainder of this section I shall outline the problem of availability from a regional standpoint. The picture concerning both aspects of reclassification will then be elaborated in the following chapter.

ii. *Regional Availability*

The manner in which the regional availability of social movements helped shape the ideologies of *intelligenty* is well illustrated by the careers of the pioneer Bundists. It will be recalled that the pioneers were quite assimilated: the mean degree of embeddedness of their families of orientation in the Russian class structure was 2.9, almost exactly the same as the Mensheviks'. The question therefore arose as to why the pioneers should have developed an ideology with Jewish-nationalist overtones, while the Mensheviks were almost all anti-Jewish nationalist. The answer, I submit, — or at least the major part of it — is that the spontaneously-developing Jewish workers' movement was responsible for the re-crystallisation of Jewish identity on the part of the pioneers.

The idea of propagandising among Jewish workers scarcely occurred to Jewish *intelligenty* during the populist era. (See, however, Sapir, 1938; Kirzhnitz in Dimanshtein, 1930: 206–37 for exceptions.) As one *narodnik* recalled, '[w]e were all convinced assimilationists' (M. Vinchevsky, quoted in Goldhagen, 1974: 484). Nor could it have been otherwise. For in order to conceive of propagandising among Jewish workers it was necessary to believe that the latter were indeed capable of radical action. But this became readily apparent only with the growth of the strike movement in the final decades of the nineteenth century.

The strike movement, as one early Bundist remarked, 'had to attract the attention of the revolutionary and especially of the Marxist *intelligenty* and bring them closer to earth, to the real life of the Jewish worker' (Peskin, 1939: 548). However, in order for the assimilated pioneers to forge ties with Jewish workers they had to undergo radical changes in their thinking. Specifically, they came to the conclusion that their old strategy of 'propaganda' ought to be replaced by what they termed 'agitation'. The earlier propaganda strategy had involved 'developing cadres for the *Russian* revolutionary movement and acquainting them with *Russian* culture' (Kopelson in Dimanshtein, 1930: 71; my emphasis) — in short, acquainting workers with the rudiments of natural science, history, Russian language, political economy and socialist theory in order that they might become part of the larger movement. But given the limited human and material resources of the *intelligenty* and the inherent difficulties bound up with having artisans attend study and discussion circles after an exhausting thirteen to sixteen hour working-day, this involved the training of only a small number of labour 'aristocrats' (Gozhansky in Dimanshtein, 1930: 81–2; Martov, 1923: 144). Moreover, the propaganda strategy had the unintended consequence of producing educated workers who wanted to leave their class (and therefore the class struggle) in order to become master craftsmen or 'worker-*intelligenty*' concentrating their efforts on cultural matters.

The growth of the strike movement offered the pioneers the opportunity to overcome these problems by extending their activities among what they called the 'broad masses'. And this in turn led to the development of the notion that the Jewish worker could play an *independent* role in the Social

Democratic movement.[12] The seeds were thus sown for the creation of Bundist ideology. The new policy of agitation was aimed at encouraging the workers' fight for better working conditions and higher wages in the expectation that political demands would eventually grow out of the economic struggle. But working among the 'broad masses' was not without its problems, the most conspicuous of which was that the average worker knew no Russian while the pioneers knew next to no Yiddish. The pioneers therefore had to learn Yiddish and to recruit former *yeshiva* students and *externs*, who knew not only the language but also Jewish life as 'insiders', as a bridge to the workers (Litvak in *Roiter pinkas* . . ., 1921–4: vol. 1, 5–30; Mill, 1946: vol. 1, 106–8) — which, incidentally, explains the difference between the social origins of pioneers and later recruits to the Bund noted in Fig. 7. Exigencies created by the strike movement thus caused the pioneers to adopt a new strategy which involved sinking roots in the Jewish working class; and this set in motion an extended process whereby the pioneers' ethnic identity was recrystallised. As Henry Tobias notes, by '1892 . . . ethnic identification had proceeded to the point where one could claim to fight as a Jew along with other nationalities without apology — and the intellectuals were willing to accept that proposition' (1972: 32). In following years threats posed and attacks launched by other groups — notably the Polish Socialist Party and the left-Zionists — forced the pioneers to develop an even stronger sense of ethnic identity. But these forces merely accelerated a more fundamental and chronologically prior process: the Jewish working class itself was the major force underlying the pioneers' becoming Jews again. As ties between the relatively assimilated pioneers and the workers hardened, so did the pioneers' sense of being Jewish. One *intelligent* explained it well when he wrote in 1895 that 'life itself forced us to change our tactics . . . [B]y placing the mass movement at the centre of our programme we had to adapt our propaganda and agitation to the mass, i.e., to make them more Jewish' (Martov, 1922 [1895]: 85).

Of the thirteen pioneers eight were born in the province of Vilna while the others were born in the neighbouring Lithuanian provinces of Grodno and Kovno. Their reclassification occured in the city of Vilna, the centre of a region where the overwhelming majority of Jewish workers were located. Such pioneers as Arkady Kremer, Motl Srednitzky and Isai Izenshtat had earlier been active in the Russian movement in the interior of the Empire. But the police had them sent back to their home town under supervision. Had they been able to remain in St Petersburg they would in all likelihood have become Mensheviks since they would have been able to attach themselves only to Russian workers. In Vilna, however, the most numerous and vigorous section of the working class was Jewish. When in the 1890s the opportunity to become attached to these workers presented itself, the three radicals took advantage of it. In spite of the fact that they were relatively assimilated, the availability of social movements in their immediate social environment led them to take their first steps toward the creation of Bundism.

This process was by no means restricted to the pioneers. Vladimir Medem, Ilya Vilenkin and Yakov Kaplan were also assimilated Jews (although Kaplan less so than the others; see Medem, 1923; Hertz, 1956–8: vol. 1, 256–8, 316–18). They pursued their studies and their revolutionary activities in the city of Kiev until apprehended by the police. The police proceeded to supervise the radicals' return to their home town of Minsk, another Jewish workers enclave. If they had been able to remain in Kiev they, too, might have joined the Menshevik party; but circumstances led them to become Bundists. Medem, who had been baptised at birth in the Russian Orthodox church, noted in his memoirs that a 'major factor' in his becoming a Jew again was 'the direct influence of the Jewish workers' movement' (Medem, 1923: vol. 1, 175). Actually, this was probably the decisive influence.

The dynamic analysed above also worked in reverse. Before the creation of the Bund in 1897, the pioneers had formed an organisation known as the Group of Jewish Social Democrats in Russia, or simply the Vilna Group. Since they viewed themselves at this early stage as no more than an adjunct of the general Russian movement the pioneers trained and supplied a host of radicals for centres outside the northern provinces of the Pale (Wildman, 1972). Significantly, 'the majority of the activists who arrived in the South no longer returned to the Jewish labor movement, but remained in the general Social Democratic movement' (Mishkinski, 1969: 39–40). Even someone like Lyuba Axelrod-Ortodoks, the daughter of a Vilna rabbi, could become a Menshevik after leaving the northern Pale. In doing so she followed a well-worn path taken by Emil Abramovich, Nikolai Vigdorchik, Boris Ginzburg (Kon *et al.*, 1927–31: vol. 5, 5–7, 42–4, 796–9, 1261–7) and, according to a leading worker in the Bund, 'many others' (Tzoglin in Dimanshtein, 1930: 145). One of these others was Boris Gorev (Gorev, 1924; Levin, 1976), whose brother, Mark Liber, although from similar social origins, remained behind in Vilna and became a leading Bundist. Another was Julius Martov who, after leaving Vilna, became the leader of the Menshevik party (Kremer in *Arkady* . . ., 1942: 367–71; Martov, 1923: 129–85). The fact that workers with certain characteristics (to be discussed in greater detail below) were located predominantly in the northern Pale made that area — and only that area — a Bund stronghold. Moving into the region could make one a Bundist, moving out could make one something else.

In most cases the cultural orientations developed as a child, in consequence of one's degree of embeddedness in the Russian class structure, coincided with the ideological requiremeñs imposed by available sections of the workers movement. For example, those who developed a strong sense of Jewish identity were normally located in areas where they could attach themselves to Jewish workers while those who viewed themselves as Russians tended to be situated in regions where a strong Russian workers movement was available. On the other hand, the character of available movements sometimes did not 'fit' one's ideological propensities. In such cases, a number of which were mentioned above, ideologies were often accommodated to the demands imposed by available movements; and, if more than one movement were available, the *intelligent* tended to join the one most congenial to his cultural standards. This does not mean that radicals' ideologies were so plastic that coming into contact with a different type of worker necessarily resulted in the transformation of ideological viewpoints. To be sure, such transformations did occur, particularly when the differences between the various movements were not yet fully articulated and when one's own ideology was not yet fully crystallised. When these conditions obtained it was not even necessary, in order for ideological accomodation to occur, that *intelligenty* be forced (by, say, police supervision) to remain in areas where the degree of fit was low. Most often ideological accommodation could occur slowly and imperceptibly precisely because ideologies were not yet fully crystallised. But since *intelligenty* were to some degree geographically mobile (this was of course less true from the Pale to points outside than for points within the Pale) they could, if the disjuncture between their initial orientations and the ideological requirements of local work were great, move to locations where the character of mass movements more closely fit their ideological propensities. The 1906 decision on the part of a group of top Poalei-Zion *intelligenty* to move from Poltava in the Ukraine (where there were next to no Jewish workers) to Vilna in Lithuania (where there were many) is only the most striking example of the lengths to which radicals would go in order to achieve this fit (Zerubavel, 1938: 63). There were, then, three ways in which the reclassification process combined with the classification process to produce ideologies. First, the ideological consequences of both aspects of embedding could coincide. Second, there could be poor fit between the two processes and a low degree of ideological crystallisation, in which case the ideological impact of reclassification prevailed to a large degree over the impact of classification.[13] And third, poor fit could, particularly if the level of ideological crystallisation were high, result in movement, the purpose of which was to achieve closer fit.[14]

This analysis, which has focused on the question of ethnic identity, suggests that if we are to gain an adequate understanding of the ideology formation process in general, it is first necessary to find out where *intelligenty* were recruited to the Social Democratic movement and then outline those regional variations in the character of the working class in Russia which had an impact on their ideologies. In the remainder of this chapter I shall merely describe these variations; the ideological consequences for *intelligenty* of being embedded in different segments of the working class will be discussed in the following chapter.

First, the problem of recruitment. Fig. 9 cross-classifies data on (a)

Fig. 9. Reclassification: *Intelligenty* by Party and Region of Recruitment
(%)

region	party			
	Bolshevik (n = 19)	Menshevik (n = 24)	Bund (n = 89)	Poalei-Zion (n = 46)
Northern Pale (excl. Minsk)	10.5	8.3	59.6	28.3
Minsk province	0	0	13.5	28.3
Southern Pale	21.1	45.8	18.0	39.1
Provinces outside Pale and west of St Petersburg-Astrakhan line	21.1	22.9	9.0	3.2
Provinces east of St Petersburg-Astrakhan line	47.4	22.9	0	1.1
total	100.1	99.9	100.1	100.0

Notes: (a) For sources and method of construction, see Technical Appendix.

　　(b) $x^2 = 86.3$, sig. at $< \cdot 001$, d.f. $= 12$.

where *intelligenty* in my sample first became party members; and (b) which party they joined. The data clearly reveal substantively and statistically significant differences with respect to the regional basis of recruitment — and this despite the fact that the operationalisation of the independent variable is rather crude. (Ideally one would want information on the type of worker with whom each *intelligenty* tended to be engaged in radical activities, and not merely on the type of worker most conspicuous in his region of recruitment. Limitations on the quality of my data necessitate this roundabout solution to the measurement problem and thus some information loss. See, for example, Aronson, 1961: 47 ff.).

　　The comments made above about the Bund being restricted largely to the northern Pale are borne out by Fig. 9. Over 73 per cent of the Bundists in my sample were recruited to their party in the north (including the province of Minsk; see map, Fig. 10) and only 18 per cent in the south. In contrast, Poalei-Zionism appears to have been much more of a southern phenomenon, with nearly 40 per cent of the party's *intelligenty* having been recruited in that region and just over 56 per cent in the north (including Minsk).

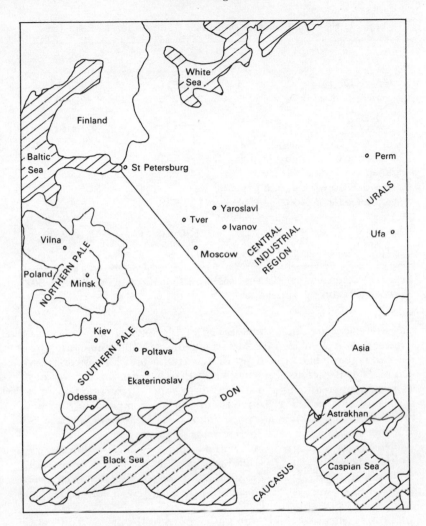

Fig. 10. European Russia

Notes: (a) Regions are indicated by capitals and solid lines.
   (b) Scale: 1 inch = 333 miles; 1 cm. = 222 km.

What Jewish workers in the two regions had in common we already know: 90 per cent of them were employed in small artisans' workshops and the remainder in small unmechanised factories; the vast majority worked in ethnically homogeneous establishments; and virtually all were employed by fellow Jews. The relevant differences between Jewish workers in

Fig. 11. Selected Statistics on Social Composition of Pale, 1897

	north	south
a. Jewish workers	173,978	207,148
b. Jewish non-workers	228,724	363,625
ratio a:b	0.76:1.00	0.54:1.00
c. Jewish workers and persons engaged in personal service	244,662	306,733
d. non-Jewish workers and persons engaged in personal service	105,938	1,030,267
ratio c:d	2.30:1.00	0.30:1.00

Sources: Compiled from data in (Rashin, 1954: 164; Rubinow, 1907: 502).
Note: See Technical Appendix.

the two regions are summarised in Fig. 11. These differences concern the relative weight of the Jewish proletariat in the class and ethnic structure of the two regions. The ratio of Jewish workers to Jewish non-workers was considerably higher in the northern Pale than in the south (in 1897, 0. 76: 1. 00 as compared to 0.54 : 1.00). And the ratio of Jewish to non-Jewish workers was higher still (2.30 : 1. 00 in the north as compared to 0. 30 : 1. 00 in the south). The Ukrainian city of Poltava—home town of Ber Borokhov and Yitzkhak Ben-Tzvi and therefore the single most important source of Poalei-Zionist ideology—was 'without industry and without a proletariat' (Ben-Tzvi, 1956: 14) and thus represents an extreme case. But, generally speaking, Poalei-Zionism was stronger than Bundism where Jewish workers were fewer in proportion to both Jewish non-workers and non-Jewish workers.

Further evidence of this relationship is provided by the 'deviant' case of Minsk province. Although located in the northern Pale, Minsk appears to have been a more important recruitment base for the Poalei-Zionist than the Bundist party: over 28 per cent of the Poalei-Zionists in my sample, but under 14 per cent of the Bundists were recruited there. Given the posited relationship between relative size of the Jewish proletariat, on the one hand, and strength of Poalei-Zionism and Bundism, on the other hand, one would expect Minsk, unlike other areas of the north, to have had relatively few Jewish workers. In actuality it is only a slight exaggeration to claim that the city of Minsk was 'without industry . . . [and] significant industrial masses' (Litvak, 1945: 191, 197): there were at the turn of the century only 2,500 Jewish workers in the city of Minsk, or .5.3 per cent of the city's Jewish population (compared to 5,800 in the city of Vilna — many of whom were employed in larger tobacco and bristle factories and tanneries — or 9.1 per cent of the city's Jewish population; calculated from data in *Encyclopaedia* . . ., 1971 – 2: vol. 12, 52; vol. 16, 144; *Materialy* . . ., 1906: 86).

But Poalei-Zionism was strong in Minsk not just because there were relatively few Jewish workers there. Also important was the fact that its mass base was in considerable measure comprised of non-proletarian elements. One historian thus points out that Minsk Poalei-Zionism 'did not have an influence on the lower levels of the masses. Their people were drawn mainly from the educated groups and the master craftsmen' (Zinger, 1944: 38). Little wonder, then, that the statutes of Minsk Poalei-Zion clearly stated that 'non-workers' can join the party 'when their activities are of use' (Loker, 1928: 186). (In contrast, the statutes drafted by the Moscow Trades Council stated that '[a]ll unions must preserve their proletarian character; mixed unions of employers and workers are inadmissible; joint unions of high- and low-paid workers are undesirable'. Quoted in Turin, 1968 [1935]: 88.)

From this brief description we may conclude that in its formative years Bundism thrived where Jewish workers were relatively numerous (the northern Pale), while Poalei-Zionism prospered where there were relatively few Jewish workers and/or where non-working class elements formed a large segment of the party's mass base (the southern Pale and Minsk): an interesting pattern which I shall have occasion to analyse later.

Once we turn to the recruitment of Bolshevik *intelligenty* we must direct our attention far to the east of the Pale. For over 47 per cent of the Bolsheviks in my sample were recruited to the east of a line joining St Petersburg and Astrakhan, the remainder being distributed more or less evenly throughout the other regions (excluding Minsk).

Theodore Dan once observed that 'the mainstay of Bolshevism became the textile centre of the country [i.e., the Central Industrial Region around Moscow, Tver, Yaroslavl and Ivanovo] and the backward metallurgical industry of the Urals [around Perm and Ufa]' (1964 [1946]: 256). Contemporary research (esp. Lane, 1969) validates his statement. Workers who supported the Bolsheviks during the period dealt with here were typically employed in giant Russian-owned factories located predominantly in the eastern part of European Russia. These factories were, from the point of view of capital investment and technological sophistication, and in comparison with foreign-owned industry further to the west, relatively backward. Workers in these plants were relatively unskilled and mainly of Great Russian origin. And, most significantly, they retained especially strong ties to the land.

It will be recalled that many industrial workers in Russia were what I have termed protoproletarians. Fig. 12 provides us with several indices of where the latter were concentrated. There were 32 per cent more workers employed in non-urban factories in Bolshevik areas than in Menshevik (increasing to 87 per cent more if we consider only highly industrialised provinces). Some 47 per cent more persons received the kind of internal passport necessary to return to the countryside for seasonal work or extended visits in Bolshevik areas than in Menshevik (250 per cent more in highly industrialised provinces). And 45 per cent more rural residents worked part-time in industry in Bolshevik areas than in Menshevik (120 per cent more in highly industrialized provinces). Thus, no matter which index of working-class urbanity is used, it appears that workers in areas of Menshevik strength tended to be relatively highly urbanised while workers in Bolshevik strongholds tended to be of the protoproletarian type.

Fig. 12. Indices of Working Class Urbanity (highly industrialised provinces only in brackets)

index	a. Menshevik areas	b. Bolshevik areas	b-a as % of a
of factory workers employed outside cities per 1,000 factory workers, 1902	484 (338)	639 (632)	32 (87)
of short-term internal passports issued per 1,000 population, 1906–10	78 (42)	115 (147)	47 (250)
of rural residents with part-time industrial work per 1,000 rural population, 1897	62 (46)	90 (101)	45 (120)

Source: Compiled from data in (Rashin, 1958: 209, 328, 342–3).
Note: See Technical Appendix.

The geographical distribution of protoproletarians may be explained largely as a consequence of variations in the requirements of industry. Thus, in the iron ore industry of the Urals (Bolshevik territory), 'the work force could fluctuate harmlessly according to the needs of agriculture, since iron ore was easily stockpiled'. But metallurgy and coal-mining, 'the two staples of southern industry, . . . demanded permanent full-time laborers, some of them highly skilled. Blast furnaces burning twenty-four hours a day seven days a week for years at a time cannot follow the cyclical vagaries of planting and harvesting' (McKay, 1970: 254–5).

Fig. 13. Selected Characteristics of the Parties' Industrial Bases

party	area(s) of predominance	characteristic type of worker	ethnic composition
Bolshevik	east of St Petersburg-Astrakhan line	unskilled, strong ties to country-side, employed in large, relatively backward industry	Great Russian
Menshevik	outside Pale and west of St Petersburg-Astrakhan line; southern Pale	more highly skilled, weak ties to countryside, employed in large, modern industry	Ukrainian, Great Russian, White Russian, Georgian, Tatar
Bund	northern Pale (where Jewish workers were relatively numerous)	artisans, unskilled workers in unmechanized factories	Jewish
Poalei-Zion	southern Pale; Minsk (where Jewish workers were relatively few)	artisans, master craftsmen	Jewish

The south was Menshevik territory. Menshevism was strong where industry was more modern and foreign-owned; where workers were more highly skilled, paid, educated and westernised; where workers had relatively few, weak ties to the countryside; and where the working class was ethnically heterogeneous: comprised of Ukrainians, Great Russians, White Russians, Tatars and Georgians. Industrial workers with these characteristics were concentrated in the southern Pale (the Ukraine), the Don Basin, the Caucasian oil fields and, to a lesser degree, St Petersburg.[15] A full 68.7 per cent of the Mensheviks in my sample were recruited in these regions — outside the Pale and to the west of the St Petersburg-Astrakhan line, or in the southern Pale.

Since the characteristics of the parties' industrial bases will frequently be referred to in the following chapter, I have for purposes of convenience summarised the above discussion in Fig. 13. Although subject to all the criticisms which must be lodged against any set of generalisations, the figure does offer a rough picture of the parties' industrial supporters. Clearly, *intelligenty* were reclassified in segments of the Russian working class which were markedly different from one another, and these differences were strongly associated with variations in party affiliation. As I have hinted here, and as I seek to demonstrate at greater length below, these variations, together with variations in classification, go a long way towards explaining why *intelligenty* developed radically different ideologies.

Only one aspect of ideology — ethnic identity — has been examined in this chapter because identity is usually regarded as the most fundamental element of internalised political culture (Verba, 1965: 529). If the embedding process could alter such a basic element of ideology it stands to reason that other less fundamental features of consciousness were at least equally susceptible to the impact of classification and reclassification. This cannot however be accepted on faith. Let us therefore see how the embedding process helped shape attitudes toward those issues which are generally regarded as representing the points of greatest ideological divergence among the four parties.

4 Strangers and Rebels

It is well known that both absolutely and proportionately there were far fewer Jewish Bolshevik *intelligenty* than Mensheviks, Bundists and Poalei-Zionists. Poalei-Zionists and Bundists were all — or nearly all (Zerubavel, 1967: 352–65) — Jews. But, judging from the list of participants in the 1907 Russian Social Democratic Labour Party (R.S.D.L.P.) congress, about 23 per cent of the Menshevik leadership and only 11 per cent of the Bolshevik leadership was Jewish. Moving up the echelons in the latter two parties, Jewish representation increased but the ratio of Jewish Mensheviks to Bolsheviks remained about the same — two to one. Thus, two of the seven top Bolsheviks and five of the eight top Mensheviks in the period 1903–7 were Jews (Lane, 1969: 28, 44).[1]

To oversimplify matters considerably, this chapter may be viewed as an attempt to explain these variations by applying the embedding model to an analysis of ideological differences among the parties. In all cases aside from the Bolshevik this can be done by examining the writings of Jewish ideologues only. But since there were few Jewish Bolshevik ideologues of any importance in the period dealt with here I shall consider some of Lenin's writings to be fairly typical of Bolshevik views. (This procedure is in no way problematic since only those aspects of Bolshevism which were points of internal party consensus will be discussed; and since the character of the party ensured considerable ideological homogeneity in any case.[2])

Ideological differences among the parties centered on three questions: What should happen to the Jewish community now that the period of its socio-economic usefulness in Russia has expired? How much importance should be assigned the intelligentsia in the revolutionary overthrow? Who, other than the intelligentsia, should be demarcated revolutionary agents and what are the implications of this demarcation for the character of the revolution? As I shall seek to demonstrate, the pattern of responses to these questions indicates that the embedding process led only a few *intelligenty* to become ideal-typical 'rebels', while it led the vast majority to retain elements of the 'stranger' mentality characteristic of Russian Jewry and thereby directed them towards other ideological viewpoints.

A. The Jewish Question

Alexander Helphand (Parvus): Today nationalism is meaningless. Even the manufacture of my coat demonstrates the international character of the world: the wool was taken from sheep pastured in Angora; it was spun in England; it was woven in Lodz; the buttons came from Germany; the thread from Austria . . .

Nakhman Syrkin: And the rip in your sleeve comes from the pogrom in Kiev!

an exchange at a meeting of the Russian-Jewish Scientific Society, Berlin, about 1890

Different degrees of embeddedness in the Jewish community were associated not only with variations in strength of Jewish identity, as suggested in the preceding chapter, but also with exposure to different ideological systems. In the course of two or three generations, the members of a typical family whose occupational ties to the Jewish community were weakening might first find their attachment to traditional Judaism waning; then develop keen interest in the liberal Jewish enlightenment (*haskala*); then be guided by various western political ideologies; and, finally, espouse more strictly Russian political views. Fig. 14 provides a rough indication of which ideological clusters tended to be associated with each degree of embeddedness in the Jewish community: in other words, with a picture of which *intelligenty* were influenced by which culture patterns.

It appears that most Poalei-Zionists or their parents had at one point been followers of the *haskala*, which provided by far the most important ideological avenue leading away from traditional Judaism from the middle of the nineteenth century on. After having first appeared during the French Enlightenment and then made their way to Germany, the teachings of the *haskala* moved eastward via the crossroads of commerce between the latter country and Russia (Cannon, 1974; Dawidowicz, 1967: 113–42; Greenberg, 1930; Lilienthal, 1915; Mahler, 1971 [1952–61]: 536–601; Raisin, 1914; Tzitron, 1921–2; Tzunzer, 1905). This is anything but astonishing, for the *haskala* was a thoroughly liberal current and was therefore first espoused by well-to-do merchants enjoying the trade boom with the west, by their intellectually-inclined kin and by intellectuals in their pay. Such persons not only began to integrate into the Russian class structure themselves, but also promoted the integration of their co-religionists with full civil rights. Traditionally, Jews had considered themselves to be in 'Exile' and longed to a greater or lesser degree for the day when the Messiah would appear and lead them back to 'Zion'. For those who

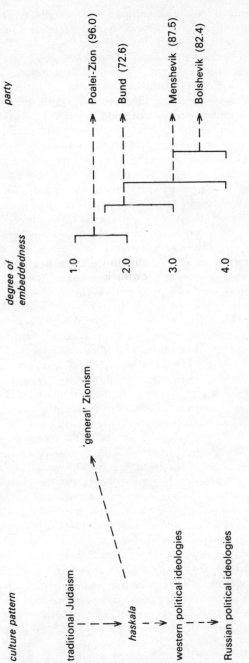

Fig. 14. Cultural Influences on *Intelligenty* by Party and Degree of Embeddedness in Russian Class Structure

Source: Fig. 7.
Notes: (a) Figures in brackets indicate percentage of each party's intelligentsia included in each range.
(b) See Technical Appendix.

became advocates of *haskala*, on the other hand, Exile was denied and Zion denuded of any historical or geographical significance: the Zion of the *maskilim* (enlighteners) came to be thought of as 'any place in the Diaspora which the Jews wished to think of as home' (Halpern, 1969 [1961]: 100). Having begun to integrate structurally, the *maskilim* soon discarded any pretence of a desire to leave their 'host' country.

For many *maskilim*, the pogroms of 1881–2 changed all this since the horrors of those years demonstrated that the integration of Jews in Russian society had proceeded just about as far as possible under existing social conditions. English liberals could point proudly to a Benjamin Disraeli and claim that 'it is possible . . . for the man whom Nature alone has made great, to win his proper station' (Junior, 1869). But in Russia there were few 'careers open to talent', especially as far as Jews were concerned. Thus, middle-class fear of Jewish competition on the market; the reluctance of the state to accept Jews as citizens with equal rights; the silence of still-timid liberal intellectuals concerning the pogroms; the complicity of a large segment of the populist intelligentsia in the advocacy of these excesses; and the historically conditioned antipathy of the peasantry to the Jewish middleman caused at least some *maskilim* to rethink the concepts of Zion and Exile and create the ideology of middle-class (or, as it was then known, 'general') Zionism. The 1880s were years of world depression and they therefore hastened liberalism's secular decline. Where liberalism was weak — and this was especially the case in Russia with its tiny bourgeoisie — anti-Semitism flourished[3] and Zionism appeared in re-action.[4] *Der Judenstaat* was Herzl's *Anti-Dühring*. In Russia, middle-class Zionism first struck root among those disillusioned *maskilim* who, significantly, were not yet 'too detached from the community' (Halpern, 1969 [1961]: 62–3). (Arthur Hertzberg [1959] provides biographical sketches of ten Russian Zionists born in 1865 or earlier who were not members of any of the Poalei-Zionist groups. The mean degree of embeddedness of their families of orientation in the Russian class structure was 1. 2.) By the early years of the twentieth century, general Zionism began to find supporters among the Jewish lower middle class (Leshchinsky, 1928: 2).[5] And it was propounded as a means of reconstituting these relatively intact yet threatened groups on new, national foundations.

The traditional notion of Zion and all that it implied had rarely been taken literally. For the Jew in pre-capitalist eastern Europe was, as Simmel recognised, not a 'stranger' in the sense we usually understand the term ('the wanderer who comes today and goes tomorrow') but was more like 'the man who comes today and stays tomorrow — the potential wanderer, so to speak'. The Zionists, however, were forced to become strangers 'in the usual sense of the term' (Simmel, 1971: 143). As Leon Pinsker, one of the most important of early Russian Zionists wrote in 1882, the Jews

are not a living nation; they are everywhere aliens; they are therefore despised . . . The proper and the only remedy would be the creation of a Jewish nationality, of a people living upon its own soil, the auto-emancipation of the Jews; their emancipation as a nation among nations by acquisition of a home of their own (Pinsker in Hertzberg, 1959: 198).

The influence of this idea was an aspect of many labour-Zionists' upbringing which distinguished them from virtually all other *intelligenty*. Some of the most important labour Zionists — including Ber Borokhov (Zerubavel, 1926), Yitzkhak Ben-Tzvi (1956), Zalman Shazar (1967 [1950]), Berl Katzenelson (1941), Shlomo Kaplansky (Zinger, 1971) and Avraham Ravotzky (Tarnopoler, 1970) — had fathers who were active general Zionists. But it would be mistaken to claim that this difference in upbringing — a consequence of what I have termed classification — was the sole distinction between Poalei-Zionists and others. For in order to adhere to the Zionist idea it was sufficient for many (particularly unassimilated) *intelligenty* who lacked the parental model to be reclassified in the southern Pale or the province of Minsk: strongholds of the Zionist movement.

It has been said that, all other things being equal (degree of organisation, control over resources), size itself is an important determinant of group power (Bierstedt, 1974: 220–41; but see Brym, 1977e); to which one might add the proposition that power is *the* determinant of ideological predominance. Viewed in this way it is no mystery that general Zionism had considerable influence on non-middle-class Jews where members of the Jewish middle class were most numerous. Even the results of the 1918 municipal elections clearly reveal a concentration of Zionist strength in Minsk and the southern Pale (Aronson in Aronson *et al.*, 1969: 23–4). And, incredibly, the vast majority of persons with Russian backgrounds in Israel's 'power elite' in the late 1960s came from the southern Pale or had parents who did. Lithuanians 'are conspicuous by their absence' (Rosenzweig and Tamarin, 1970: 32).

Jewish workers in the southern Pale formed a relatively small group compared to both Jewish non-workers and non-Jewish workers, in consequence of which they tended to come under the ideological influence of the latter two groups: as Chaim Weizmann noted in 1901, Jewish workers in the south were either Zionist or Russian Social Democratic ideologically (Weizmann, 1968–76: vol.1, 193). In Minsk, where there were relatively few Jewish workers compared to Jewish non-workers, and where members of the Poalei-Zion party were often from the lower middle class, Jewish workers also tended to be more prone to accept the Zionist idea than in the rest of the northern Pale. And in both Minsk and the south, the relative lack of Jewish workers offered unassimilated *intelligenty* certain 'degrees and freedom' in their thinking which their counterparts in the rest of the Pale lacked. In the rest of the Pale, the relatively large number of working class Jews forced *intelligenty* to pay more attention to class, rather than national issues. 'North of Kiev', writes Wildman with only slight exaggeration,[6] 'the nationality problem seldom came within . . . [the Jewish intelligentsia's] field of vision' (1972: 76). But in the south and Minsk, the paucity of Jewish workers allowed unassimilated *intelligenty* to place greater emphasis on national concerns. Even a brief sojourn in Vilna could make a socialist-Zionist whose views were still in flux, such as Berl Katzenelson, have doubts about the Zionist idea (Katzenelson, 1941: 24).

If the socialist-Zionists became Zionists due to these consequences of classification and reclassification, the embedding model also provides us with an explanation as to why the socialist-Zionist 'sons' were more radical than the general Zionist 'fathers'. First, between the first sproutings of Zionism in the early 1880s and the formation of the first socialist-Zionist groups nearly two decades later, the Jewish working-class movement had appeared. It was now possible to express one's discontent in other, more radical ways than Jewish nationalism pure and simple due to this change in the structure of available movements. Second, as one of the 'fathers' noted in his memoirs, his 'was the last generation of the Jewish student youth to enjoy the benevolence of the . . . regime' (Levin, 1967: 246). The promulgation of the 1887 *numerus clausus*, increased legal disabilities, the expulsion of the Jewish communities from St Petersburg and Moscow in 1891 and the outbreak of particularly shocking pogroms in Kishinev and Gomel during the early years of the new century indicated that whatever possibility had once existed for middle-class integration was now gone. The middle-class Zionists grew up when there was still hope, the socialist-Zionists when there was none.

The changed political atmosphere following the pogroms in Kishinev and Gomel did not, however, merely radicalise the 'sons'. It also politicised the 'fathers' (who were originally opposed to work aimed at improving conditions in the Diaspora); heightened Jewish awareness among some assimilating *intelligenty*; and produced a sense of urgency among all Zionists which led to the emergence of what came to be known as 'territorialism'. Diplomatic attempts to procure a charter for a Jewish homeland from Abdul Hamid, autocrat of the Ottoman Empire, had been made ever since the World Zionist Organisation held its first congress in 1897. After six years, negotiations had proved fruitless (Mandel, 1965: 105). A perturbing question therefore arose in the minds of many Zionists: 'Why Palestine?' (Kivin in Zerubavel, 1928: 36). The notion was now entertained of settling the Jews in *any* available territory, not just in Palestine (Gutman and Zilberfarb in *Roiter pinkas . . .*, 1921–4: vol. 1, 113–73; Patkin, 1947: 222–8, 237–41; Weisbord, 1968).

Territorialism posed a grave threat to nascent Poalei-Zionism, with its emphasis on Palestinian colonisation: Until 1903 left-wing Zionism consisted of little more than a disconnected set of ideologically hetero-geneous groups. But by 1906 three distinct and competing tendencies emerged. Aside from the Poalei-Zionists proper, there came into existence a territorialist, Marxist party by the name of the Zionist-Socialist Workers Party (Z.S.) and the Jewish Socialist Workers Party (S.E.R.P.), also territorialist but closer to the populist tradition. The threat posed by the more numerous territorialists (see Fig. 15) obviously required some appealing new ideological justification for Palestinian colonisation. This rather elaborate construction was provided by Ber Borokhov.

Fig. 15. Approximate Memberships of Selected Radical Parties in Russia (incl. Poland), 1905–7

Bolshevik	46,000	Poalei-Zion	16,000
Menshevik	38,000	Z. S.	26,000
Bund	33,000	S.E.R.P.	13,000

Sources: (Abramovich, 1949: 389; Keep, 1963: 288).

Marx had viewed progress as the resolution of contradictions which develop within social systems — specifically, between a society's class structure ('relations of production') and its productive apparatus ('forces of production'). When the productive appratus is hampered in its growth by the class system the latter structure is, Marx argued, rent by class conflict. a subordinate 'class-in-itself' is transformed into a conscious 'class-for-itself' which eventually overthrows the old, dominant class. Occasionally Marx also suggested that the social 'mode of production' — a blanket term which includes both the forces and relations of production — can assume different forms in different regions due to variations in natural environment. Borokhov's solution to the Jewish problem was based on an elaboration of the latter point.

According to Borokhov, peoples differ from one another because they work in different 'conditions of production', the most important aspect of which is the character of the territory in which they reside. And just as a class-in-itself is transformed into a class-for-itself due to contradictions between forces and relations of production, so peoples are transformed into nations due to contradictions between forces and conditions of production. Shorn of its perhaps antiquated terminology, the argument boils down to this: When the middle class of a people finds that its economic expansion is blocked due to lack of territory it seeks to consolidate its area of residence as a nation-state. The nation-state serves in turn as a basis for capturing a larger share of the world market. Moreover, the working class, too, has an interest in territory, for territory provides workers with a place of employment. When their place of employment is endangered — through national oppression or the immigration of foreign workers, for example — a form of proletarian nationalism develops (Borokhov, 1972 [1937]: 135–66).

What, then, are the implications of this argument for the Jews? The Jews lack their own territory. Moreover, they are being driven out of their places of residence because their traditional economic functions are being taken over by 'native' middle classes. Even those former merchants who managed to become involved in small industry are now facing a mounting threat from large competitors. And because Jewish workers are employed almost exclusively in small Jewish-owned establishments they face the same problem: both the Jewish petit bourgeoisie and the Jewish proletariat are being robbed of the most general prerequisite for their existence — a 'strategic base' or territory for industrial growth and employment. Emigration, it is true, provided the Jewish workers with a temporary solution. But even such countries as England are, Borokhov noted, now saturated with workers. (The Aliens Bill, restricting immigration in England, had in fact just been passed.) This means that the Jewish masses require 'concentrated immigration into an undeveloped country . . . Jewish migration must be transformed from immigration into colonisation' (ibid.: 191).

But why colonise Palestine? Simply because there is no alternative. International population flow, said Marx, follows international capital flow. Borokhov agreed but pointed out that both population and capital were being redirected from developed countries which now had their own surpluses of capital and labour, such as the United States, to predominantly agricultural countries, such as Argentina and Canada. The latter countries are, however, totally unsuited to Jewish settlement. Because they are characterised by government-directed colonisation and large-scale lending to a multitude of homesteaders, there is no room there for the petty capital of the small Jewish businessman. Moreover, because the Jews are a 'city-bred people' they are unable to compete with persons coming from an agricultural background for jobs. Therefore, what is necessary for the Jews is a country to which 'Jews alone will migrate . . . separated from the general stream of immigration. The country will have no attraction for immigrants from other nations' (ibid.: 201). Such a country is Palestine.

Whether or not the United States, Argentina and Canada could in fact absorb the Jews is quite immaterial here.[7] What is important is Borokhov's insistence that not Jewish tradition, nor geographical proximity, nor even availability made Palestine the ideal location for a Jewish colony. Rather, Palestinian colonisation by the Jews was the inevitable outcome of blind socioeconomic development. The Poalei-Zionists might pursue general working-class interests, both political and economic, while in Russia; but gains won in the Diaspora were viewed as mere 'palliatives'. Unlike the industrial worker, who can bring the economic life of the country to a standstill, the artisan cannot in any case play an important role in the making of the revolution. His only hope is to follow Jewish capital to Palestine where a sound 'strategic base' will be constructed, thus transforming him into an industrial worker. Once this occurs the Jewish worker's nationalism will vanish and class conflict will progress along normal lines. This will eventually culminate in a socialist revolution in Palestine.

This brief overview suggests that, like other strata still firmly attached to the community, Poalei-Zionist *intelligenty* reacted to the fact that they stood (as I put it in Chapter 2) between two social epochs by taking their stranger status literally. Even while actively participating in the 1905 revolution many felt compelled to ask themselves: 'Why am I here and not there? [i. e., in Palestine] (Ben-Tzvi, 1966: 62)'? As might be expected given their different mobility patterns, *intelligenty* in the other parties viewed the matter rather differently.

Unlike so many leading Poalei-Zionists, the pioneer Bundists did not have fathers who were active in the general Zionist movement. As we have seen, only *maskilim* with relatively strong ties to the Jewish community were transformed into middle-class Zionists in the 1880s and 1890s; and the pioneers' fathers, although all *maskilim*, were already too firmly embedded in the Russian middle class to be much affected by the new current. They therefore continued, albeit at a slower pace than before 1881, to assimilate culturally, to deny both traditional and Zionist notions of Zion and Exile and to develop a relatively strong sense of being part of Russian society. These sentiments were effectively transmitted to their offspring.

Not that this was the only difference between Poalei-Zionists and Bundists. Especially during the final third of the nineteenth century the ideas of the *haskala* began to filter down to students in the Jewish school system. Their outmoded religious beliefs were thus replaced by an ideological posture which constituted a set of scathing criticisms against tradition, an introduction to the secular culture of the west and a bridge to more radical forms of thought. (For early examples, see Rappaport, 1951 [1939]; Litvak in *Roiter pinkas* . . ., 1921–4: vol. 2, 80–106). Later recruits to the Bund *and* a considerable number of Poalei-Zionists were among those who followed this route. Fig. 14 indicates that both groups passed directly from the *haskala* to membership in their respective parties without any mediating .Zionist influence. The critical difference between these Poalei-Zionists and second-generation recruits to the Bund thus had little to do with early socialisation patterns. What distinguished the two groups was, as mentioned above, a difference in the character of social movements to which they could become attached. The social composition and power of available movements tended to be reflected in the ideologies of the two groups of *intelligenty*: the Bundists were less Jewish-nationalistic because they were reclassified in a region where the Jewish bourgeoisie was comparatively weak.

The fact remains that the ready availability of Jewish workers did manage to promote at least the recrystallisation of the pioneers' sense of

Jewish identity. Already by 1892 they considered themselves able to join the revolutionary movement as Jews — a significant change in thinking from earlier years. By 1895 the need felt for a Jewish socialist party, separate from the general Russian movement, was growing, although this was still motivated more by simple expediency than by national sentiments *per se*. In fact, the emergence of such sentiments actually post-dated the founding of the Bund in 1897, becoming evident only in the period 1899–1903. This development was hastened by two forces. First, labour Zionism began to make significant inroads among Jewish workers and in order to counter this threat the Bundists had to become more nationalistic. Second, and not unrelated to the successes of labour Zionism, was the fact that heightened oppression in the early years of the new century led nearly the whole Jewish community to become more concerned with specifically Jewish problems.

It was in 1901, at its fourth congress, that the Bund took its first official step away from its old position on the Jewish question (which involved nothing more than the demand for equal civil rights). A resolution was passed stating that Social Democracy was obliged to oppose not just class and state oppression, but also oppression

by one nation over another, the domination of one language over another.

The congress recognizes that a state such as Russia, which consists of many different nationalities, should in the future be reorganized into a federation of nationalities, each with full national autonomy, independent of the territory which it inhabits.

The conference recognizes that the concept 'nationality' is also applicable to the Jews.

Considering it still too early, under existing conditions, to put forth the demand for national autonomy for the Jews, the conference considers it sufficient for the present to fight against all discriminatory anti-Jewish laws; to publicize and protest against the oppression of the Jewish people; but also to take care not to fan national feeling, which can only cloud over the class consciousness of the Jewish proletariat. (Quoted in Aronson *et al.*, 1960–6: 180–1.)

Two things are noteworthy about the resolution. First, it clearly signified the Bundists' growing preparedness to argue that the Jewish worker was not merely a worker, but also a Jew; and that recognition of this fact necessarily entailed making special non-class demands. But any similarity to Poalei-Zionism ended with the willingness of both parties to refer to the Jews as a nation: whereas the term meant a territorial entity to the Poalei-Zionists it meant only a cultural entity to the Bundists; and whereas the Bundists feared the transformation of national awareness into 'chauvinism', the Poalei-Zionists considered proletarian nationalism a progressive force, at least for the moment. Second, in practical terms the resolution departed in no way from traditional practice. 'Full national autonomy' was yet an ultimate and poorly defined goal with no strategic ramifications.

By the time the fifth Bund congress was held in 1903, the person fast becoming the party's leading spokesman on the national question, Vladimir Medem, was able to muster considerable support for a more active approach to what was now called 'national cultural autonomy' (*Materialn . . .*, 1927a; 1927b). Medem sought to steer a clear course between what he regarded as the twin evils of nationalism and assimilationism, between the position of the general and labour Zionists, on the one hand, and the Mensheviks and Bolsheviks, on the other. The middle course — what Medem referred to as 'neutralism' — displayed neither of these 'dangers'. Whether or not the Jews would continue to exist as a nation cannot be known in advance, Medem claimed. This only history can decide. A neutral position regarding the Jewish question insists that history be given free reign, that neither forced assimilation nor some artificially induced nationalism be allowed to distort the Jews' unknowable course of development. At the congress, and even more so in a series of articles written the following year (Medem in *Vladimir Medem . . .*, 1943: 173–219), Medem drew the logical conclusion from this set of postulates (and thereby changed his 'neutralist' stance to one which at least implicitly opposed assimilationism): both now and after the revolution the Bund must actively pursue the goal of national cultural autonomy. By this he meant that the Jewish people itself should exercise complete control over all areas 'in which national life as such is expressed . . . that is, in the area of cultural questions' (ibid.: 217). At the sixth Bund congress in 1905, this principle — the active and independent encouragement of, and control over Jewish cultural development — was accepted as the basis of the Bund's position on the Jewish question (Tobias, 1972: 331).

The growing particularism which this demonstrated was closely bound up with the Bund's attempt to alter its relationship to the R.S.D.L.P. At the first R.S.D.L.P. congress in 1898, the Bund was content to be referred to as an 'autonomous' section of the larger party (Carter, 1970: 36); by 1901 it sought 'federative' status since it had come to view itself as a national party which could claim to be 'the representative of the Jewish proletariat' (Aronson *et al.*, 1960–6: 181); and by 1903 the Bund's self-definition was strengthened to 'sole representative of the Jewish proletariat'.[8] As we shall see in the following section, this move towards greater independence went against the grain of centralising tendencies then taking hold of other segments of the R.S.D.L.P. This conflict between Bundists and Russian Social Democrats was at least in part responsible for the formal withdrawal of the Bund from the larger party at the second R.S.D.L.P. congress in 1903.

It would, however, be mistaken to believe that Menshevik/Bolshevik opposition to the Bund was motivated solely by differences of opinion concerning the 'organisation question'. True, Martov appeared to be arguing solely about organisational matters when he claimed that granting the Bund federative status might encourage other groups to follow suit and thereby reduce the R.S.D.L.P. to a fragmented and disorganised body incapable of taking unified and decisive action (*Vtoroy* . . ., 1959 [1904]: 53–7). But if this were the only issue at stake one would expect those who opposed the Bund to have been united whenever the question of party organisation arose. Such unity did not, however, obtain. As is well known, it was precisely the organisation question which sparked the Menshevik-Bolshevik split. This suggests that the tortuous debate which ensued at the second R.S.D.L.P. congress over the Bund's place in the party was not merely a subordinate element of a larger debate. At least as far as the Jewish protagonists were concerned, the debate was equally about the fate of the Jewish community.[9]

This perhaps implicit motive for the debate can best be appreciated if we ask what Trotsky meant when he asserted at the congress that Jewish *intelligenty* in the Russian section of the R.S.D.L.P. 'considered and [still] consider themselves [to be] representatives of the Jewish proletariat as well' as the non-Jewish proletariat (ibid.: 57). Clearly, he did not intend this to be taken literally. As Mark Liber, chief spokesman for the Bund, pointed out, Trotsky and the other Jews in the Russian section had had no contact with Jewish workers (ibid.) and so could hardly be considered representatives in the formal sense of the word. A more credible interpretation is that Trotsky considered Jews in the Russian section to be representing Jewish workers' true interests.

Trotsky and the other *intelligenty* soon to become Mensheviks and Bolsheviks typically came from families standing on the periphery of the Jewish community. One the one hand, because of their upbringing, they considered themselves more Russian than Jewish and prescribed the path they had followed — assimilation — as the only credible first step toward solving the Jewish problem. On the other hand, they had escaped the powerful forces which kept most Jewish *intelligenty* firmly anchored in areas of Jewish working-class predominance. Even *intelligenty* who managed to receive an education outside the Pale were required by law to return when their studies ended; and if they chose to live illegally in St Petersburg or Moscow they were more often than not taken under police supervision back to the Pale, where, 'with almost no alternative they would then turn to the Jewish worker' (Katzenelson in Reznichenko, 1948: 57). But Mensheviks and Bolsheviks, due either to their determination to remain identified with the non-Jewish world or to sheer accident, were not reclassified in this manner. They therefore continued to believe that the assimilation of Jewish workers would ensure working class solidarity; that this in turn would hasten the overthrow of the autocracy, the eventual destruction of capitalism and the advent of socialism; and that socialism, as

Marx himself had argued in his essay *On the Jewish Question*, was ultimately the only solution to the Jewish question. Once this line of reasoning was accepted it followed that the encouragement of Jewish cultural development and the formation of a party invested with the right to act as 'sole representative of the Jewish proletariat' were regressive steps. Assimilation, together with a party acting only as the organisational representative of the R.S.D.L.P. among Jewish workers, was all that was required.

To a considerable degree, then, the debate over the Bund's place in the R.S.D.L.P. was a struggle

> within the Jewish people itself. It was a struggle over the question of whether or not the Jewish people would assimilate; whether or not there was a need to develop within the Jewish worker a separate Jewish culture, language and literature; and whether or not there was a need for a separate Jewish workers organization in order better to guarantee the interests of the Jewish masses (Abramovich, 1944: 115).

Stated otherwise, *intelligenty* were, depending on their mobility patterns, more or less optimistic about the fate of the Jewish community in the Diaspora. Bolsheviks and Mensheviks accepted without question the proposition that Jews would eventually integrate in the Russian social structure without much problem. After all, had they not done so themselves (cf. Shibutani and Kwan, 1965: 532)? Bundists, too, accepted this argument — but with qualifications. More firmly embedded in the community and therefore more sensitive to its travails, they felt that integration, although possible, could be accomplished only if special precautions were taken to safeguard Jewish interests. Moreover, they believed that structural integration did not necessarily imply cultural assimilation. They certainly did not want to emigrate: Bundists considered it 'unethical . . . for a socialist to leave Russia' as long as he was not being hunted by the police (Katz-Blum 1940: 37). In contrast, Poalei-Zionists, who were more a part of the community than any other group, rejected *in toto* the idea of integration. This, as anyone in their position could clearly see, was not happening. Nor could it be expected to occur before the laws of capitalist development drove the Jews to Palestine. Bundists could still proclaim that they 'are not strangers here and not guests' (from a 1903 Bund pamphlet, quoted in Tobias, 1972: 252). For the Poalei-Zionists, their stranger status was as evident as the horrors of the last pogrom (cf. Shibutani and Kwan, 1965: 517).

Not just Trotsky, but all members of the intelligentsia felt that they were representing Jewish workers' true interests. In light of the above discussion it is not difficult to understand why. Each group of *intelligenty* had its own interests and expectations, defined by its members' mobility patterns. These interests and expectations were simply projected on the Jewish worker. *Intelligenty* did not place 'ideals before interests' (Malia, 1961: 9) or 'cultural considerations above social' (Parsons in Rieff, 1963: 4). As is the case with most people most of the time, their interests shaped their ideals.

This conclusion follows quite obviously from the discussion of Jewish identity in Chapter 3. But what of other elements of ideology? In the next section I want to examine how the embedding process shaped attitudes regarding a second point of ideological divergence — the question of the intelligentsia's proper role in the Social Democratic movement.

B. The Role of the Intelligentsia

> A workers movement cannot be created from the top down [but] must arise from below . . . The task of the . . . intelligentsia is only to illuminate this massive current . . . to remove obstacles, to help, to serve.
>
> *Vladimir Medem*

> Social Democratic consciousness among the workers . . . could only be brought to them from without . . .[T]he working class, exclusively by its own efforts, is able to develop only trade union consciousness . . . The theory of socialism, however, grew out of the . . . bourgeois intelligentsia.
>
> *Vladimir Lenin*

When in 1902 Lenin wrote a pamphlet on 'the question of the relationship between consciousness and spontaneity' (Lenin, 1960–70 [1925–6]: vol. 5, 374) he pinpointed an issue which was to distinguish fundamentally between Bolshevism and other forms of Russian Marxism. The question he addressed was this: Will workers become Social Democrats on the basis of their own *spontaneous* development with the intelligentsia playing only a helping role, or will it be necessary for Marxism to be brought to the workers largely from without — that is to say, by the politically *conscious* intelligentsia? Although the answers formulated by members of the various parties were by no means so clear-cut and invariant as is often assumed, it may safely be said that the Bolsheviks came to favour 'consciousness' while, at the other extreme, Bundists were partial to 'spontaneity'. Between these two poles the Mensheviks stood closer to the Bundists and the Poalei-Zionists to the Bolsheviks. But, in general, Jewish radicals tended to favour the principle of spontaneity.

They were undoubtedly predisposed to adopt this position by their socialisation patterns. Fig. 14 shows that the liberal Jewish enlightenment, or *haskala*, figured prominently in all Poalei-Zionists' and Bundists', a good many Mensheviks', but no Bolsheviks' backgrounds or parents' backgrounds. The significance of this fact in the present context can be appreciated only if we recognise that the *haskala* was very much a western ideology, deeply appreciative of the scientific and humanistic accomplishments of Europe. As Yehudah Slutzky remarks, 'the face of the *haskala* movement was turned to the west, and mainly toward the lands of Germany' (1960: 115); and as Jacob Raisin points out, when the *haskala* 'took root in Russia it was purely German for fifty years and more' (1914: 191). Little wonder, then, that its Russian adherents were commonly known as *Berliner* or *Deutscher*. Many of the Mensheviks' families, it is true, were already far removed from the *haskala*. But they still developed a strong appreciation for the west since in most cases they were brought up and reclassified in the most westernised sections of the Empire (particularly the southern Pale) where the Russian and Jewish middle classes were strongest. Typically, Mikhail Beltman, who linked the cosmopolitanism of his home town of Odessa to its strong bourgeoisie, could speak fondly of its western atmosphere, its European character (*Deyateli* . . ., n.d. [1925–7]: pt. 2, 99).

Because most *intelligenty* imbibed the teachings of the *haskala*, or at least a strong dose of westernism, they developed a propensity in their youth to look westward for sources of ideological inspiration. Medem spoke for the vast majority when he once unequivocally stated that 'we associate ourselves with western European culture' (*Materialn* . . ., 1927: pt. 1, 93). At least two other sets of circumstances reinforced this orientation. First, migration to western universities was much more widespread among Jews than non-Jews due to the operation of the *numerus clausus*: at the turn of the century only about 7 per cent of university students in Russia were Jews, but in Switzerland Jews constituted roughly half the Russian student body. This gave Jews greater exposure to western culture and enabled them to learn first-hand the theories and methods of European Social Democracy. Second, Russian anti-Semitism inevitably led many Jewish radicals to form a deep-seated aversion to things Russian and a corresponding attraction to the west and all for which it stood. In Isaac Deutscher's words, 'especially on the Jewish intelligentsia, that part of the world which knew no pogroms, no pale, and no *numerus clausus* exercised immense fascination' (1965 [1954]: 20).

While Jewish radicals had never fitted comfortably into the populist movement with its peasant orientation and its Slav spirit (Cherikover, 1939: 131–2, 135–7, 152–72; Deich, 1922: 56–60, 304; Stepniak, 1890: 47), the advent of Marxism in Russia permitted them to feel more at ease with their radicalism. For this innovation in ideas represented what one Jewish Menshevik called the '"europeanisation" of Russian socialism' (Dan, 1964 [1946]: 166). The model for Russian Marxism was at first provided by German Social Democracy. This immediately established an affinity between the western orientation of Jewish radicals and the new ideology. These urbanised youths consequently flocked to the theory of urban revolution in far greater numbers than to any other radical system of thought (Brower, 1972–3). And they continued to think in western terms throughout their careers (e. g., Getzler, 1967: 124). As Berl Katzenelson wrote of Russian-Jewish Marxists: 'Before their eyes there was always a human ideal-type — the Berlin Social Democrat, who was also "the last word" in western culture, the master who had to be looked up to' (in Reznichenko, 1948: 62). Thus, when the question arose of 'whether to draw closer in spirit and structure to the great legal labor parties and trade unions of the West' or 'to prepare for early armed uprising under the leadership of a self-selected, rigidly centralized, secret and conspirative band of revolutionary intellectuals' (Wolfe, 1948b: 160–1), Jews would opt overwhelmingly for the former alternative, for the spontaneously developing working class over the conscious intelligentsia.

Not so the Bolsheviks. Unlike other *intelligenty*, they were too integrated in the Russian class structure to be thoroughly westernised. As Fig. 14 indicates, they were from an early age exposed mainly to the offerings of Russian culture so that they developed a propensity in their youth to look to Russia's radical tradition, not Germany's for a model of political behaviour. Since such populists as N. G. Chernyshevsky and Peter Tkachev provided them with the prototype for the Bolshevik brand of revolutionary action (Karpovich, 1944; Utechin, 1960; 1968; Weeks, 1968) it will prove worthwhile to devote a few words to the ideas of these men.

The question of how important 'the people' would be in the destruction of the old order and the creation of the new had been a recurrent problem of Russian populism. Attempts to minimise the peasantry's independent significance in the revolutionary overthrow had periodically flowered, particularly when concerted efforts to rouse the peasantry ended in utter failure. This was most evident when the fiasco of the 'go to the people' movement was followed by a wave of political terrorism in the second half of the 1870s — a reaction which indicated that the intelligentsia wanted to speed up history by taking things into its own hands. But the socialist intelligentsia had by then been in existence for three decades and the peasantry had proven to be immune to its ideas throughout this period. In consequence, the 'conscious' intelligentsia had, well before the 1870s, formulated a theory of revolutionary elitism with which the names of Chernyshevsky and Tkachev are usually associated.

Chernyshevsky maintained that only those persons who are fully conscious of their own interests know what is best for society as a whole (1953: 49–135). Such persons, he wrote, may be 'few in number, but they put others in a position to breathe who without them would have been suffocated' (Chernyshevsky, 1961 [1863]: 241). These *intelligenty* form a fully conscious elite obliged to shape the people's interests (as the latter are incapable of doing themselves) and lead them in their struggle for freedom.

Tkachev, who acknowledged Chernyshevsky as 'the genuine father and founder of the socialist revolutionary party in Russia' (quoted in Venturi, 1960 [1953]: 465), took this argument one step further. Whereas Chernyshevsky submitted that the intellectual elite's elevated sense of morality derived from the unconscious strivings of the people (Bowman, 1954: 195 ff.), Tkachev came close to denying the latter any importance at all in creating the new society. 'The people', he wrote, 'if left by themselves will build nothing new' (quoted in Weeks, 1968: 75). The 'revolutionary minority' is therefore 'no longer willing to wait but must take upon itself the forcing of consciousness upon the people' (quoted in ibid.: 77). A highly disciplined and centralised party (Tkachev in Burtzev and Kravchinsky, 1897: 135) must seize state power at the earliest possible opportunity. Capitalism is taking root in Russia, Tkachev observed, and the chance to proceed directly to socialism may well be missed. 'That is why', he concluded, the intellectual elite 'cannot wait' (quoted in Weeks, 1968: 123): delaying until the masses have been adequately prepared or sufficiently agitated to rise in mass revolt is futile.[10]

Such elitist ideas were available to Jewish Bolsheviks only because they were highly Russified. Due to the fact that they were firmly embedded in the Russian class structure the Bolsheviks tended to formulate their ideology by drawing heavily on Russian political culture. Because there were relatively few fully-assimilated Jews in turn-of-the-century Russia, and because there were few who lived in unwesternised regions, there were relatively few Jewish Bolsheviks. Less divorced from the Jewish community and from western culture, the far more numerous Jewish radicals in the other parties were able to draw more heavily on the western political tradition, to favour a mass democratic movement on the German model which, they reasoned, would spontaneously grow with and finally destroy the capitalist system.

Preferences for sponaneity or consciousness were, however, determined less by early socialisation patterns and regional variations in recruitment than by the *temporal* availability of the workers' movement This becomes evident if one examines the manner in which the level of intelligentsia elitism fluctuated within and between parties over time. For it appears that the principle of consciousness was stressed only when links between *intelligenty* and workers were weak. When *intelligenty* were more firmly embedded in the working class, spontaneity was emphasised.

Contrary to the suggestion of many writers, the Russian intelligentsia did not always hang suspended between classes: the available memoir literature and a substantial body of historical research indicate that, during certain periods at least, ties binding *intelligenty* to workers were dense. That is to say, there were both times when contact between the two groups — in 'propaganda' circles, party organisations and so forth — was very close and times when it was not.

Generally speaking, the 1890s were years of close contact. This was a decade of heavy foreign investment, rapid industrial expansion and relatively low unemployment. It witnessed not only a mounting wave of labour unrest, but also a concerted attempt on the part of many workers to have the intelligentsia help organise, educate, propagandise and agitate. 'This time', wrote one Jewish *intelligent*, 'it was not us who sought out the workers, but the workers who sought out us' (Gorev, 1924: 24). *Intelligenty* viewed with pride the 'continuous growth of our connections to factories and workshops' (ibid.: 33) and the rapidly increasing number of workers in party organisations (Akimov, 1969 [1904]).

The strike movement, and with it increased contact between workers and *intelligenty*, originated in Poland, spread to the Pale of Settlement and then moved eastward to central Russia. And, significantly, a new strategic idea was diffused precisely along the route blazed by the strikers. During the late poulist era, *intelligenty*, ignored by the peasants, felt the need to 'give history a push' and engage in individual acts of political terror. But now things were developing quite nicely on their own. As contact between workers and *intelligenty* strengthened, the latter consequently developed a strategy which played down their own role in the revolutionary movement and emphasised that of the workers. The Social Democratic movement was to be, as its name implied, democratic; *intelligenty*, it was argued, must be careful not to take things into their own hands.

Acceptance of the new strategy in Russia was signalled by the publication in Vilna of Arkady Kremer's *On Agitation* (1893) — a pamphlet which provided the whole Social Democratic movement with strategic foundations sound enough to last some eight years. The core of Kremer's argument was that the strike movement is an 'elementary school' for the training of worker Social Democrats. By participating in strikes the individual worker's 'struggle for petty demands' will broaden to a conflict between the entire working class, on the one hand, and 'all the higher classes' together with the government, on the other. This, Kremer reasoned, will culminate in the overthrow of the autocracy. But for the moment, until workers are sufficiently organised and educated to ac-complish this task, the struggle must be waged chiefly on the economic front. True, the strike movement was to be guided by *intelligenty*. But the latter were admonished to keep their fingers 'on the pulse of the masses' and merely assist in the gradual unfolding of workers' class consciousness. For in the final analysis, Kremer submitted, only the workers themselves are capable of overthrowing the regime (Kremer in *Arkady . . .*, 1942: 293–321).This set of ideas, which stressed the leading role to be played by the movement's *demos*, soon swept the Empire. Even Lenin, who would only a few years later develop quite the opposite viewpoint., claimed in 1895 that the role of the intelligentsia is merely 'to *join up with* the workers' movement, to bring light into it, to *assist* the workers in the struggle they *themselves* have already begun to wage' (Lenin, 1960–70 [1925–6]: vol. 2, 112; my emphasis).

By 1901, however, several forces caused many *intelligenty* to discard such opinions. Two of these — one economic, the other political — may be emphasised here.[11] First, recession struck late in 1899 with disastrous consequences for the strike movement or, more accurately, for strikers in large industry (see Fig. 16). It is not always the case that increased labour unrest is associated with upswings in the business cycle and quiescence with downswings (Bouvier, 1964; Hansen, 1921; Hobsbawm, 1952; Perrot, 1968; Rees, 1952; Smith, 1972; Walsh, 1975; Weintraub, 1966); but very often it is, and Russia appears roughly to have followed this pattern (Johnson, 1975).[12] At the turn of the century, few gains could be registered on the economic front since the recession compelled workers to concentrate

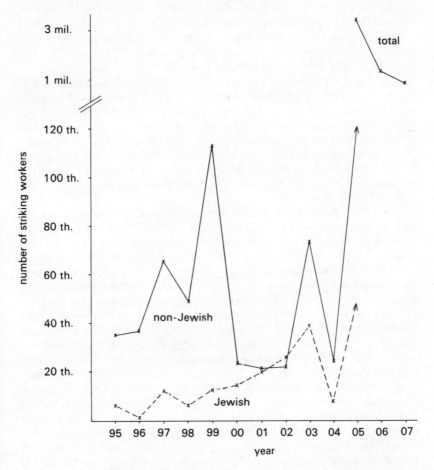

Fig. 16. Number of Striking Workers, Jewish and non-Jewish, in Russia, 1895–1907

Sources: Compiled from data in (Borokhov, 1923: 29, 41; Haimson, 1964: 627; Turin, 1968 [1935]: 187).

Note: See Technical Appendix.

more on survival than revolution, to give up participation in both strikes and party activities for the more mundane goal of finding enough to eat. Due to unique local conditions Moscow may have represented an extreme case, but in essence the situation was little different wherever there was large industry: until 1905 the intelligentsia 'was unable to reestablish close ties with the factory masses and thus to exert a directing influence on the . . . labor movement' (Schneiderman, 1976: 74). Peter Garvi, who was actively involved in party work in the southern Pale and in Moscow during this period, noted in his memoirs how he 'invariably ran up against one and the same phenomenon'. Aside from *intelligenty*, party organisations contained 'mainly green, fervent, resolute, young workers, but weakly connected to the working masses and uninfluential in industrial enterprises' (1946: 440; also Wildman, 1967: 90).

As Allan Wildman and Jeremiah Schneiderman have recently emphasised, at least equally important a cause of the growing rift between workers and *intelligenty* was the political — more precisely, the police — activity of the regime. This was manifested in heightened rates of political arrests, increased police brutality and intensified attempts on the part of police agents to infiltrate party organisations. Less obvious than the way in which *provocateurs* could destroy revolutionary organisations is the manner in which police brutality encouraged the intelligentsia to lose sight of the working class:

The year 1901 saw the culmination of a political awakening on the part of educated 'society' (ibid.: 209 ff.; Orlov, 1938). The familiar cycle of government repression leading to increased intelligentsia radicalism leading to further repression, etc., was the principal cause. University students in the capital, having been subjected to a particularly strong display of arbitrary action on the part of the authorities, took part in large-scale demonstrations in 1899. Temporarily quelled by police whips, the students were soon joined by other protesters across the country. The regime reacted by meting out harsh punishment: in St Petersburg and Kiev alone over two hundred students were press-ganged into military service. The enraged students now redoubled their efforts, which culminated in the assasination of the Minister of Education, still more protests and another dose of police brutality. Even the liberals now began openly to sympathise with the students, to protest against the actions of the regime and to join in the widespread street demonstrations of 1901. Ever since the central tenets of Russian Marxism had been formulated by Plekhanov the Social Democrats had believed that they were, at least until such time as a liberal-democratic regime could be established, the allies of the liberals. It now seemed possible to realise this belief, to go not just to the workers, but 'to all classes of the population' (Lenin, 1960–70 [1925–6]: vol. 5, 424). All opposition groups — liberal, populist and Marxist — denounced the autocracy in unison. The intelligentsia's sense of self-importance grew as attention shifted from workers to educated society:

In this heightened revolutionary atmosphere, ideological lines often became somewhat blurred. The image of the worker's position at the forefront of the revolutionary movement began to fade into the background and in its place emerged the heroic radical intelligentsia, the repository of the highest ideals of the nation and courageous champion of human dignity against police truncheons, the drafting of protesting students and other humiliating abuses (Wildman, 1967: 209).

All in all, a fascinating conjuncture of events. Because worker militance was fuelled by one set of contradictions (*see above*, 13–23, 91) and the intelligentsia's radicalism by quite another, autonomous set (*see above*, 47–53, 92), the two groups could converge (as they had to if revolution were to occur) or diverge (as they did at the turn of the century; cf. Althusser, 1970 [1965]; Godelier, 1967 [1966]; Zelnik, 1972–3). At this particular conjuncture the intelligentsia's radicalism and self-confidence blossomed at precisely the same moment that the workers' movement declined. In consequence, 'those techniques which had brought intellectuals and workers into intimate contact were rapidly falling into disuse' (Wildman, 1967: 218). Ties established between factory workers and *intelligenty* in the course of the preceding decade were now to a very large extent snapped. Because industrial workers now became 'temporally unavailable' to the intelligentsia the ground was prepared for a reassertion on the part of future Mensheviks and Bolsheviks of their own importance in the revolutionary overthrow (consciousness) and a corresponding diminution of the workers' (spontaneity).

Under the leadership of the editors of *Iskra*, those who were to become Mensheviks and Bolsheviks in only a few years built up a highly centralised organisation for purposes of dominating the activities of Russian Social Democracy (Wildman, 1964). *Iskra*'s organisational plan, worked out by Lenin, was based on the notion that workers by themselves are capable of developing only 'trade-union consciousness' and cannot reach the point of demanding the overthrow of the autocracy. The ideas of Social Democracy must therefore be brought to the workers completely 'from without' by a centralised party of 'professional revolutionaries'. This organisation was to consist of both *intelligenty* and workers who had been raised to their level of consciousness. The intelligentsia was, in other words, not to join the workers (as Lenin had claimed in 1895); a few of the more advanced workers were to join the intelligentsia. It was later explained that two 'centres' would exercise ultimate authority over the party — a Central Organ, located in western Europe and 'responsible for ideological leadership', and a Central Committee, located in Russia and responsible for 'direct and practical leadership' (Lenin, 1960–70 [1925–6]: vol. 6, 236). The members of both bodies were to be self-selected and 'in complete harmony with one another'. Below the two centres, and totally dependent on them, were to be the local committees of each town. Analogously, the local committees would consist of self-selected members to which a plethora of lower-level groups, such as factory cells, would be subordinated. Authority was therefore to flow only from the top down; responsibility only from the bottom up. It was fully realised that, since leaders were to be self-selected, there existed a danger that the centres and local committees might 'include an incapable person invested with tremendous power' (ibid.: 242). How, then could the membership get rid of such a person? Not elections — organisational democracy was at this point in time viewed by the Russian Social Democrats as mere 'striving after effect' (ibid.: vol. 5, 482) — but only 'comradely influence' could oust an incompetent or dangerous leader. In a word, there was to be no institutionalised check on authority. To some degree, centralisation of power, secrecy and the use of the 'selective principle' was necessary in a police state: but the Russian Social Democrats failed to recognise that this could also allow leaders to develop authoritarian tendencies inimical to the members' interests.

Having been written in 1902, this reassertion of the conscious intelligentsia's sense of self-importance was not without its ironies. For just as the future Mensheviks and Bolsheviks lost their faith in the working class, large-scale strikes and demonstrations broke out — quite spontaneously — in the southern Pale and the Caucasus (Wildman, 1967: 246 – 7). Russian workers demonstrated that they were indeed capable of demanding the abolition of the autocracy and of thinking along Social Democratic lines rather than being limited to mere 'trade-union consciousness'. They would do so again, even more resoundingly, in 1905 (Anweiler, 1974 [1958]: 20 – 96). But both in 1903 and at the outset of 1905 the Bolsheviks and, to a very large degree, the Mensheviks were oblivious to the workers' activities. For these *intelligenty* were far too busy centralising the movement, re-establishing intelligentsia hegemony and participating in stratospheric party squabbles to notice the rumblings below.

Until 1903 there were virtually no theoretical differences between leading Mensheviks and Bolsheviks (Haimson, 1955: 129, 171). And until 1905 differences between the two groups were *only* theoretical. Practically, they behaved alike because the Mensheviks, like the Bolsheviks, were 'isolated from the broad working masses' (Garvi, 1946: 519; also Keep, 1963: 147) until the 'dress rehearsal for the Russian revolution' took them both by surprise.

Some of the leading Mensheviks did, however, begin awakening to their theoretical misgivings concerning the Bolshevik view of party organisation during the second R.S.D.L.P. congress in 1903. That they began to decrease their emphasis on the role of the conscious intelligentsia before the Bolsheviks did was decided mainly by the fact that they were better-schooled in the tradition of German Social Democracy and could therefore go along with the Bolsheviks only up to a certain theoretical point.[13]

At the 1903 congress both Mensheviks and Bolsheviks agreed that a high degree of centralisation in the party was vital — that, in Trotsky's words, the party had to maintain a sense of 'organisational distrust' concerning its members in order to function under Russian conditions (*Vtoroy* . . ., 1959 [1904]: 169). But although both groups understood that the ease with which *agents provocateurs* could disrupt party work required centralisation of authority and secrecy, they differed over the question of degree. Thus, the Bolshevik proposal for the membership clause of the party constitution stated that a member is one who recognises the party's programme and 'supports the party through personal participation in one of the party's organisations' (ibid.: 262). The Mensheviks suggested that a member be defined as one who recognises that party's programme, 'supports the party by material means and gives it regular personal assistance under the guidance of one of its organisations' (ibid.: 425). Characteristically, the Menshevik version was copied from the statutes of the German Social Democratic party (Haimson, 1955: 175). The difference between the two clauses undoubtedly appeared minor even to many of the delegates but its significance was profound. For the Bolsheviks the party was synonymous with the organisation of professional revolutionaries, the contours of which had been outlined in Lenin's *What Is To Be Done?* But for the Mensheviks the conspiratorial organisation and the party were distinct entities; and the latter was to be as broadly based as possible. In Martov's words,

> the wider the title of party member is spread the better. We could only rejoice if every striker, every demonstrator . . . were ablt to declare himself a party member. A conspiratorial organization makes sense to me only insofar as it is enveloped in a broad, Social-Democratic workers party (*Vtoroy* . . ., *1959* [1904]: 263; also Martov, 1963 [1904]).

Twelve days earlier Alexander Martynov had argued at some length that the Bolsheviks were afraid of spontaneous mass action (*Vtoroy* . . ., 1959 [1904]: 108–19). It became apparent that the Mensheviks were prepared — now in principle, by 1905 in practice — to admit the 'fear-evoking' masses into the party so as to prevent the intelligentsia from actually becoming the party. One of Menshevism's cardinal principles — the encouragement of spontaneous working class development, of workers' initiative and participation — was beginning to become evident. This precipitated a split in the R.S.D.L.P. between Mensheviks and Bolsheviks.

Before turning to the events of 1905 let us see how the 'question of the relationship between consciousness and spontaneity' was resolved by Bundists and Poalei-Zionists. The Bundists never reached the same heights of intelligentsia elitism as the Mensheviks and Bolsheviks. For although at the turn of the century *intelligenty* in all parties reacted to the political awakening of educated 'society' and the relatively disorganised state of the whole labour movement by making a concerted attempt to gain greater control over its activities and politicise it,[14] the Bundists' mass base did not disappear from sight: in contrast to the non-Jewish strike movement, the movement among Jews continued to grow. This is illustrated by Fig. 16. The graph indicates that the number of Jewish strikers *per annum* increased steadily from 1895 to 1903, while the number of non-Jewish strikers *per annum* dropped quickly after 1899. In 1902 — the year in which *What Is To Be Done?* was published — there appear to have been fewer non-Jewish than Jewish strikers although Jews could claim to make up only 10 per cent of all those in the Empire who, according to the 1897 census, were engaged in 'mechanical and manufacturing pursuits' (Rubinow, 1907: 500).

Although both groups of workers were of course affected by the depression which began late in 1899, the Jews were able to continue their strike activities unabated, probably because they were better organised. But whatever the cause, the overall effect of the Jewish strike-movement's continued growth was that it indicated to the Bundists that the worker was still very much a force to be reckoned with. Any pretence of ignoring the spontaneously evolving labour movement could not possibly persist for long in such an atmosphere. Bundists therefore continued arguing that 'it is better to go along with the masses in a not totally correct direction than to separate oneself from them and remain a purist' (Kossovsky in *Vladimir Medem . . .*, 1943: 133). Before 1905 the actions which such words implied were anathema to Bolsheviks, Mensheviks — and Poalei-Zionists.

The Poalei-Zionists were not similarly affected by the mounting wave of Jewish labour unrest because, as I mentioned in Chapter 3, the leading *intelligenty* in the party were before 1906 located in Poltava, a town in the southern Pale entirely devoid of workers. Their weak ties to the working class permitted the Poalei-Zionists to develop elitist ideas in some ways reminiscent of Bolshevism. Ber Borokhov thus complained in late 1904 or early 1905[15] that 'we are too much involved in pleasant and lofty discussions on Zionism as a "movement of the people"' (Borokhov, 1955: 52). Labour Zionism, he insisted, is a movement of politically conscious pioneers (*khalutzim*) drawn from the intelligentsia, who must undergo tremendous personal sacrifice in preparing Palestine for colonisation. But, as noted in the preceding section, Borokhov forgot entirely about this elite vanguard of *intelligenty* within a year or so. Palestinian colonisation was by 1906 viewed as the inevitable outcome of spontaneously developing socio-economic forces affecting not *intelligenty* but the Jewish masses. As Borokhov wrote in that year, 'the radical revolution in Jewish life will be produced not through the force of *consciousness* . . . but by the power of a *spontaneous* process' (quoted in Frankel, 1961: 391; my emphasis).

What prompted this ideological *volte-face*? Principally, the fact that between early 1905 and 1906 the knit of social ties between Poalei-Zionist *intelligenty* and Jewish workers became more dense. During the 1905 revolution intelligentsia elitism receded into the background as worker militance surged ahead. In 1906 the party leaders became convinced that their headquarters should be transferred to Vilna, the centre of the Jewish labour movement. One worker-leader who made the move from Poltava explained how in Vilna 'there opened up a world with new impressions and influences . . . We felt the pulse and rhythm of the political movement' (Zerubavel, 1956: 122–3). In Vilna, Poalei-Zionist *intelligenty* developed closer ties to the working class. This could not but result in increased emphasis on the role of labour and decreased emphasis on the role of the intelligentsia.

The events of 1905 had a similar effect on the Bolsheviks. In 1903 their stress on the role of the conscious intelligentsia reached a plateau which was maintained for two years. Thus, the Bolshevik proposal for the definition of party member, defeated at the 1903 congress, was incorporated in their party constitution as late as the third (Bolshevik) congress in April 1905 (Carter, 1970: 56). Nor did the 1905 congress discuss the advisability of undertaking trade union work, in contrast to the All-Russian Menshevik conference, held concurrently, which advised its party organisations to 'undertake extensive agitation among the workers for the organisation of trade unions' (ibid.: 75–6). But the Bolsheviks' adamant refusal to admit the spontaneous labour movement into its ranks did not last the year. For 1905 was a year of revolution during which over 550 per cent more workers went out on strike — first to make economic, then political demands — than during the whole preceding decade. Political liberties, including the legalisation of trade unions, were finally wrested from the autocracy, at least for a time. And by September the Bolsheviks (and the Mensheviks) 'ceased to be a sect' (Keep, 1963: 165), having once again sunk roots in the the working class.

As in the 1890s ideological accommodation to the exigencies of the moment now took place. By November, Lenin admitted that conditions had so changed that much of the analysis in *What Is To Be Done?* was 'outdated'. He therefore called for the establishment of a political centre 'with deep roots in the people' (Lenin, 1960–70 [1925–6]: vol. 10, 22); demanded 'the full application of the democratic principle in party organisation' (ibid.: 33); and even went so far as to claim that 'the working class is instinctively, spontaneously [!] Social Democratic' (ibid.: 32). To be sure, the Bolsheviks still insisted that the secret apparatus of the party be kept intact while the Mensheviks pressed for the full legalisation of the party. But although Bolshevism remained the most elitist form of Russian Marxism, Lenin's position in 1905 nevertheless amounted to a major revision of earlier Bolshevik views. The workers in that year demonstrated that their spontaneity had been transformed into consciousness, in consequence of which the Bolsheviks considered it necessary to broaden somewhat their notion of party organisation and make it more democratic. This is undoubtedly what Trotsky meant when he wrote that 'the revolution . . . forestalled the work of political consciousness' on the part of the intelligentsia (1971 [1909]: 124).

In concluding this section it may be mentioned in passing that this discussion throws some light on the question of whether or not the authoritarian degeneration of Bolshevism after 1917 was, as is often claimed (e. g., by Billington, 1966), the inevitable outcome of Russian *cultural* development or the result of the *structural* forces outlined here (cf. Carlo, 1973). Billington suggests that Russian political culture had always been anti-democratic and that this tendency, as manifested in the typical Bolshevik personality, prevented the realisation of the revolution's democratic goals. Carlo, on the other hand, notes that world and civil wars combined with foreign invasions to destroy half of Russia's industrial labour force and demoralise the remainder. When in 1912–14 and in 1917 labour militance surged ahead there was very little question as to who would carry out the revolution's goals.[16] But when in the mid-1920s the decimated remains of the working class proved to be incapable of accomplishing the task, the Party once again substituted itself for the proletariat. Carlo thus suggests that, because of weak ties between workers and *intelligenty*, consciousness emerged victorious and the revolution was lost.

The problem with Billington's view is that an important empirical consequence of his hypothesis does not hold. If it were the authoritarian tendencies inherent in Russian political culture which led to the failure of the revolution, then one would expect persons who did not imbibe this culture not to have developed such elitist attitudes. Here the Poalei-Zionists provide us with an interesting test case. As Fig. 14 indicates, they were almost to a man unexposed to Russian political culture as they grew up. Yet, as noted above, they were nearly as elitist as the Bolsheviks until 1906; and as Jonathan Frankel points out, even after 1906 some of them tended to favour Bolshevik principles of party organisation over Menshevik (1961: 384). This would suggest that culture was a less important factor: it was more the degree to which *intelligenty* were embedded in the working class over time which determined the outcome of their efforts.

It thus appears that intelligentsia elitism fluctuated over time and among the parties in accordance with the temporal availability of different segments of the working class.[17] Periods of heightened labour militance and close ties between workers and *intelligenty* were associated with the democratisaton of ideologies, while declines in the workers movement and weak ties between the two groups led *intelligenty* to assert their own importance in making the revolution.[18] Such variations were, it is true, produced also by primary socialisation patterns, regional differences in recruitment and autonomous developments within the intelligentsia itself. But it nevertheless appears that an 'iron law of democracy' was operative. The major force capable of preventing the resurgence of intelligentsia elitism and its degeneration into outright authoritarianism was the working class itself.

Let us now consider how the principles of spontaneity and consciousness were in 1905 used to define the revolution's agents and character in accordance with the *regional* availability of different working-class strata.

C. The Agents and Character of the Revolution

The further east one goes in Europe, the more cowardly, mean and politically weak is the bourgeoisie, and the greater are the cultural and political tasks confronting the proletariat. The Russian working class must and will bear on its own sturdy shoulders the cause of winning political freedom . . . The Russian proletariat will throw off the yoke of autocracy, and thus with greater energy will continue the struggle against capitalism and the bourgeoisie for the complete victory of socialism.

Manifesto of the R.S.D.L.P., 1898

The Manifesto of the R.S.D.L.P. left unanswered a vital question concerning the character of the impending revolution: If the weakness of the Russian bourgeoisie meant that the proletariat had to play a leading role in overthrowing the autocracy, then should the proletariat go so far as to seize state power immediately? If it did not, the 'cowardly, mean and politically weak' middle class might prove incapable of carrying out the democratic tasks of a bourgeois revolution. If it did, a working-class regime would find itself in the ideologically and practically difficult position of controlling a country where capitalism was not fully developed. In this section I want first to outline the manner in which the intelligentsia sought to resolve this dilemma; and then to propose an explanation as to why different solutions were formulated by different groups.

Before 1905, the opinions of Georgi Plekhanov regarding this issue were widely accepted by members of all parties. In his debate with the populists in the mid-1880s Plekhanov had characterised as hopelessly utopian their belief that Russia could pass directly to socialism without going through a period of capitalist development. Basing himself on what he believed were firm Marxist principles,[19] he argued that the level of a country's economic development determines its preparedness for true democracy and socialism. A socialist revolution in a backward country like Russia was, he insisted, out of the question for the moment — which left him with the thorny problem of indicating what the conscious intelligentsia might do until capitalism, and with it the working class, spontaneously matured. His answer was that the working class could first be organised to play a leading role in the prior bourgeois revolution. Second, because Marx and Engels had claimed in the *Manifesto of the Communist Party* that the German bourgeois revolution would be the 'immediate prologue to the workers' revolution', Plekhanov further submitted that the existence of a still weaker middle class in Russia meant that the period between the bourgeois

and proletarian revolutions in the latter country would be of proportionately shorter duration. He neglected to mention how long this
period would be, and thereby managed to synthesise two apparently
contradictory views. On the one hand, he offered a deterministic refutation
of populist voluntarism by seeking to demonstrate that capitalist development could not bypass Russia; on the other, he suggested a means of
immediately utilising the revolutionaries' fervour by showing how their
efforts could bear fruit in the not-too-distant future. The principles of
conscious action and spontaneous development were thus temporarily
fused (Plekhanov, 1974 [1960]: 49–357).

As we have seen, tensions between these two principles were evident
from the 1890s on, but were reflected only in the debate over party
organisation. The year 1905, however, witnessed a qualitative shift in the
character of this debate. The principles of spontaneity and consciousness
took on a new colouring, being now used to define the revolution's class
character. Would socialism have to wait until capitalism and the working
class spontaneously matured? Or could some politically conscious alliance
of class forces seize state power and begin immediately the task of
constructing a socialist society? These were the issues at stake in 1905.

The Menshevik position, which was in all essential respects identical
with that of the Bundists and Poalei-Zionists,[20] was clarified at an April
1905 party conference. The Mensheviks undertook to emphasise the
revolution's bourgeois character by resolving that 'the objective conditions
of social development' demand the 'liquidation once and for all [of] the
monarchial regime' and the 'direct acquisition of power' by 'elements
of . . . politically liberated bourgeois society'. Social Democracy, continued the Menshevik resolution, must merely 'strive to retain . . . a
position which would best afford [it] the opportunity of furthering the
[bourgeois] revolution'. This was to involve putting pressure from below
on the new government. Specifically, the Social Democrats must neither
participate in the provisional government nor seize state power on their
own since a bourgeois revolution cannot be made by a working class
wishing to adhere to its socialist ideals. Rather, Social Democracy must
'remain the party of the extreme revolutionary opposition' and force the
government not to falter in carrying out its historically assigned tasks
(Carter, 1970: 72–3). This could be accomplished by creating an
alternative to the recently proclaimed State Duma (parliament) capable
of functioning as a 'revolutionary self-government'. The details of this
plan, worked out by Martov,[21] were as follows: Workers organisations
would take the initiative in promoting the election of 'people's agitational
committees' comprised of all strata of the population dissatisfied with the
Tsar's half-hearted Duma reform. These committees would campaign for
democratic candidates. At the same time, 'the committees seek to create,
aside from the legal representation, an illegal representation which at a
certain moment would appear before the country as a provisional organ of

the people's will' (Martov, 1905a: 2, col. 1). By establishing this system of 'dual power' the Mensheviks would thus be able to transform themselves from a sect into a mass party, to encourage the liberal bourgeoisie to effect democratic reforms and, at the same time, give capitalism free reign to develop.

Not all Mensheviks were in 1905 as sympathetic to the liberals as Pavel Axelrod, who called outright for a coalition between working and middle classes (Ascher, 1972: 236–7). But the Mensheviks unanimously agreed to 'renounce a comprehensive struggle with all bourgeois society' (Martov, 1905b: col. 5)[22] and abstain from power. Even if some Mensheviks temporarily fell short of regarding the middle class an ally, few ever went so far as to consider members of that class opponents. It was, after all, a middle-class revolution that was at hand.

Another envisaged coalition of class forces led the Bolsheviks to a radically different (and vaguer) set of predictions. In 1902, the structure of available social movements had changed dramatically as large-scale peasant uprisings broke out after years of relative quiescence. Those *intelligenty* who, as we shall see, stood closest to the Russian radical tradition and to the peasants adjusted their hopes and expectations accordingly. A revivified populist voice was born in the form of the Socialist-Revolutionary party; and the Bolsheviks 'discovered' the peasantry (Dan, 1964 [1946]: 293; Haimson, 1955: 205 ff.). The Bolsheviks' call in 1905 for a 'revolutionary-democratic dictatorship of the proletariat and the peasantry' represented a major accommodation to this altered opportunity structure, an attempt to harness the peasants' discontent by offering to feed their land hunger.

The Bolshevik slogan rested on a distinction between two stages in the revolution. The first democratic stage was to involve a coalition of the proletariat and all peasants against the autocracy; the second socialist stage, a coalition of only the urban and rural proletariat against the whole (urban and rural) bourgeoisie. The rural poor were thus to fight 'with the peasant bourgeoisie for democracy, with the urban proletariat for socialism' (Lenin, 1960–70 [1925–6]: vol. 8, 87). It was during the first stage, that a worker-peasant alliance would form a 'provisional re-volutionary government' — the Bolshevik reply to the Menshevik notion of 'revolutionary self-government' — by seizing state power through an armed uprising. This act was necessary because no force other than the worker-peasant alliance was viewed as capable of carrying through with the revolution's first democratic stage. The bourgeoisie, argued the Bolsheviks, 'stand in too great need of tsarism . . . to want it to be destroyed' (ibid.: vol. 9, 56). Thus, while the Mensheviks saw reason to be hopeful of middle-class strength the Bolsheviks saw none; and where the Bolsheviks were sensitive to the peasantry's power the Mensheviks were blind.

Did the Bolshevik call for a 'revolutionary-democratic dictatorship of the proletariat and the peasantry' imply that Russia was on the eve of a socialist revolution? Their answer was none too clear. True, it was claimed that any such talk was 'absurd' and 'anarchist gibberish' since 'the degree of Russian economic development . . . and the degree of class-consciousness and organisation of the proletariat' presumably rendered socialism unrealisable for the time being (ibid.: 28, 49). The worker-peasant dictatorship was, then, 'only a transient, temporary socialist aim' (ibid.: 86). But this raised a further problem: What was to prevent the worker-peasant dictatorship from holding on to state power if, by definition, no other classes possessed sufficient strength to seize it in the first place? Did this contradiction not imply that a Bolshevik victory would entail striving for a retention of state control and a rapid or even immediate transition to stage two of the revolution? In fact, the Bolsheviks said as much on several occasions. Anticipating a position which they would accept fully only in 1917, it was argued that a victorious revolution in Russia might well be the prologue to a socialist revolution in western Europe. A socialist West could offer economic aid and political support to backward Russia, thus enabling the two stages of the revolution to be collapsed. 'We stand', wrote Lenin in September 1905 'for uninterrupted revolution' — that is to say, for the immediate extension of the revolution to its second socialist stage (ibid.: 237; also 82, 84; vol. 8, 100, 303). Some Mensheviks had argued along similar lines in March of that year, but did so reluctantly, viewing this outcome of something of a last resort (Martov, 1905b: col. 8). Moreover, their eagerness soon dissipated. The Bolsheviks were a good deal more sanguine.

This thumbnail sketch permits us to conclude that the two dominant characterisations of the revolution worked out in 1905[23] were rooted in different perceptions of the Russian class structure. The Mensheviks, along with the Bundists and Poalei-Zionists, predicted a bourgeois revolution because they regarded Russian merchants, industrialists and liberal intellectuals as relatively strong and progressive politically, and the peasantry as possessing little radical potential. The Bolsheviks foresaw, albeit dimly, a socialist revolution because they perceived the Russian bourgeoisie to be weak and the peasantry to be a major revolutionary force.

This difference in perceptions is often explained in terms similar to those that might be derived from the classification aspect of the embedding model (cf. Carr, 1956): In this connection it must be recalled that, in the course of the nineteenth century, only a handful of Russian intellectuals — socialist, liberal or conservative — had viewed the middle class and its values in a favourable light. This is only to be expected given Russia's retarded economic development and the stunted growth of its bourgeoisie. Here one could find very little of a middle-class nature worthy of admiration; only if one were thoroughly westernised could the accomplishments of a middle class — i.e., the western bourgeoisie — be appreciated.

In fact, even if one goes back to the roots of the 'westernising' tradition in nineteenth-century Russian intellectual history one can detect a degree of ambivalence concerning the western bourgeois world.[24] If equivocation can be found here, one can imagine how much more anti-bourgeois the vast majority of Russian intellectuals were. Thus, as several students of the subject have remarked, Russian literature of the last century is riddled with disdain for the middle class (Bill, 1956; Gorev, 1976 [1917]). And among radicals such contempt was, especially after 1848, taken for granted since the assistance of the European middle class in defeating the revolutions of that year suggested to Russian *intelligenty* the need to re-examine the revolutionary potential of their own country rather than expect radical change to emanate from the west (Barghoorn, 1949). As they began 'turning away from German ideas to Russian facts' (Masaryk, 1919 [1913]: vol. 2, 3) they became convinced that the peasantry might well represent Russia's only hope. Only then did populist ideology take root in Russia (Herzen, 1956: 336–506).

E. H. Carr once wrote that French utopian socialism and German left-Hegelianism 'had to be transformed and reabsorbed into the Russian environment and the Russian tradition' before Russian populism could fructify (1956: 377). In the twentieth century not all Russian Social Democrats were in a position to effect an analogous transformation in Marxist doctrine. The Bolsheviks, who, because of their mobility patterns were the only completely Russified group of Jewish *intelligenty*, were able to take the long-standing attitudes of the Russian intelligentsia to heart by proclaiming the impotence of the Russian middle class, its inability to seize state power. Members of the other parties, whose mobility patterns ensured that they would imbibe a more substantial dose of westernism, were rather more confident in the middle class, less sensitive to the peasantry and consequently able to predict a bourgeois revolution. They proved to be wrong because they were unable to 'transform and reabsorb into the Russian environment and the Russian tradition' the teachings of German Marxism. M. Tomsky once accused Pavel Axelrod of 'viewing Russia through German spectacles' (quoted in Ascher, 1972: 265), of being a 'stranger' in the land. The same accusation could have been lodged against the vast majority of Jewish *intelligenty* with considerable justice.

Although this traditional argument throws some light on why *intelligenty* thought what they did in 1905 it is not without its problems, the most conspicuous of which is that it fails to explain how internalised values were reinforced and acted upon. Accepted beliefs are frequently forgotten or later denied; and wide discrepancies may exist between thoughts and actions. If elements of culture accepted at one point in time are later to be actualised, certain structural conditions must facilitate their transmission over time and their eventual realisation; in order to be able to say that a given *cultural* tradition will survive 'we have to know which of the *social* causes that have maintained it for such a long time will survive'

(Durkheim, 1972: 221). Below, the decisive social fact which led *intelligenty* to translate their perceptions of class structure into political actions will be examined: regional variations in their reclassification.

We may begin with what appears to be a quite trivial incident. In 1905, Y. Sverdlov, a Jewish *intelligent* who headed the Bolshevik organisation in the Urals, wrote a pamphlet entitled 'What is a Workers Party?' It was apparently intended for distribution among 'backward' workers. Not only was its style simple, but its content was readily understandable to a factory worker with strong ties to the peasantry: the typical Bolshevik supporter. This is evident from the fact that Sverdlov was prompted to define capitalist exploitation as 'a new form of *corvée*' and liken workers to serfs (Sverdlov, 1957–60: 5). In order to propagandise among workers who might still own a plot of land in the countryside or even work it on a seasonal basis *intelligenty* had frequently to talk in peasant terms and to some extent adapt to their way of thinking. In the case mentioned above this involved only an allusion to serfdom, the memory of which was kept very much alive in the mind of the protoproletarian by the continued existence of various obligations dating back to the 1861 reforms. If one did Social Democratic work where the protoproletarian type was particularly numerous — as only Bolsheviks did — one had, in other words, to think peasant.

Workers who shifted back and forth between factory and village quite literally led *intelligenty* to rural Russia. The latter thus came in contact with and were, like Sverdlov, influenced by the peasantry's presence. In some Bolshevik strongholds 'more than half . . . the industrial labour force lived in the countryside; the workers went there almost weekly and constantly met their countrymen in the city' (Morokhovetz, 1925b: 68). These workers facilitated the spread of Social Democratic ideas among the peasants by 'taking proclamations and "the message" home with them' (Lane, 1969: 112; Morokhovetz, 1925b: 60–1). The ground thus prepared, *intelligenty* began, in some cases as early as 1902, to help establish in outlying settlements and semi-industrialised rural areas both workers groups and committees designed specifically for propaganda among the peasants (Lane, 1969: 68, 99, 152; Morokhovetz, 1925a: 56).

That *intelligenty* working in rural areas were affected by their proximity to and contact with peasants is indicated by their willingness in some locations to use for propaganda purposes literature published by the neo-populist Socialist-Revolutionary party (Lane, 1969: 100; Morokhovetz, 1925a: 57–8). More important, the very existence of peasant committees indicates that the availability of radicalised peasants in the immediate social environment of Bolshevik *intelligenty* led the latter to believe in the revolutionary potential of the countryside: already in 1902 the idea of a proletarian-peasant alliance was beginning to germinate. Thus, the typical Bolshevik worker, because of his intermediate position between factory and village, acted as a sort of structural transmission belt which conveyed the revolutionary significance of peasant unrest to the intelligentsia.

As is frequently noted, the overall impact of Bolshevik ideas on the peasantry was not great in 1905. Social Democratic influence in general was, it appears, largely restricted to areas surrounding industrial centres and regions where capitalist agriculture was highly developed and had therefore called into existence a substantial rural proletariat (Morok-hovetz, 1925a – 1925e). Moreover, the Mensheviks played an important role in the peasant movement in some areas such as Georgia; and even the Bundists sent some agitators to the countryside in White Russia (Perrie, 1972: 135). But what is more important in the present context is the influence of the peasantry on the Bolsheviks. There can be little doubt that it was considerable. The Bolsheviks appear almost certainly to have taken the lead in forming permanent peasant committees and generally establishing links with rural Russia. Particularly in the Urals and the Central Industrial Region Bolshevik peasant committees had by 1904 or 1905 sprung up in 'a whole series of peasant districts' (Lyadov, 1926: 184; see 24–39, 184–92). This is only to be expected given the fact that Bolshevik *intelligenty*, unlike those in other parties, were connected mainly to workers who were themselves tied to the peasantry. In Odessa, where workers were generally more highly urbanised and had severed their rural ties, one Jewish Bolshevik worker recalled that 'the question of getting in touch with the peasantry . . . was not raised' (Piatnitsky, 1933 [1925]: 106).[25] Little wonder that Odessa was located in a region of Menshevik predominance.

It may thus be suggested that before and during the 1905 revolution Bolsheviks were more sensitive to the peasantry not only because of their upbringing, but also because of the class ties they forged during late adolescence and early adulthood. In 1904 Martin Lyadov was undoubtedly not alone as he began to grow conscious of the peasantry's revolutionary potential. He remarked in his memoirs that 'often in conversations peasants praised the workers: "They are fed up with their suffering, they have already begun to fight. We peasants ought to take their example to heart"'. The peasants, reasoned Lyadov, 'were far from so downtrodden as we usually think of them', and concluded from this that Russia was on the eve of revolution — although not the kind of revolution non-Bolshevik *intelligenty* had in mind (Lyadov, 1926: 29, 32, 30).

Few Jews could arrive at precisely the same sort of conclusion for the simple reason that residence restrictions and the watchful eye of the police prevented them from living in the Russian interior and thus becoming reclassified in a working class stratum capable of leading them in this ideological direction. Undoubtedly the highly urbanised and westernised Jewish *intelligent* also found the idea of working among the peasants quite out of step with his ideological training. And peasant anti-Semitism reinforced such propensities. In any event, only a tiny minority of Jewish *intelligenty* came from a background and were in a position to envisage a 'revolutionary-democratic dictatorship of the proletariat and the peasantry' and thereby become ideal-typical 'rebels'.

The reclassification of Bolshevik *intelligenty* in the lower strata of the working class had a second important consequence for the ideology of that party: it sometimes forced *intelligenty* to adopt extremist tactics, even against their better judgement. But an important qualification is in order before this theme can be developed. One ought not to conclude that peasants and protoproletarians were everywhere so rebellious as Lyadov makes them out to be. True, the protoproletarian in particular eventually became the most radical worker in the Empire for reasons outlined in Chapter 2. But this, it must be emphasised, occurred on a large scale only *after* 1905. Thus, if we measure radicalism by the frequency with which workers took part in the strike movement we find that workers in areas of Bolshevik strength — where the protoproletarian was most conspicuous — were in 1905 less radical than workers in areas of Menshevik strength: on the average, each worker in the former region went out on strike nearly twice in 1905, each worker in the latter region nearly two and a half times (calculated from data in Amalrik, 1955: 174, using the same geographical boundaries as in Fig. 12; figures for highly industrialised provinces only are almost identical). The main reason Menshevik workers were more radical was that discontent among them was aggravated by national antagonisms, the strike movement thus assuming its most widespread form in the Baltic region and the Caucasus. Moreover, in many instances peasants and peasant/workers displayed only profound respect for the Tsar and shock at any suggestion that they might endeavour to undermine his rule (Woytinsky, 1961: 70ff.). The grip of Tsarist paternalism over the mind of God-fearing and illiterate (Rashin, 1951) rural Russians certainly weakened in 1905, particularly after the events of 'Bloody Sunday', but its hold did not relax completely until later. Only after the regime demonstrated repeatedly its disregard for wishes of the Russian people were the institutions which made the protoproletarians the most radical of Russian workers able to function at peak efficiency as crucibles of discontent.

Yet one incident did reveal the drift of future events quite clearly and so deserves to be mentioned. This was the Moscow uprising of 1905. The Moscow uprising involved a ten day long series of clashes between several hundred revolutionaries and government troops. It was the most violent event of the year, the closest the Bolsheviks came to realising their much-hoped-for 'armed uprising', and it provided a model for the transfer of power from the old regime to the new. Was the uprising merely a consequence of the fact that Bolsheviks were predominant in Moscow and encouraged workers there to engage in an insurrection? Or did the workers in the city push the Bolsheviks in that direction? The evidence I have inspected indicates that, in large measure, the impetus came from below.

Early in December 1905 the Moscow Bolshevik Committee came to realise that 'the mood among the masses was such that if we did not call a [general] strike, it would break out by itself. Nobody doubted that a [general] strike would inevitably turn into an armed uprising' (Lyadov, 1926: 124). In the Moscow Soviet of Workers Deputies, over which the Bolsheviks had quickly gained ascendance,[26] this impression was soon confirmed. Not *intelligenty*, but 'the worker delegates . . . most strongly advocated calling for a general strike and armed uprising' (Slusser, 1963: 109). Many Bolshevik *intelligenty* realised that they were inadequately prepared for an insurrection. They therefore tried to stall matters by deciding to discuss the issue with factory workers in an organised manner and only then come to a final decision. But on 5 December a conference of between 500 and 900 worker delegates (reports vary) decided unanimously to call a general strike and strive to transform it into an armed uprising. At the risk of losing workers' support if they backed down, those Bolshevik *intelligenty* who had previously opposed this move now 'became convinced that the mood of the workers permitted no turning back' (ibid.: 112).

Who precisely were the workers capable of pushing the Bolsheviks in this direction? Police records show that ninety-one persons were arrested for participating in the Moscow uprising. The social composition of this group probably represents a fairly accurate cross-section of the insurrectionists. A mere five of the ninety-one (or just over 5 per cent) were students. Only seven (or under 8 per cent) were listed as workers. The largest single category of persons arrested — including forty-six individuals (or nearly 51 per cent of the total) — were peasants who were working or had recently been working in Moscow factories (Lane, 1969: 128). In Moscow at least, the protoproletarian had clearly demonstrated his radicalism.

Further indirect evidence that Social Democratic doctrine in Moscow was more the result of local workers' militance than the upbringing of *intelligenty* may be derived from the behaviour of Mensheviks in the city. Although the Mensheviks were generally more restrained in their actions than the Bolsheviks, they were not, as contemporary Soviet historiography would have us believe, opposed to the armed uprising even though this was contrary to official Menshevik policy. Moreover, at the first session of the Moscow Soviet, then under Menshevik control, a resolution was adopted calling for an alliance of the working class with the peasantry. The liberal bourgeoisie was not even mentioned as a possible ally. Robert Slusser (1963: 76) concludes from these facts that the Moscow Mensheviks 'were far from conforming to the general Mensheviks strategy in the revolution, and surprisingly close to what later came to be regarded as the orthodox Bolshevik line'. But is this really so surprising? If the Moscow Mensheviks had chosen to ignore their demands, all influence over local workers would have been lost. In other words, the Mensheviks were so radical in Moscow probably because workers in that city forced them to be. Some Moscow Mensheviks were actually prompted to form an extremist left wing which collaborated closely with the Bolsheviks. It is perhaps not accidental that the leader of this group, Peter Garvi, was attached to workers in 'Red Presnia' (Garvi, 1946: 605 ff.), the most radical section of town and one noted for its unusually large number of protoproletarians.

But one would have to wait another seven years before the full effect of the protoproletarian on Bolshevik ideology became visible. For in 1912 the business cycle began an upward swing; Russian industry rapidly expanded; scores of thousands of protoproletarians were recruited from the countryside; and the Bolsheviks increased their following among the new industrial recruits as quickly as the Mensheviks lost ground (Haimson, 1964). These workers, along with workers and peasants in uniform, were the driving forces behind the events of 1917. During that year the liberal bourgeoisie proved to be quite as weak as the Bolsheviks had expected. As one Menshevik later put it, the

> Menshevik conception of the 'pressure' of the working class on the bourgeoisie with the aim of revolutionizing it and pushing it into power . . . proved to be unfeasible — primarily because the presumed object of the 'pressure' was simply not there (Dan, 1964 [1946]: 340).

The Mensheviks, along with the Bundists and Poalei-Zionists, thus grossly miscalculated the course of events that year, in part because the working class strata to which they were attached did not lead them to believe in the possibility of insurrection and seizure of power by a worker-peasant coalition. John Kenneth Galbraith once said that the man who breaks through a rotting door acquires an unjustified reputation for violence; some credit ought to be given the door. He might have added that neither is the man's violence solely a result of his individual predilections: it also depends on whether or not he is embedded in a segment of a class which allows him, or even compels him, to become a 'rebel' capable of such extremes.

The non-Bolsheviks did rather better when it came to assessing the problems inherent in the Bolshevik seizure of power. Although the degeneration of Boshevik elitism into outright authoritarianism was not, as suggested in the preceding section, always inevitable, it was always a very real possibility. And it did become inevitable once the Russian working class was decimated. In addition, the Bolshevik seizure of power by virtue of peasant support raised a further problem which the non-Bolsheviks perceived quite clearly: giving land to the peasants created a large class of individual proprietors in a country whose government was avowedly socialist. Stalinism was not the inevitable result; but it became increasingly likely when revolution in the west failed to materialise. Once tractors from the west were not forthcoming it became more and more difficult gradually to convince individual landholders of the value of socialism, and more and more tempting for an authoritarian regime to eliminate them as a class.

The Bolsheviks were thus in a position to see more or less accurately the shape of events in 1917. The non-Bolsheviks were able to perceive the consequences of these events. But, it may be added, no *intelligenty* foresaw at all clearly the problems of the other 'successful' ideology — Poalei-Zionism. The constant hue and cry of non-Zionist radicals was that the Poalei-Zionists were undermining the basis for victory by threatening to leave Russia in droves. The criticism was misdirected for two reasons. First, the Poalei-Zionists believed that Palestinian colonisation would be an extended process and that Jewish workers should in the meantime take as active a role as possible in the Russian revolutionary movement. In point of fact, few Poalei-Zionist workers left Russia before 1917. Thus, in 1905–6 there was a grand total of between 400 and 550 organised Jewish workers in Palestine, at least half of whom had been *intelligenty* before they migrated, only 60 of whom were members of the Poalei-Zion party, and not all of whom had come from Russia (Ben-Tzvi in Reznichenko, 1948: 106ff.; Laqueur, 1972: 282). Second, as Borokhov had emphasised, the artisan was in any case a minor revolutionary force: the revolution was made by industrial workers, military men and peasants, not by Jewish tailors and bristle-makers in Vilna and Minsk. The migration of Poalei-Zionists to Palestine thus had an insignificant impact on the course of the revolution.

The members of all parties failed to realise that the central flaw in the Poalei-Zionist programme had nothing to do with Russia, but rather with Palestine. For although the Poalei-Zionists' characterisation of the Russian revolution corresponded with that of the Mensheviks and Bundists (they all thought it would be bourgeois), their proximity to the Jewish community, and hence their Zionist beliefs, led them to envisage a bourgeois revolution in the Middle East as well. They expected that the agents of this revolution would be Jewish immigrants — in alliance with the Arab *felaheen*. Material and cultural benefits would, they submitted, accrue to the Arabs of Palestine as a result of Jewish immigration; and there was an identity of interest between Jews and *felaheen* as against the *effendi* and the Ottoman regime (Ro'i, 1968: 203). This argument led them to believe that Arab nationalism, the emergence of which they were fully aware (Borokhov, 1920: 282 ff.), would have little impact on the Palestinian scene. They even went so far as to claim that 'the *felaheen* will fuse with us to the point where there will be no difference' between Jew and Arab (Borokhov, 1955: 149). Ironically, the Poalei-Zionists proposed for the Arabs of Palestine the 'solution' which Mensheviks and Bolsheviks proposed for the Jews of Russia: assimilation.

Neither in Russia nor in Palestine did the proposal work. Which permits me to conclude that the Jews, having been situated between lord and serf in medieval Poland, and between feudalism and capitalism in nineteenth-century Russia, faced a return to their age-old predicament when they became 'strangers' again in the Middle East.

5 Rootless Cosmopolitans?

The relationship between the intellectuals and the world of production is not as direct as it is with the fundamental social groups but is, in varying degrees, 'mediated' by the whole fabric of society and by the complex of superstructures, of which the intellectuals are, precisely, the 'functionaries'. It should be possible both to measure the 'organic quality' [*organicita*] of the various intellectual strata and their degree of connection with a fundamental social group, and to establish a gradation of their functions from the bottom to the top (from the structural base upwards).

Antonio Gramsci

Before outlining some of this work's broader theoretical implications it may be useful briefly to summarise the foregoing chapters. Fig. 17, which presents in schematic form the explanatory model developed in the course of this study, should simplify the task.

In Fig. 17 we are dealing with three groups at three points in time: the Russian-Jewish community in about 1850, the Russian middle class in about 1895 and the Russian working class in about 1905. Each group is comprised of several segments, symbolised by letters of the alphabet. Solid lines represent structural ties, or bonds of occupational association among segments; broken lines represent paths of social mobility followed by *intelligenty*.

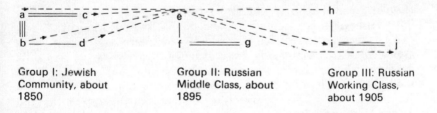

Group I: Jewish Community, about 1850

Group II: Russian Middle Class, about 1895

Group III: Russian Working Class, about 1905

Typical Mobility Paths

Poalei-Zionists: a——►h
Bundists: b——►h
Mensheviks: c——►i
Bolsheviks: d——►j

Fig. 17. The Embedding Process

Consider first Group I, the Jewish community. In Chapter 2 we saw that most Jews in pre-capitalist eastern Europe were middlemen; and that artisans, persons engaged in the transmission of culture, and so forth, formed important appendages to this basic class. Whatever their occupations, Jews were highly dependent on each other for credit and/or employment and/or markets. But capitalist development changed all this, for it provided some Jews with the opportunity to break occupational ties with their co-religionists. For example, a wealthy merchant who had previously extended credit to smaller merchants and artisans now found it more profitable to alter his traditional pattern of investment by pooling his capital with that of a German banker in order to finance the construction of railroads. In the process he not only ceased to supply the credit necessary for the livelihood of some fellow Jews, but also rendered some of their functions (e.g., estate management) anachronistic by speeding the development of capitalism. Similarly, the partial modernisation of the educational system allowed a handful of Jews to engage in occupations (e.g., engineering) which did not directly service the Jewish community.

As these and other categories of persons departed from the community structurally they tended to leave it culturally as well. That is to say, they tended to assimilate into the cultural milieu of the non-Jewish world to the extent that they were relatively independent from other Jews in the search for a livelihood.

The families which comprised the Jewish community in mid-nineteenth century were ranged along a continuum of embeddedness in the community; and the greater one's degree of embeddedness, the stronger one's sense of Jewish identity. This is illustrated by Fig. 17. The solid lines which symbolise bonds of occupational association among community segments 'a' through 'd' indicate that segment 'a', with a total of five ties to other segments, was most securely integrated in the community structurally, and therefore culturally; segment 'b' was next with four ties; followed by segment 'c' (two ties); and segment 'd' (one tie). Poalei-Zionist *intelligenty* tended to be recruited from segment 'a'; Bundists from segment 'b'; Mensheviks from segment 'c'; and Bolsheviks from segment 'd'.

That the mean degree of embeddedness of each party's intelligentsia was associated with variations in later ideological views was most readily apparent when attitudes towards the Jewish question were discussed. Bolsheviks, who in most cases considered themselves more Russian than Jewish, wanted the Jews completely to assimilate into the larger society. So did the Mensheviks, although here one can find certain individuals, such as Pavel Axelrod and David Shub, who hedged on the issue. But the Bundists, who eventually clearly identified with the Jews, wanted the Jewish community to remain intact culturally. And the Poalei-Zionists, whose sense of Jewish identity was strongest, endeavoured to have the community reconstituted on new national foundations. Thus, strength of Jewish identity, and therefore views on the Jewish question, were largely a function of the degree to which radicals' families of orientation were structurally embedded in the community.

As the broken lines in Fig. 17 indicate, the *intelligenty* all experienced social mobility as they entered the Russian or Jewish school systems. But although they were on their way to becoming members of the 'new middle class' they instead became radicals. Why they did so can be readily understood once we realise that turn-of-the-century Russia, more than any other European country, trained intellectuals but provided them with few occupational opportunities which allowed them to propound liberal ideas. The emergence of a strong liberal-democratic intellectual stratum was therefore blocked to a considerable degree — and the development of intellectual dissidence encouraged. This situation was exacerbated in the 1860s and 1870s when there was a quantitative over-supply of educated persons relative to the number of jobs available for them. By the end of this period the inability of Russian society to integrate its intellectuals into institutions where liberalism could thrive resulted in the emergence of a new occupational role — that of professional revolutionary. This signified that an entire social institution — a 'school of dissent' to use David Brower's term — had been created to employ persons who were poorly embedded in the middle class. This situation is illustrated in Fig. 17 by the lone social tie binding segment 'e' to its class.

It is of some interest that the proportion of radicalised intellectuals among a given category of persons appears to have varied inversely with the degree to which persons within that category were tied, or anticipated being tied to the middle class: the lower the degree of actual or anticipated middle-class integration, the higher the proportion of radicals. Thus, students, who by definition possessed no occupational ties to the middle class, contributed a larger proportion of recruits to the intelligentsia than employed professionals even though there were many more employed professionals than students in Russia. Actual and perceived blockages in social mobility were higher among Jews than among other categories of the student body due to widespread ethnic discrimination. This is the principle reason why Jewish students were more over-represented in the ranks of the intelligentsia than students in general.

The fact that *intelligenty* were poorly embedded in the middle class did not mean that they were destined always to hang suspended between classes. For, to varying degrees, they were able to forge concrete social ties with members of the Russian working class who, they believed, possessed the capacity to give vent to their discontent. Now the character of the Russian working class — its ethnic composition, its level of power *vis-à-vis* other classes, the degree to which its members still retained social ties to rural Russia — varied regionally. And as Fig. 17 shows, *intelligenty* were recruited to different segments of the working class. Not that their degree of embeddedness in the working class remained constant over time. On the contrary, different segments of the working class were prepared to engage in revolutionary activities (and thereby keep in touch with *intelligenty*) at different points in time, depending on the way in which their industries were organised and the phase of the business cycle. And *intelligenty* sometimes lost sight of the working class and formed an inflated sense of their own importance in the revolutionary overthrow. The latter development was closely associated with levels of government repression which, when moderately high, tended to increase the level of intelligentsia radicalism.

All this is significant because variations in the regional and temporal availability of workers exercised a profound impact on the ideologies of *intelligenty*. Recall the following example. Non-Jewish members of the Russian working class were, in the late nineteenth and early twentieth centuries, in the process of being transformed from peasants into workers. Particularly in the eastern part of European Russia workers were in fact half-peasants because they might still own and, on a seasonal basis, work plots of land in the countryside, because they very frequently journeyed to their villages to visit family, and so forth. Jewish Bolsheviks tended to be recruited to the revolutionary movement in this region. And by virtue of the fact that they thereby became attached to protoproletarians, they began, in some cases as early as 1902, to form political organisations among the peasants, to whom they were led by their protoproletarian associates. Little wonder, then, that it was about this time that the idea of an alliance between the working class and the peasantry began to germinate among the Bolsheviks. No other *intelligenty* were able to conceive of such an alliance because they tended to be attached to more urbanised workers and therefore remained relatively divorced from the realities of the countryside. Bolsheviks were, in other words, able to envisage the combination of class forces which would topple the regime in 1917 partly because of the character of the segment of the working class to which they were attached.

Regional variations in the character of the working class had other ideological consequences as well. Particularly when they first set out on their careers, assimilated *intelligenty* could find their sense of Jewish identity recrystallising if they engaged in radical activities in regions where the ratio of Jewish to non-Jewish workers was relatively high. Unassimilated *intelligenty* were likely to become more Jewish-nationalistic if they worked in areas where the ratio of Jewish workers to Jewish non-workers was relatively low. *Intelligenty* tended to be more westernised if they were recruited to the revolutionary movement where the Russian and Jewish middle classes were strongest. And *intelligenty* recruited in regions where the protoproletarian type was most conspicuous could become — and in some cases were eventually compelled to become — more radical than most because they were connected to the most solidary group of workers in the Empire ('j' in Fig. 17).

The temporal availability of workers was no less influential in determining the ideological tendencies of *intelligenty*. This is clearly revealed by the manner in which elitism waxed and waned among *intelligenty*. For intelligentsia elitism appears to have varied among the four parties and over time in accordance with the degree to which *intelligenty* were tied to the working class. When such ties were strong — when, that is, the ratio of workers to *intelligenty* in party organisations was relatively high — the intelligentsia tended to minimise its own importance in the revolutionary movement. When, on the other hand, the ratio of workers to *intelligenty* in party organisations was relatively low, the intelligentsia sought to give history a push, to take things into its own hands, to minimise the importance of workers in the revolutionary process.

This summary gives some indication of how the ideologies of *intelligenty* were shaped by the degree to which they were embedded in various social groups over time. Russian-Jewish Marxists were recruited from groups which had been jettisoned to varying degrees from the Jewish community; they became very poorly embedded in the Russian middle class; and they were finally re-embedded more or less securely in different segments of the Russian working class. Views on the Jewish question; levels of intelligentsia elitism; the demarcation of revolutionary agents; and other elements of ideology were produced largely by differences in the mobility patterns of *intelligenty*.

There is a very long tradition behind the notion that the nineteenth-century Russian intelligentsia was a 'rootless' or 'classless' group. Among Russian social thinkers this view was given its most consistent form by the *narodnik* sociologist, Ivanov-Razumnik, and it has been accepted without question by most western historians, led perhaps by Martin Malia. I doubt that many sociologists in the west have been directly influenced by this line of thought. But the concept of the relatively unattached intellectual is certainly a recurrent theme in the works of western sociologists from Karl Mannheim to Rolf Dahrendorf. Parallel to this emphasis on the rootlessness of intellectuals in general and the Russian intelligentsia in particular, students of Jewish history have tended overwhelmingly to view the objects of their study as eternal wanderers: unattached persons whose very survival was contingent upon their ability to pick up and leave when circumstances demanded. In literature we discover the same theme — Thomas Mann's simile 'as unfettered as a Jew' in *The Magic Mountain* provides a nice example. Nor has the idea been restricted to academic circles. 'Rootless cosmopolitans' became a term of opprobrium in twentieth-century ideological parlance. Andrei Zhdanov used it to explain why Jewish intellectuals had no place in Mother Russia; David Ben-Gurion to explain why they had no place in the Diaspora.

High degrees of consensus sometimes lull social thinkers into a false sense of intellectual security. Nowhere is this clearer than in discussions of intellectuals, Russian *intelligenty* and Jews. One ought not to reject out of hand the proposition that Russian Jews were marginal men and the *intelligenty* among them *déclassé*; but I have sought to demonstrate that the explanatory gains are considerable if one recognises that the rootlessness of Russian-Jewish *intelligenty* was a variable, not a constant. For the assumption that they were immutably divorced from social structure already determines by conceptual fiat not just our research agenda, but also some questionable conclusions regarding the problem of ideological divergence. Perhaps the most common argument advanced by those who maintain that *intelligenty* were held together not by some social similarity but 'solely by ideas' (Berdyaev, 1948 [1937]: 19) is that we had best concern ourselves with the evolution of culture patterns; and that culture itself played the major role in determining the thoughts and actions of *intelligenty*. A second, less idealistic alternative is to claim that, from a structural point of view, ideological divergence is pretty much a random process. As Eric Hoffer (1951: 25) put it, when

> people are ripe for a mass movement, they are usually ripe for any effective movement, and not solely for one with a particular doctrine or program . . . In the overcrowded pale of Czarist Russia the simmering Jewish population was ripe for both revolution and Zionism. In the same family, one member would join the revolutionaries and the other the Zionists.

The historians, Isaac Levitats and Ezra Mendelsohn, have made a similar point[1]: how can one claim that the selection of ideas was structurally determined when brothers — i.e., persons from what appears to be precisely the same social location — sometimes followed different ideological paths? Finally, ignoring the fact that *intelligenty* do have social roots has led some scholars to adopt a voluntarist position. Thus Shlomo Avineri (1957: 277):

> The intellectuals are a social group determined as such by society to possess the individual power of choice . . . There is no *a priori* determination [of ideas], as in the case of the capitalist or the worker. Choice is the very embodiment of the intellectual's determined social being.

All three alternatives undoubtedly have some validity. We are of course influenced by ideas every day, as the cultural determinists suggest. But when it comes to ascertaining which ideas influence which groups of people and to what degree, it is important to gauge receptivity in terms of social location. Thus, only certain *intelligenty* were strongly influenced by the *haskala*, only certain others by the Russian radical tradition. Above all else, what determined one's particular exposure to culture was the degree to which one's family of orientation was embedded in the Jewish community. Those who take the random variation approach have a point too, albeit a less convincing one. There are always individual exceptions to any sociological generalisation, persons who act and think in a manner not covered by our 'laws': I have, for example, no idea as to why Shimon Dimanshtein, an unassimilated *intelligent* active in the northern Pale, became a Bolshevik. It is, however, important to distinguish between what is genuinely exceptional and apparently exceptional; and to note that the line between the two types of exceptions can be drawn only in terms of the explanatory power of our generalisations since greater theoretical specificity usually renders 'lawful' what at first sight appears to be random. Take the case of the two brothers who followed divergent ideological paths. Were they, as Hoffer, Levitats and Mendelsohn claim, from the same social location? I think not. Families, like all social structures, are constantly in flux, as are their environments. A person born into a family at one point in time may be socialised in a milieu and confronted with a set of opportunities for mobility quite different from the milieu and opportunities faced by someone born into the 'same' family at another point in time. Only if we recall Heraclitus' dictum that one can never step into the same river twice can we explain why, say, Boris Gorev became a Russian Social Democrat and his brother, Mark Liber, a Bundist (*see above*, 64), or why Chaim Weizmann became a general Zionist and his brother, Shmuel, a revolutionary (Weizmann, 1966 [1949]: 13).

The voluntarists' contribution is to guard us against mechanistic interpretations of social behaviour which portray men as empty vessels, the actions of which are solidly moulded by society and into which pour a defined assortment of beliefs, symbols and values. I expect that my critics will accuse me of having fallen victim to this distortion, of emphasising context at the expense of creativity. To some degree the point is justified. But I must claim in my defence that if (as Lenin put it after the second R.S.D.L.P. congress) I 'bent the stick too far in the opposite direction', this was entirely warranted by the current state of research on the Russian intelligentsia. As persons who endeavoured to destroy their society root and branch, Russian *intelligenty* are usually portrayed as having been men and women who made history just as they pleased. Their social context is often ignored and this, I submit, is a serious shortcoming. We stand to profit a great deal from examining what Simmel (1955 [1922]: 168) would have called the 'network of overlapping group-affiliations' of *intelligenty*. Only in this way can we develop further the research programme outlined in this chapter's frontispiece.[2]

Notes

Chapter 1

1. The following definitions are employed in this study: (a) 'Intellectuals' comprise an occupational group within, and ideologically supportive of the middle class. Their role is to produce, distribute and exchange ideas (cf. Eagleton, 1976: 59–76; Lipset and Dobson, 1972: 137–8). (b) Although it departs somewhat from the meaning of the Russian original (see Pollard, 1964) it will be useful to define the 'intelligentsia' as an occupational group of persons who (i) are structurally divorced from the middle class and (ii) produce, distribute and exchange ideas which are supportive of non-dominant classes. Following the Russian original, one member of the intelligentsia is referred to as an *intelligent*, more than one as *intelligenty*. Both are pronounced with a hard 'g'.
2. Although erring in the opposite direction is probably just as common. See, for example, (Shub, 1944).

Chapter 2

1. 'As it Christians, so it Jews.'
2. Historians frequently point out that western European feudalism was in many respects quite unlike the eastern European serf system and therefore reserve the term feudalism only for the west (see Blum, 1961: 90 ff.; Florinsky, 1947: vol. 1, 108 ff.). In order to avoid the disputes concerning this issue, I shall, following Dobb (1963 [1947]: 35), use the term feudalism as a synonym for serfdom.
3. On earlier settlements, see (Dubnow, 1916–20: vol. 1, 13–43).
4. Taking the case of northern medieval Europe to be typical, many have ignored the widespread participation of Jews in agriculture and crafts in other times and places. (See Wischnitzer, 1965).
5. The remainder were employed as clerks and assistants to Jewish businessmen, in religious occupations such as rabbi, scribe, beadle and the like, as professionals (notably doctors), as craftsmen and even as agriculturalists.
6. A computation by Weinryb (1972: 153) of blood libel accusations, charges of profanation of the holy wafer, pogroms, etc., for the period 1542–1717 reveals that such excesses were concentrated in western urban areas, thus indicating a close 'connection between false accusations plus pogroms and the competitive struggle for livelihood between burghers and the Jews'.

The thesis that anti-Semitism grew with the rise of indigenous bourgeoisies in Europe was first advanced by W. Roscher (1944 [1875]). For a favourable appraisal of his argument, see (Kisch, 1944). For a critique, see (Oelsner, 1958–9).

7. Later, when declining opportunities in the mercantile sphere necessitated the growth of Jewish artisanry, apprentices could turn only to Jewish masters, restricted as they were from Christian guilds. Thus, the concentration of Jews in particular branches of production took on a certain momentum of its own.

8. Gerschenkron (in Habbakuk and Postan, 1941–67: 706–7) argues that 'there is little evidence that in the decades preceding the emancipation the institution of serfdom had become incompatible with the growth of agricultural output'. Rather, the two main motives behind Emancipation were (a) the state's desire to increase production after humiliating defeat in the Crimean War; and, more important, (b) its desire to be saved from the dangers of peasant unrest. The reasons for Emancipation were, then, of a political rather than an economic character.

   The problem with Gerschenkron's view is that it involves a misunderstanding on the argument I employ in the text. The contention that contradictions between forces and relations of production resulted in the abolition of serfdom does not mean that existing class relations blocked *all* growth of *agricultural* output, as Gerschenkron interprets it; it means that the growth of output *as a whole* was *hampered* by existing class relations. The evidence he cites is therefore not a refutation of the explanation I employ. (In fact, he adds weight to what he calls 'the usual sweeping generalisations' by demonstrating how serfdom acted as a 'trammel upon industrial development' [ibid.: 715; also Gerschenkron, 1962: 17]). Furthermore, it is undoubtedly true that the state wished to increase productivity in order to catch up with the great powers and that it feared increasing peasant unrest. Such motives clearly played an important role in the decision to emancipate the serfs. However, it could be argued that both low productivity and peasant unrest were produced by the inefficiencies of the institution of serfdom itself. Political motives, in other words, derived from this social (not merely 'economic') fact.

9. Notably, an important role in the early industrialisation of Russia was played precisely by those able to escape such obligations – the religious schismatics or 'Old Believers'. They fled to the Russian hinterland, beyond the reach of the bureaucracy, when the remnants of Church democracy were being destroyed by Archbishop Nikon. Persecution caused the Old Believers to withdraw into self-sufficient communities and 'to accumulate the money which provided their only protection and power' according to Blackwell. The parallel with the Jewish community is striking. See (Blackwell, 1968: 212–40; also Gerschenkron, 1970: 1–61; Bill, 1959: 18–108).

10. All this applies only to the peasants who belonged to private landowners — about 40 per cent of the total number of peasants. No attempt will be made here to discuss the complex legislation affecting the remainder. Attached to the state and the royal family, the latter were, generally speaking, rather less harshly dealt with in terms of both the size and valuation of their allotments. Nevertheless, it may safely be said that they greeted Emancipation with little more enthusiasm than the others.

11. This impression was substantiated by Professor Robert Johnson in conversation with the author (in Toronto, 10 Aug 1976).

12. After three partitions (1772, 1793 and 1795) Poland's territory was divided among Russia, Prussia and Austria. Having succumbed to Napoleonic forces at Jena in 1806, Prussia's share of the spoils was next transformed into the

Duchy of Warsaw. The subsequent defeat of Napoleon led to the establishment of Congress Poland in 1815 as a kingdom attached to Russia. Finally, after an unsuccessful uprising in 1831, Congress Poland was incorporated into the Russian Empire. In this way Poland became Russia's Ireland.

13. My own views regarding this matter have been influenced by (Berkowitz, 1976).

14. In not a few cases — such as that of the Brodsky brothers, the sugar barons — wealthy Jews entered industry by first subsidising factories owned by indebted landlords and then taking over production completely.

15. Only the very wealthy could establish banks, while in railroad financing 'only the powerful and experienced railway "kings" were able to obtain the shares' (Westwood, 1964: 68). Jews with middling capital were, however, able to invest in co-operative credit associations and non-interest loan societies (Dijur in Frumkin *et al.*, 1966: 138).

16. Wealthy Jews also stopped buying goods produced by the Jewish community. The products made by the Jewish artisan were generally of low quality, while religious articles were no longer purchased because the wealthy tended to assimilate into Gentile society.

17. A study by the Jewish Colonisation Association (Evreyskago . . ., 1904: vol. 2, table 41) reports 500,986 Jewish artisans in the whole Pale (i.e., including Poland). Margolin (1908: 245) has convincingly argued that due to faulty data-gathering techniques a more accurate figure would be at least 600,000. While I agree with Margolin's argument, I have accepted the 500,000 figure as an estimate for the Pale exclusive of Poland.

18. Even within the Pale itself many of the large factories were, as Olga Crisp writes of the Ukrainian metallurgical industry, 'set up amidst the wild steppe' (1959: 83) where Jews were forbidden to reside. (Although Jewish *entrepreneurs* were of course able to form joint-stock companies, retain controlling interest in their enterprises and conduct their affairs from the city [Yuditzky, n.d. (1930?): 69].) For further discussion of why Jews did not enter large industry, see (Brym, 1976: 85–7; Leshchinsky, 1906; Mendelsohn, 1970: 20 ff.).

Chapter 3

1. By assimilation I mean the process by which one transfers one's identity from one ethnic community to another.

2. Ioffe was actually a member of the Karaite sect. The Karaites differed from other Jews in that they rejected the oral tradition (the Talmud). But given the fact that Karaism was even stricter in the demands it placed on adherents than rabbinism and that it embodied most of the key beliefs of traditional Judaism, it seems acceptable to categorise Ioffe as Jewish. The fact that his wife recently emigrated from the Soviet Union to Israel leads one to suspect that some level of Jewish consciousness, however weak, persisted in his family. (See 'Soviet Emigrant . . .'.)

3. Nor should one attribute the non-assimilation of some wealthy Jews living within the Pale to the high social density of Jewish communities there. The wealthy 'Rothschilds' of Pinsk, for example, did not assimilate as much as one would predict on the basis of some crude measure of class position; but this probably had a great deal to do with the fact that Pinsk suffered from a lack of

workers so that Jews were employed in the mechanised factories there. In this and other cases (e.g., that of the Ginzburg family, which continued to employ many Jews in their business operations) apparent exceptions prove the rule that assimilation was largely a function of occupational contact. See (Ginzburg, 1937; Mendelsohn, 1970: 28; Rabinovich, 1970).

4. Some degree of acculturation (as opposed to assimilation; see Gordon, 1964, for an explanation of the distinction) could and did sometimes take place even without structural integration because the objective possibility of structural integration led some Jews to go through a process of what Robert Merton (1968 [1949]: 319 ff.) calls 'anticipatory socialization'.

5. The Eastman/Deutscher view that Trotsky was completely assimilated has recently been challenged by Nedava, who insists that Trotsky's upbringing was 'typical of all Jewish children at the time'. However, much of Nedava's argument is based on dubious inferences. He thus establishes that Trotsky did know the Yiddish language to some degree; but it is problematic to conclude from this that he learned it as a child since he may have acquired some competence in the language much later in order to read about and engage in polemic with the Bund. Other elements of Nedava's argument have no basis in known facts. Thus, the claim that Trotsky had a 'typical' Jewish education (the typical education involved twelve hours of Bible study per day and the subsequent acquisition of expertise in Talmudic dialectic) clearly contradicts the only source of information on Trotsky's early life (his memoirs): Trotsky led for the most part an untutored country life in which a Russian mechanic was his main 'teacher', and he later acquired an exceptionally liberal education in Odessa. In this manner, Nedava overstates his case. See (Deutscher, 1965 [1954]: Eastman, 1925; Nedava, 1972; Trotsky, 1970 [1930]).

6. Tobias (1972: 11) lists all thirteen pioneers, but the information I had on one (Tzemakh Kopelson) was not sufficiently detailed to categorise him with any degree of confidence, so that Fig. 7 contains data on only twelve of the group.

7. Compare the degree of class embeddedness of the two most important groups of intellectuals of the period — the conservative Slavophiles (who remained close to Schelling's philosophy) and the radical Westernisers, such as Herzen and Bakunin (who did not). Both groups were comprised almost exclusively of men from noble origins. But the Slavophiles, as several historians have noted, 'remained well-integrated members of their class unlike . . . [those] who made up the camp of the Westernisers' (Malia, 1966: 285; also Edie *et al.*, 1965: vol. 1, 323). The typical Slavophile, because he lived the leisured life of the landlord on his estate, was able to retain a clear-cut sense of his class interests and therefore remained conservative. The typical radical Westerniser, on the other hand, having become, say, a freelance journalist, was only tenuously bound to the nobility, in consequence of which he found his class interests, *qua* nobleman, blurred. For reasons outlined in the text, he soon found his newly-acquired middle-class interests blurred as well.

8. Professor Austin Turk suggested to me (in correspondence, 16 Oct 1976) that there exists a positive correlation between repressiveness and radicalisation, but I think it necessary to qualify this observation along the lines indicated by the Tillys: historically, *extreme* repressive measures have tended to stop radical activities.

9. That eastern European Jews had a lust for learning is well known (Zborowski, 1949), but given the fact that Russians did too (Anweiler in Katkov *et al.*, 1971: 301; Gorky, 1949: 429–616) it would seem advisable to offer a structural rather than a normative explanation for high rates of Jewish enrolment in educational institutions.

10. The much more restricted question of whether or not Jews were drawn in any particular ideological direction has, however, been addressed. According to Lev Deich (1922: 52–60), Jewish populists displayed a marked tendency to engage in 'peaceful activities'—e.g., to become Lavrovists rather than Bakuninists in the first half of the 1870s. This interpretation deserves to be mentioned here because similar arguments are often made concerning Jewish revolutionaries at the turn of the century (Lichtheim, 1951: 301; Singer, 1937: 310). Even before Deich's book was published, the notion that Jews were predisposed to engage in non-violent activities had been contested by his friend, Pavel Axelrod (Sapir, 1965: 366). And on the basis of evidence amassed by Cherikover (1939; see also Menes, 1949; Talmon, 1970), it seems that there were quite as many important Jewish Bakuninists as Lavrovists (although, it is true, no known Tkachevists). Moreover, Cherikover has shown that in the second half of the 1870s, 3 of the 28 people who founded the terrorist People's Will party were Jews (i.e., 10.7 per cent of the total). And of the 154 terrorists tried and sentenced from 1880 to 1890, 22 (or 14.3 per cent) were Jews. By comparing this last figure with the data presented in Fig. 3 for the years 1880–90, we see that Jewish representation among the terrorists was higher than their representation in the revolutionary movement as a whole. Jews were, then, quite capable of taking part in violent activities. If they tended to oppose Russian Jacobinism (both in its Tkachevist and, in the 1900s, Leninist manifestations) then the explanation must be sought not in the 'fact' that they 'shrank from violence' but in the character of the embedding process. The populist case cannot of course be considered here; but the low rate of Jewish participation in the Bolshevik party is explained in the following chapter.

11. This is not to deny that there were elements of continuity between the populist and Marxist periods. See (Barghoorn, 1942–3; Pipes, 1960).

12. Reports from such centres as St Petersburg, Moscow, Odessa and Kharkov indicated that the movement in these cities was far less advanced than in Vilna. This led the Vilna radicals to believe that they could expect no rapid growth in the larger centres and should therefore display a degree of independent initiative. This facilitated the switch to agitation. See (Martov, 1923: 171).

13. Regardless of the degree to which they were assimilated, *intelligenty* attached to Jewish workers tended to resolve the intra-personal conflict which this could involve with little difficulty. But only the most assimilated of those attached to non-Jewish workers were similarly fortunate. The remainder—*intelligenty* who retained traces of Jewish identity yet became members of the Russian movement—faced special problems. They were often afflicted with a complex syndrome which, in varying blends, might include vacillation concerning the Jewish question, self-hatred, a sense of guilt for ignoring the Jews and, in not a few cases, the desire to fight especially zealously against any sign of Jewishness in oneself or others (cf. Sartre, 1948 [1946]; Shibutani and Kwan, 1965: 502–33). Even so assimilated an *intelligent* as Martov appears to have

experienced *Selbsthaas*. After all, he was 'tainted' with having been active among Jewish artisans in Vilna for a time and of being among the first to suggest that Jewish workers required a separate party. After leaving Vilna to join the movement in St Petersburg, he became one of the Bund's worst enemies however. And, as his biographer (Getzler, 1967: 143) suggests, Martov's extreme and unswerving internationalism regarding matters that had nothing to do with the Jewish question probably originated in his denial of his earlier attachements and sympathies. The same may be said of Trotsky. His distance from the Jewish community permitted him to become the most internationalist of all *intelligenty* (Deutscher, 1968); at the same time, his internationalism was partly a reaction against his Jewish background (Nedava, 1972; but see above note 5). Nobody else in Trotsky's position could have created the theory of permanent revolution. On the other hand, the theory of permanent revolution could only have been created by someone in Trotsky's position. For additional examples, see (Aronson, 1962: 249–54; Ascher, 1965; Axelrod, 1924; Barzilai, 1968a; Shub, 1970: vol. 1, 56; Gitelman, 1972: 26).

14. There were, of course, a host of other, theoretically less interesting causes of geographical mobility. More important, it should be noted that *intelligenty* did not experience as much inter-regional mobility as one might imagine. To cite only two examples: Martin Lyadov was born in Moscow, joined the R.S.D.L.P. in Saratov and did party work mainly in the Central Industrial Region and the Urals; Y. Sverdlov was born in Nizhni-Novgorod, joined the party there and, like Lyadov, spent most of his early party life in Russia working east of a line (the importance of which will become clear shortly) joining St Petersburg and Astrakhan (*Deyateli* . . ., n.d. [1929–31?]: pt.1, 346–50; pt. 3, 13–25). This pattern of remaining in one's region of original recruitment, at least once ideologies were more or less crystallised, was the norm for *intelligenty* in all parties.

15. According to Lane (1969) working class support in St Petersburg was fairly evenly divided between Bolsheviks and Mensheviks in the pre-1908 period. In my sample, two Bolsheviks (10.5 per cent of the total) and nine Mensheviks (37.5 per cent of the total) were recruited in that city.

Chapter 4

1. I have added Trotsky to Lane's list of top Mensheviks.

2. I do not, however, wish to suggest that the Bolsheviks were all unswerving followers of Lenin who held no views of their own. This charge has been lodged against even so important a figure as Zinoviev — and even by other Bolsheviks such as Lunacharsky (1967 [1919]: 75–82). For a critique of this view, see (Hedlin, 1975; Woytinsky, 1961: 121).

3. This does not mean that anti-Semitism (or, for that matter any form of racism) emerges only during downturns in the business cycle, but only that anti-Semitic outbursts are normally associated with high degrees of competition for scarce resources and opportunities. For discussion of this point (as well as the related one of why particular groups are singled out for attack), see (Andreski,

1964; Blalock, 1956; 1957; Schweitzer, 1944). A careful reading of these sources should dispel any willingness to accept Walter Laqueur's misgivings concerning 'the' socio-economic theory of anti-Semitism (Laqueur, 1972: 29ff., 276, 591).

4. Jacob Katz (1970: 13) denies that this was the case. 'Not the need created the idea, but the idea created the need', he writes. 'If ever there were anywhere an idea which preceded its social utility', he continues, 'it was here.' Katz's argument is based on the view that such figures as Hess, Kalischer and Alkalai developed Zionist ideas in the middle of the nineteenth century, a time which saw the 'flourishing of Middle European liberalism'. The decline of liberalism and the anti-Semitic consequences of this decline cannot properly be viewed as the chief forces leading to the emergence of Zionism, he concludes.

There are at least two problems with Katz's argument. First, Hess, Kalischer and Alkali were not Zionists in the proper historical sense of the term: as Katz himself points out elsewhere (cited in Halpern, 1969 [1961]: 60), they, unlike the Zionists of the 1880s and 1890s, wanted not to supersede but merely to complement the idea of emancipation. This is precisely why Halpern refers to them as 'proto-Zionists'. Moreover, even if for the sake of argument we grant Katz this point, it is impossible credibly to maintain that the ideological products of these men developed in a social vacuum. Thus, in 1840 — the 'real turning point in Alkalai's life' (Hertzberg, 1959: 103) — the Jews of Damascus were subjected to the old medieval charge of having slaughtered a young Gentile in ritual preparation for Passover. News of the affair spread quickly throughout Europe; and 'it convinced Alkalai (as it half-convinced his younger contemporary Moses Hess) that for security and freedom the Jewish people must look to a life of its own, within its ancestral home' (ibid.: 104). Hess's convictions were strengthened, as were those of both Alkalai and Kalischer, by another *cause célèbre* — the forced conversion of six year old Edgar Mortara of Bologna in 1859. All this occured, moreover, in the context of rising nationalist movements in Europe. One need only recall the title of Hess's *magnum opus* to realise that the example of Mazzini was very much in the foreground of his thinking as he sought to grapple ideologically with the Damascus and Mortara affairs. Kalischer was 'particularly aware' of nationalism ('the major force of European history during the whole of Kalischer's adult life'; ibid.: 109) because he lived in Posen, a most advantageous observation post for viewing the manifestations of Polish nationalism in the uprisings of 1830–1 and 1863. Signs that the emancipation of the Jews would not succeed were thus becoming evident in an era when nationalism provided those who tended to be attached to the Jewish community (Kalischer and Alkalai were both rabbis; Hess, whom Marx referred to as 'the communistic rabbi' had, unlike Marx, a traditional Jewish education) with ready answers. Later ideological developments were merely more pessimistic extensions of the belief that Jews could not integrate into European society — extensions occasioned by the unfolding of those same social conditions which prompted Hess, Kalischer and Alkalai to anticipate Zionism. The idea most certainly did not antedate the social need.

5. There is no evidence to support Katz's (1970: 11) claim that Zionism had no class roots. As contemporaries pointed out time and again in their writings (e.g., Geffen, 1969–70: 191–4; Levin, 1967: 206, 225–6, 242; Weizmann,

1966 [1949]: 75, 115), Zionism was generally opposed by the wealthy and by fully assimilated professionals and intellectuals. Prosperous Jews typically acted with hostility to any suggestion that they leave Europe for the economic wasteland of Ottoman Palestine, while assimilated professionals and intellectuals were so closely identified with European and Russian culture that a return to the fold more often than not struck them as absurd.

6. Wildman neglects to mention the case of Minsk, and fails to note the fact that, generally speaking, there were a good many Zionists and socialist-Zionists in the north (albeit not nearly so many as in the south). In fact, the Central Committee of the Russian Zionist Organisation was transferred to Vilna in 1905 while the official organ of the World Zionist Organisation was moved there from Cologne three years later (Cohen, 1943: 352–3).

7. Although it might be noted in passing that actual immigration figures up to the mid-1920s did not support Borokhov's analysis. It was only after 1924 that restrictive U.S. immigration laws combined with the worsening condition of the Polish and German Jewish communities to lend credibility to his argument. Migration figures will be found in (Hersch, 1929–31; Leshchinsky, 1944; Ruppin, 1973 [1934]: 43–67).

8. This further implied that 'any activity in the name of the whole proletariat in an area where the Bund, as well as other party organisations, is active, is permissible only with the participation of the Bund' (from a resolution passed at the fifth Bund congress, quoted in Tobias, 1972: 201).

9. Thus, Martov, who spoke against the Bund, argued that the R.S.D.L.P. should be organised essentially as the Bund was — an apparent contradiction which can be resolved only if one keeps in mind the two distinct motives involved in his thinking.

10. Tkachev stood on the periphery of the populist movement during the first half of the 1870s. One of the two dominant strategies of the period was worked out by Peter Lavrov (Lavrov, 1967 [1870]; Pomper, 1972), who argued that the people had to be *prepared* by the intelligentsia to engage in the revolutionary overthrow; the other was developed by Bakunin (Bakunin, 1967 [1873]; Carr, 1937), who encouraged the intelligentsia to *agitate* the people to the point at which they would perform this act. Thus, although they disagreed on means, both were, unlike Tkachev, convinced that the revolution would be made mainly by 'the people'.

11. For those unfamiliar with the history of Russian Marxism it may be useful to point out that the agitation strategy, discussed above, tended to depoliticise and decentralise the Social Democratic movement to the point at which its 'organisational fragmentation' (Akimov's phrase) further encouraged the centripetal reaction on the part of the intelligentsia analysed in the text. On the 'workers opposition' movement, the 'Economist' controversy and 'police socialism' — all phenomena which to some extent grew out of and further aggravated this situation — see (Akimov, 1969 [1904]; Brennan, n.d. [1964?]; 1970; Frankel, 1963; Loker, 1928; Mendelsohn, 1970; Mishkinski, 1960; Wildman, 1967; Wolfe, 1948a).

12. My impression is that much of the literature on the relationship between the business cycle and strike activity is too narrowly economistic in its orientation — i.e., it fails to take into account political developments (notably the kinds of crises which result from the rapid de-legitimisation of state

authority) which both promote industrial unrest and cause such unrest to develop into explicitly political discontent. Rather than an economic bargaining model, this suggests the need for a *power* model of working class discontent which would focus on the degree to which particular groups are able to mobilise resources (including symbolic resources) to pursue their interests under given economic and political conditions. I hope to take up this theme in a future work on industrial unrest in Canada.

13. Lane (1969: 185–6) has suggested that workers who were members of ethnic minority groups — White Russian, Georgian, Ukrainian, and so forth — were attracted to Menshevism partly because it offered a higher degree of autonomy and self-expression than did Bolshevism. It would be interesting to frame the reverse of this argument as a research hypothesis: Did the demands of workers from ethnic minority groups for greater autonomy and self-expression lead *intelligenty* attached to them to accept a greater degree of decentralisation in their party organisations?

14. Thus, the Bundists greatly increased the power of their Central Committee, encouraged political demonstrations, stopped the publication of many local party journals and stepped up the circulation of literature written by their top leaders. Among the Poalei-Zionists a successful battle was fought against 'Economism' and the forces of centralisation were by 1906 able to unite many loosely connected groups into one unified party. (There were unique circumstances in the Poalei-Zionist milieu which led to increased intelligentsia politicism at this time, however. First, an important change in the recruitment pattern of Poalei-Zionist *intelligenty* occurred: the 'Economist' elements in the party, concentrated mainly in Minsk, were recruited largely from the middle-class Zionist movement while the beginning of politicism was associated with an increase in the number of former Bundists in the ranks of the Poalei-Zionist intelligentsia. Second, the Kishinev and Gomel pogroms forced many Poalei-Zionist *intelligenty* to recognise the importance of the political struggle in the Diaspora. See (Weizmann, 1968–76: vol. 3, 182; Zar in Volhiner, 1927: 25; Zinger, 1944: 295.)

15. According to the editors of Borokhov's collected works (Borokhov, 1955: 400) this article appeared in the journal *Evreyskaya zhizn'* between June and October 1905. However, they also note that Borokhov wrote the article between the sixth and seventh Zionist congresses (i.e., between 1903 and July 1905) which means that the section from which I have quoted (the fourth of nine sections) was probably written in 1904 or very early in 1905.

16. It does seem that there was a partial return to the pre-1905 Bolshevik position during the years 1908–11, when the strike movement declined rapidly. See (Zinoviev, 1923: 82). However, the resurgence of elitism was not to the best of my knowledge widespread because large numbers of *intelligenty* left their parties entirely during this period (see, e.g., Woodhouse and Tobias, 1965–6) so that the ratio of workers to *intelligenty* in party organisations did not fall as much as one might otherwise have expected.

17. The reader might object that this proposition fails to take into account that *intelligenty* in the Russian colonies of the west were never in contact with Russian workers; to which one would have to reply that they most certainly were, but in a more attenuated fashion than *intelligenty* in Russia. The appropriate unit of analysis here is not the individual *intelligent*, but the whole

network of party organisations which extended from Zurich to St Petersburg, Geneva to Vilna, etc.

18. The periodic unavailability of a mass base had other ideological consequences which cannot be dealt with here. See, for example, McNeal's (1971–2) discussion of how women acted as an ideological surrogate for the politically inert peasantry during the populist era.

19. Actually, Marx's views on the subject were rather more complex than Plekhanov was prepared to recognise. See (Marx, 1964 [1857–8]).

20. A qualification regarding the Poalei-Zionists is introduced below.

21. See also Axelrod's plan for a 'workers congress', discussed by (Ascher, 1972: 233 ff.)

22. Only column numbers are indicated for this article since the photostatic copy I procured from Columbia University does not include page numbers.

23. There were few persons who adhered to Trotsky's and Parvus' 'theory of permanent revolution' in 1905. Trotsky, like the Mensheviks, favoured the principle of spontaneity when it came to the issue of party organisation; but, even more so than the Bolsheviks, he favoured the principle of consciousness as far as his definition of the revolution's character was concerned (Trotsky, 1969 [1906]; 1918; also Zenan and Scharlau, 1965). For although he wanted to see the creation of a broadly-based Social Democratic party and denied that the peasantry was an important revolutionary force, he considered the Russian bourgeoisie too weak to seize state power. He further argued that it was 'utopianism' to believe that the Social Democrats would hand over state power to the liberals once democratic reforms had been effected. State power, he proclaimed, would be invested in the hands of the working class alone — but not just Russian members of that class. For Trotsky's schema was based on his feeling that the Russian revolution would almost inevitably encourage the success of the proletarian movement in western Europe. This would enable the revolution in Russia to be extended *in Permanenz* to its socialist culmination. As suggested above (notes 5 and 13, Chapter 3), this extreme internationalist vision is profitably viewed as a function of Trotsky's social position.

24. In 1836 Peter Chaadaev publically proclaimed that Russia did not 'amount to a thing in the intellectual order' (Chaadaev, 1969: 39) and had to accept the western bourgeoisie as a teacher, thus initiating the most important intellectual debate of the 1840s — between Westernisers (who expected progress in Russia to emanate from the west) and Slavophiles (who emphasised the superiority of Russian tradition; see Masaryk, 1919 [1913]: vol. 1, 237–83; Raeff, 1966). But even Chaadaev did not express unqualified appreciation of the western bourgeois world: towards the end of his life he remarked that Russia, because of its backwardness, might be able to avoid the many pitfalls of western civilisation (Chaadaev, 1969: 215). Apparently the west was not all that praiseworthy.

25. Although Piatnitsky exaggerates somewhat. See (Morokohvetz, 1925b: 71–90).

26. As in all centres, the Moscow Bolsheviks were at first opposed to participation in the Soviet.

Chapter 5

1. Levitats in conversation with the author at the YIVO Institute, New York, about 12 Jan 1975; Mendelsohn in correspondence with the author, 22 Feb 1977.
2. See (Brym, forthcoming).

Technical Appendix

Fig. 3: For six of the nine points on the graph one figure was given for a period of several years. In these cases I plotted the mid-point of the time period. The data concern all radicals, not just *intelligenty*. But I can think of no source of systematic error which would make a graph of the rate of Jewish intellectual radicalism look very much different from the one presented in the text. One might, however, raise the further objection that the anti-Semitic police went out of their way to arrest Jewish revolutionaries in particular so that the figures overestimate the rate of Jewish participation in the revolutionary movement. The fact is that probably the opposite is true: as Allan Wildman (1967: 60) emphasises, the 'barrier of language' rendered 'Jewish Social Democrats far less subject to police surveillance than their Russian counterparts'. The Jews could thus 'organize and participate in strikes almost with impunity, whereas the Russians could not'. If in error, the figures on which the graph are based are probably low. Count Witte seems to have been not very far off the mark when he informed Theodore Herzl in 1903 that half the revolutionaries in Russia were Jews (Schapiro, 1961: 148).

Figs. 4, 5 and 6: Figures are based on government censuses. Given the crudeness of surveying techniques they can offer only rough approximations to the actual distributions. The data on occupations in particular must be treated with caution for the additional reason that the division of labour was relatively underdeveloped in nineteenth century Russia. One might more accurately speak of occupational complexes than distinct occupations: the peddler might double as a mender of pots, the innkeeper as a grain trader (cf. Raba, 1960). In Fig. 6 (and throughout the book) the northern Russian Pale refers to the provinces of Vilna, Grodno, Kovno, Minsk, Moghilev and Vitebsk. The southern Russian Pale refers to the provinces of Bessarabia, Ekaterinoslav, Kherson, Taurida, Volhynia, Kiev, Poltava, Podolia and Chernigov. While Fig. 6 presents data on these fifteen provinces of the Pale only, Figs. 4 and 5 include the ten provinces of the Polish Pale under the rubric 'Pale'.

Fig. 7: Most of the data were taken from four multi-volume biographical dictionaries (*Deyateli . . .*, n.d. [1927–9?]; Hertz, 1956–8; Niger and Shatzky, 1956–8; Raizen, 1928–30). In addition, memoirs and biographies, a full list of which will be found in the Bibliography, were consulted. Sampling procedures are discussed in Chapter 1, but it should be mentioned here that data were collected if information was available on the educational background *or* what I have termed the 'reclassification' of those *intelligenty* who conform to the characteristics mentioned in Chapter 1. Thus, the total sample size is 207; but I have information on educational background for only 186 cases and on 'reclassification' for 178. The independent variable (degree of embeddedness) was operationalised as follows: Having become convinced after reading over a score of detailed biographical and autobiographical accounts of the lives of *intelligenty* that educational experience is a good index of structural embeddedness (see Chapter 3, section A), I divided this operational variable into a four-part scale for purposes of further data collection. For the *intelligenty* appear to have fallen into the four modal educational patterns discussed in Chapter 3, section A. In a few cases which suffered from a lack of precise information (but which I wanted to include because they were relatively important figures in the parties) I had to exercise some degree of subjective judgement when placing individuals into one or another category (although if the available data were very sketchy — as was the case with Tzemakh Kopelson — I did not include that case in my calculations). But when calculations were made exclusive of these cases the results differed in no significant way from those presented in the figure. The dependent variable (party affiliation) was operationalised in a much more straightforward manner: according to which party the *intelligent* joined during the period discussed in this study (i.e., before 1908). In those few cases where the *intelligent* transferred party allegiance during this period the last party membership before 1908 was used as the relevant datum. In those few cases where the *intelligent* did not join a party before 1908 the first party joined after that date was used. Again, calculations made exclusive of these small groups changed the results in no significant way. It should also be noted that for purposes of collecting data for Fig. 7 I interpreted Poalei-Zionist in its broadest possible sense — i.e., to include members of the Territorialist (Sejmist and Socialist Zionist) groups (see Chapter 4, section A). The mean degree of embeddedness of the Territorialists alone (n = 14) was 1.6. Finally, the results of the chi square test must be treated wih caution since several of the expected frequencies were less than five.

Fig. 8: I have averaged Slutzky's and Trotzky's figures for 1886 since there is a very small discrepancy between them.

Fig. 9: The discussion for Fig. 7 of sources, sampling procedures and operationalisation of the dependent variable applies here as well. The variable 'region' was operationalised by determining the provinces of the Russian Empire in which *intelligenty* were located when they became party members. In those cases where *intelligenty* joined their parties outside of Russia — in one of the *émigré* colonies of western Europe, for example — region refers to the area in Russia where they were last engaged in radical activities before joining the parties in the west. All Mensheviks and Bolsheviks who attended the second R.S.D.L.P. congress are included in the latter category. The fourteen Territorialists included in the figure with the Poalei-Zionists were distributed among the regions as follows: 14. 3 per cent in the northern Pale, 21. 4 per cent in Minsk province, 57. 1 per cent in the southern Pale, 7.1 per cent in provinces outside the Pale and west of the St Petersburg-Astrakhan line and 0 per cent in provinces east of the St Petersburg-Astrakhan line. The division between the northern and southern regions of the Pale corresponds to that used in Fig. 6. Half the persons recruited *in* St Petersburg were placed in the category 'provinces east of St Petersburg-Astrakhan line', while half were placed in the category 'provinces outside of Pale and west of St Petersburg-Astrakhan line' (see note 15, Chapter Three.) No *intelligenty* in my sample were recruited in Astrakhan.

Fig. 11: The second set of figures includes persons engaged in personal service (domestics and the like) because the latter could not conveniently be subtracted. But their inclusion could not have affected the size of the ratios very much since, regardless of region and ethnicity, those engaged in personal service appear to have made up a fairly constant proportion of the work force, ranging from just over 16 per cent to just under 20 per cent (see Fig. 4.) The division between northern and southern regions of the Pale corresponds to that used in Fig. 6.

Fig. 12: Although Lane (1969) defines areas of Menshevik strength as all territory to the west of a line joining St Petersburg and Astrakhan, I have, for reasons which should be apparent from the text, modified his definition to exclude the northern Pale. But I have accepted Lane's definition of the area of Bolshevik strength as lying to the east of the St Petersburg-Astrakhan line. Data for those provinces listed by Rashin were classified accordingly, the figures for St Petersburg and Astrakhan themselves being evenly divided between Mensheviks and Bolsheviks, as were the figures for Tula since that province is bisected by the line. The 'highly industrialised' provinces include, for the Mensheviks, those of Novorossiya plus Don and, for the Bolsheviks, those of the Ural region plus those of the Central Industrial Region minus Kaluga, the last-named not being included since it lies to the west of the St Petersburg-Astrakhan line. Here again, figures for St Petersburg were evenly divided between Mensheviks and Bolsheviks.

Fig. 14: Figures in brackets were computed by cumulating percentages from the appropriate cells (or fractions of cells) of Fig. 7. Thus, the figure for the Poalei-Zionists is 66.0 plus 30.0; for the Bundists, 17.9 plus 36.8 plus half of 35.8; for the Mensheviks, 45.8 plus 16.7 plus 25.0; and for the Bolsheviks, 11.8 plus 70.6.

Fig. 16: Turin's data (strike totals for 1895–1904) have been revised upward by 30 per cent and Haimson's (strike totals for 1905–7) by 20 per cent as the respective authors suggest in order to compensate for deficiencies in government statistics. Borokhov's data on Jewish strikers were compiled on the basis of an exhaustive search of the Jewish Social Democratic press for the years 1895–1904. Only 8.6 per cent of the newspapers were unavailable to Borokhov. Since most of these cover the years 1895–1899 I have increased the Jewish strike totals for these years by 8.6 per cent. (Increasing figures for the earlier period only is warranted in that reportage was probably less exhaustive then.) Borokhov found information on 603 strikes during the years 1895–1899 and 1,673 during the years 1900–4. But information on the number of strikers involved in each strike was available in only 42.6 per cent of the cases during the earlier period and in 52.0 per cent of the cases during the later period. Since, in each of those strikes in which the number of workers was unknown, different numbers of workers were involved, Borokhov estimated figures for the 'unknown' strikes by calculating a weighted mean. Thus, for the 1900–4 period, information was available on 81,973 strikers; but Borokhov's corrected figure is 109,000 (i.e., an increase of 33.0 per cent). This procedure was not followed for the earlier period, however. Nor does Borokhov supply the information necessary to make the calculations oneself. So I have simply increased the figures for each year during the earlier period by the same 33.0 per cent. The data, both in raw and corrected form, are probably still far from precise in absolute terms. But they undoubtedly give a fairly accurate picture of trends in the strike movement, which is all that interests me here.

Bibliography

Note: This bibliography is neither a comprehensive list of sources on the subject matters touched upon in this study nor a complete list of all sources consulted in its preparation. Rather, the bibliography includes (a) all sources of biographical information consulted on *intelligenty*; and (b) all sources cited in the text and notes.

Abramovich, R., *In tzvei revolutzies: di geshikhte fun a dor*, 2 vols (New York, 1944) vol. 1.
—— (R. Abramovitch) 'The Jewish Socialist Movement in Russia and Poland (1897–1919)', *The Jewish People: Past and Present*, 4 vols. (New York, 1949) vol. 2, 369–98.
Abramsky, C., 'A People that Shall Dwell Alone . . .', *The New York Review of Books* (12 Dec 1974) 22–4.
Adams, B., 'Interaction Theory and the Social Network', *Sociometry* (30: 1967) 64–78.
Akimov, V., *Vladimir Akimov on the Dilemmas of Russia Marxism*, J. Frankel, ed. (Cambridge, Eng., 1969 [1904]).
Alavi, H., 'Peasants and Revolution', *The Socialist Register*, R. Miliband and J. Saville, eds. (New York, 1965) 241–77.
Alston, P., *Education and the State in Tsarist Russia* (Stanford: 1969).
Althusser, L., 'Contradiction and Overdetermination', *For Marx*, B. Brewster, trans. (New York, 1970 [1965]) 89–129.
Amalrik, A., 'K voprosu o chislennosti i geogralicheski razmeshchenii statechnikov v evropeiskoi Rossii v 1905 godu', *Istoricheskie zapiski* (52: 1955) 142–85.
Anderson, K., *The Organisation of Capital for the Development of the Canadian West* (unpublished M.A. thesis, University of Regina, 1974).
Andreski, S., 'An Economic Interpretation of Antisemitism', *The Uses of Comparative Sociology* (Berkeley, 1974) 291–307.
Annan, N., 'The Intellectual Aristocracy', *Studies in Social History: A Tribute to G. M. Trevelyan*, J. Plumb, ed. (London, 1955) 241–87.
Antonovsky, A., 'Toward a Refinement of the "Marginal Man" Concept', *Social Forces* (35: 1956) 57–62.
Anweiler, O., 'Russian Schools', *Russia Enters the Twentieth Century*, G. Katkov *et al.*, eds., G. Onn, trans. (London, 1971) 287–313.
——*The Soviets: The Russian Workers, Peasants, and Soldiers Councils, 1905–1921*, R. Hein, trans. (New York, 1974 [1958]).

Arkady: zamlbukh tzum andenk fun Arkady Kremer (New York, 1942).

Aronsfeld, C., 'Jewish Bankers and the Tsar', *Jewish Social Studies* (35: 1973) 87–104.

Aronson, G., *Revolyutzionnaya yunost': vospominaniya, 1903–17* (New York, 1961).

—— *Rusish-idish inteligentz* (Buenos Aires, 1962).

—— *et al.*, eds., *Di geshikhte fun Bund*, 3 vols. (New York, 1960–6) vol. 1.

—— *et al.*, eds., *Russian Jewry, 1917–1967*, J. Carmichael, trans. (New York, 1969).

Aronson, I., 'The Attitudes of Russian Officials in the 1880s Towards Jewish Assimilation and Emigration', *Slavic Review* (34: 1975) 1–18.

Ascher, A., 'Pavel Axelrod: A Conflict Between Jewish Loyalty and Revolutionary Dedication', *Russian Review* (24: 1965) 249–65.

—— *Pavel Axelrod and the Development of Menshevism* (Cambridge, Mass., 1972).

Avakumovic, I., 'A Statistical Approach to the Revolutionary Movement in Russia, 1878–1887', *Slavic Review* (18: 1959) 182–6.

Avineri, S., 'Marx and the Intellectuals', *Journal of the History of Ideas* (28: 1957) 269–78.

Axelrod, P., 'Pogromen un di revolutzionere bavegung mit 43 yor tzurik: vi di idisher sotzialistn hobn dan farshtanen zayre oifgabe', *Di tzukunft* (29: 1924) 550–5.

Bakounine, M., *Gosudarstvennost' i anarkhiya/Etatisme et Anarchie* M. Body, trans. (Leiden, 1967 [1873]).

Balaban, M., *Yidn in Poiln* (Vilna, 1930).

—— 'Ven un fun vanen zenen di Yidn gekumen kein Poiln', *Bleter far geshikhte* (13: 1960) 3–24.

Balabanoff, A., *My Life as a Rebel* (Bloomington, 1973 [1938]).

Barghoorn, F., 'The Russian Radicals of the 1860s and the Problem of the Industrial Proletariat', *Slavonic Review* (21: 1942–3) 57–69.

—— 'Russian Radicals and the West European Revolutions of 1848', *Review of Politics* (11: 1949) 338–54.

Baron, S., 'Plekhanov's Russia: The Impact of the West Upon an "Oriental" Society', *Journal of the History of Ideas* (19: 1958) 388–404.

Barzilai, Y., 'Sikhot im Shimon Dimanshtein', *he-Avar* (15: 1968a) 216–39.

—— 'Ya'akov Sverdlov u-mehapekhat Oktober', *he-Avar* (15: 1968b) 211–15.

—— 'Adolf Ioffe — he-Yehudim v'reishit ha-diplomatia ha-sovietit', *he-Avar* (17: 1970) 207–16.

—— 'Yu. Larin — m'rishonei ha-tikhnun ha-sovieti', *he-Avar* (18: 1971) 151–60.

Baykov, A., 'The Economic Development of Russia', *Economic History Review* (7: 1954) 137–49.

Becker, H., *Through Values to Social Interpretation* (Durham, 1950).

Belinsky, V., *Selected Philosophical Works*, M. Yovchuk, ed. (Moscow, 1956).

Ben-Tzvi, Y., *Mit der tzveiter aliya* (Buenos Aires, 1956).

—— *Zikhronot u-rishimot: me-ha-ne'orim ad 1920*, R. Yanait Ben-Tzvi and Y. Orez, eds. (Jerusalem, 1966).

Berdyaev, N., *The Origin of Russian Communism*, R. French, trans. (Ann Arbor, 1960 [1937]).

Berger, B., 'How Long is a Generation?' *British Journal of Sociology* (11: 1960) 10–23.

Berkowitz, S., *The Dynamics of Elite Structure: A Critique of C. Wright Mills's Power Elite Model* (unpublished Ph.D. thesis, Brandeis University, 1976).

Berlin, I., Russia and 1848', *Slavonic Review* (26: 1948) 341–60.

—— 'A Marvellous Decade (I): 1838–48: German Romanticism in Petersburg and Moscow', *Encounter* (5, 5: 1955) 21–9.

Bierstedt, R., *Power and Progress: Essays in Sociological Theory* (New York, 1974).

Bill, V., 'The Dead Souls of Russia's Merchant World', *Russian Review* (15: 1956) 245–58.

—— *The Forgotten Class: The Russian Bourgeoisie from the Earliest Beginnings to 1900* (New York, 1959).

Billington, J., *The Icon and the Axe: An Interpretive History of Russian Culture* (New York, 1966).

Black, C., ed., *The Transformation of Russian Society: Aspects of Social Change Since 1861* (Cambridge, Mass., 1960).

Blackwell, W., *The Beginnings of Russian Industrialization: 1800–60* (Princeton, 1968).

Blalock, H., 'Economic Discrimination and Negro Increase', *American Sociological Review* (21: 1956) 584–8.

—— 'Per Cent Non-White and Discrimination in the South', *American Sociological Review* (62: 1957) 677–82.

Blum, J., 'The Rise of Serfdom in Eastern Europe', *American Historical Review* (62: 1957) 807–36.

—— *Lord and Peasant in Russia from the Ninth to the Nineteenth Century* (Princeton, 1961).

Boissevain, J., *Friends of Friends: Networks, Manipulators and Coalitions* (Oxford, 1974).

Bonacich, E., 'A Theory of Middleman Minorities', *American Sociological Review* (38: 1973) 583–94.

Borokhov, B., *Poalei-Tzion shriftn* (New York, 1920).

—— *Di idishe arbeter bavegung in tzifern* (Berlin, 1923).

—— *Geklibene shriftn*, B. Loker, ed. (New York, 1928).

—— *Ktavim*, 3 vols., M. Avidor, trans., L. Levita and D. Ben-Nakhum, eds. (n.p. [Tel-Aviv?], 1955) vol. 1.

—— (B. Borochov) *Nationalism and the Class Struggle* (Westport, 1972 [1937]).

Bouvier, J., 'Mouvement ouvrier et conjonctures économiques', *Le mouvement social* (48: 1964) 3–30.

Bowman, H., 'Revolutionary Elitism in Černyševski', *Slavic Review* (13: 1954) 185–99.

Brennan, J., *The Origins, Development and Failure of Russian Social-Democratic Economism, 1886–1903* (unpublished Ph.D. thesis, University of California at Berkeley, n.d. [1964?]).

—— 'The Origin and Nature of Economism in St Petersburg', *Canadian Slavic Studies* (4: 1970) 162–82.

Brinton, C., *The Anatomy of Revolution* (New York, 1938).

Broido, E., *Memoirs of a Revolutionary* (London, 1967 [1929]).

Brower, D., 'The Problem of the Russian Intelligentsia', *Slavic Review* (26: 1967) 638–47.

—— 'Fathers, Sons, and Grandfathers: Social Origins of Radical Intellectuals in Nineteenth-Century Russia', *Journal of Social History* (2: 1968–9).

——'Student Political Attitudes and Social Origins: The Technological Institute of St Petersburg', *Journal of Social History* (6: 1972–3) 202–13.

—— *Training the Nihilists: Education and Radicalism in Tsarist Russia* (Ithaca, 1975).

Brutzkus, Y., 'ha-Studentim ha-Yehudim ba-universita ha-moskvait', *he-Avar* (18: 1971) 63–5.

Brym, R., *Strangers and Rebels: The Russian-Jewish Intelligentsia in Marxist Social Movements at the Turn of the Twentieth Century* (unpublished Ph.D. thesis, University of Toronto, 1976).

—— 'Democracy and the Intellectuals: A Test of Karl Mannheim's Thesis', *Scottish Journal of Sociology* (1: 1977a) 173–82.

—— 'Explaining Regional Variations in Canadian Populist Movements' (paper presented at the meetings of the Canadian Sociology and Anthropology Association, Fredericton, 1977b, and the Canada-Poland Sociology Exchange Seminar, Warsaw, 1977b).

—— 'Lewis Feuer and the Generation of Ideology', *Newsletter of the International Society for the Sociology of Knowledge* (3, 1: 1977c) 1–3.

—— 'A Note on the *Raznochintsy*', *Journal of Social History* (10: 1977d) 354–9.

—— 'Power and Progress (Review Essay)', *Scottish Journal of Sociology* (2: 1977e).

—— *Intellectuals and Politics* (London, forthcoming).

Burke, P., ed. *Economy and Society in Early Modern Europe: Essays from Annales* (New York, 1972).

Burtzev, V. and Kravchinsky, S., eds., *Za sto let (1800–1896): sbornik po istorii politicheskikh i obshchestvennykh dvizheniy v Rossii* (London, 1897).

Cahan, A., *The Education of Abraham Cahan*, L. Stein *et al.*, trans. (Philadelphia, 1969 [1926–31]).

Cahnman, W., 'Role and Significance of the Jewish Artisan Class', *Jewish Journal of Sociology* (7: 1965) 207–20.

Cannon, E., *The Political Culture of Russian Jewry During the Second Half of the Nineteenth Century* (unpublished Ph.D. thesis, University of Massachusetts, 1974).

Carlo, A., 'Lenin on the Party', *Telos* (17: 1973) 2–40.

Carr, E., *Michael Bakunin* (London, 1937).

——— ' "Russia and the West" as a Theme of Russian History', *Essays Presented to Sir Lewis Namier*, R. Pares and A. Taylor, eds. (London, 1956) 357–93.

Carsten, F., 'The Court Jews: A Prelude to Emancipation', *Leo Baeck Institute Yearbook* (3: 1958) 140–56.

Carter, R., ed. *Resolutions and Decisions of the Communist Party of the Soviet Union*, 4 vols. to date (Toronto, 1970) vol. 1.

Chaadaev, P., *The Major Works of Peter Chaadaev*, R. McNally, trans. (Notre Dame: 1969).

Chamberlin, W., 'The Short Life of Russian Liberalism', *Russian Review* (26: 1967) 144–52.

Chambliss, W., 'The Selection of Friends', *Social Forces* (43: 1965) 370–86.

Cherikover, E., (E. Tcherikower) 'Peter Lavrov and the Jewish Socialist Emigres', *YIVO Annual of Jewish Social Science* (7: 1952 [1939]) 132–45.

——— 'Yidn revolutzionern in Rusland in di 6oer un 7oer yorn', *Historishe shriftn* (3: 1939) 61–172.

Chernyshevsky, N., *Selected Philosophical Essays* (Moscow, 1953).

——— *What Is To Be Done? Tales About New People*, B. Tucker, trans. (New York, 1961 [1863]).

Cohen, A., *Custom and Politics in Urban Africa: A Study of Hausa Migrants in Yoruba Towns* (Berkeley, 1969).

——— *Two Dimensional Man: An Essay on the Anthropology of Power and Symbolism in Complex Societies* (London, 1974a).

——— ed., *Urban Ethnicity* (London, 1974b).

Cohen, I., *History of the Jews in Vilna* (Philadelphia, 1943).

Coser, L., *Men of Ideas: A Sociologist's View* (New York, 1966).

——— 'The Alien as a Servant of Power: Court Jews and Christian Renegades', *American Sociological Review* (37: 1972) 574–81.

Crisp, O., 'French Investment in Russian Joint-Stock Companies, 1894–1914', *Business History* (2: 1959) 75–90.

Dan, T., *The Origins of Bolshevism*, J. Carmichael, trans. (New York, 1964 [1946]).

Dawidowicz, L., ed., *The Golden Tradition: Jewish Life and Thought in Eastern Europe* (Boston, 1967).

Debo, R., 'Litvinov and Kamenev—Ambassadors Extraordinary: The Problem of Soviet Representation Abroad', *Slavic Review* (34: 1975) 463–82.

Deich, L., *Yidn in der rusisher revolutzie: zikhroines vegn Yidn-revolutzionern*, A. Korman, trans. (Berlin, 1922).

Deutscher, I., *The Prophet Armed: Trotsky, 1879–1921* (New York, 1965

[1954]).

—— 'The Non-Jewish Jew', *The Non-Jewish Jew and Other Essays* (London, 1968) 25–41.

Deyateli SSSR i oktyabr'skoy revolyutzii, 3 pts. (n.p. [Moscow?]: n.d. [1927–9?]).

Dimanshtein, S., ed., *Revolyutzionnoe dvizhenie sredi Evreev* (Moscow, 1930).

Dinur, B., 'Dmuta ha-historit shel ha-Yahadut ha-rusit u-ve'ayot ha-kheker ba', *Tzion* (22: 1957) 93–118.

Dobb, M., *Studies in the Development of Capitalism* (London, 1963 [1947]).

Dubnow, S., *History of the Jews in Russia and Poland*, 3 vols., I. Friedlander, trans. (Philadelphia: 1916–20).

Du Bois, C., 'The Gratuitous Act: An Introduction to the Comparative Study of Friendship Patterns', *The Compact: Selected Dimensions of Friendship*, E. Leyton, ed. (St John's, 1974) 15–32.

Duncan, K., 'Irish Famine Immigration and the Social Structure of Canada West', *Studies in Canadian Social History*, M. Horn and R. Sabourin, eds. (Toronto, 1974) 140–63.

Durkheim, E., *Selected Writings*, A. Giddens, ed. and trans. (Cambridge, Eng., 1972).

Eagleton, T., *Marxism and Literary Criticism* (London, 1976).

Eastman, M., *Leon Trotsky: Portrait of a Youth* (New York, 1925).

Edie, J., *et al.*, eds., *Russian Philosophy*, 3 vols. (Chicago, 1965).

Encyclopaedia Judaica, 16 vols. (Jerusalem, 1971–2).

Evreyskago kolonizatzionnago obshchestvo, *Sbornik materialov ob ekonomicheskom polozhenii Evreev v Rossii*, 2 vols. (St Petersburg: 1904).

Evreyskaya entziklopediya, 16 vols. (The Hague: 1969–71 [1930–1]).

Eymontova, R., 'Universitetskiy vopros i russkaya obshchestvennost' v 50–60-kh godakh XIX v.', *Istoriya SSSR* (6: 1971) 144–58.

Falkus, M., 'Russia and the International Wheat Trade, 1861–1914', *Economica* (33: 1966) 416–29.

—— *The Industrialization of Russia, 1700–1914* (London, 1972).

Feis, H., *Europe, The World's Banker, 1870–1914: An Account of European Foreign Investment and the Connection of World Finance with Diplomacy Before the War* (New Haven, 1930).

Feuer, L., *The Conflict of Generations: The Character and Significance of Student Movements* (New York, 1969).

—— 'Generations and the Theory of Revolution', *Survey* (84: 1972) 161–88.

—— 'The Conversion of Karl Marx's Father', *Jewish Journal of Sociology* (14: 1974) 149–66.

Figner, V., *Memoirs of a Revolutionist*, C. Chapin *et al.*, trans. (New York: 1968 [1927]).

Fischer, G., *Russian Liberalism: From Gentry to Intelligentsia* (Cambridge, Mass., 1958).

Flacks, R., 'Review Article', *Journal of Social History* (4: 1970–1) 141–53.

Florinsky, M., *Russia: A History and an Interpretation*, 2 vols. (New York, 1947).

Francis, E., 'The Nature of the Ethnic Group', *American Journal of Sociology* (52: 1947) 393–400.

Frank, V., 'The Russian Radical Tradition', *Survey* (29: 1959) 97–102.

Frankel, J., *Socialism and Jewish Nationalism in Russia, 1892–1907* (unpublished Ph.D. thesis, Cambridge University, 1961).

—— 'Economism: A Heresy Exploited', *Slavic Review* (22: 1963) 263–84.

Frölich, P., *Rosa Luxemburg: Ideas in Action*, J. Hoornweg, trans. (London, 1972 [1939]).

Frumkin, J., *et al.*, eds. *Russian Jewry (1860–1917)* M. Ginsburg, trans. (New York, 1966).

Garvi, P., *Vospominaniya sotzialdemokrata: stat'i o zhizni i deyatel'nosti P. A. Garvi* (New York, 1946).

Geffen, J., 'Whither: To Palestine or America in the Pages of the Russian Hebrew Press Ha-Melitz and Ha-Yom (1880–90): Annotated Documentary', *American Jewish Historical Quarterly* (59: 1969–70) 179–200.

Gerschenkron, A., *Economic Backwardness in Historical Perspective: A Book of Essays* (Cambridge, Mass., 1962).

—— *Europe in the Russian Mirror: Four Lectures in Economic History* (Cambridge, Eng., 1970).

Getzler, I., *Martov: A Political Biography of a Russian Social Democrat* (Cambridge, Mass., 1967).

Ginzberg, L., *Students, Scholars and Saints* (Philadelphia, 1928).

Ginzburg, S., 'Di familie Baron Ginzburg: drei doires shtadlanus, tzadoka un haskola', *Historishe verk*, 3 vols. (New York, 1937) vol. 2, 117–59.

Gitelman, Z., *Jewish Nationality and Soviet Politics: The Jewish Section of the CPSU, 1917–1930* (Princeton, 1972).

Glaser, B. and Strauss, A., *The Discovery of Grounded Theory: Strategies for Qualitative Research* (Chicago, 1967).

Glazer, N. and Moynihan, D., *Beyond the Melting Pot* (Cambridge, Mass., 1965).

Godelier, M., 'System, Structure and Contradiction in *Capital*', B. Brewster, trans. *The Socialist Register*, R. Miliband and J. Saville, eds. (London, 1967 [1966]) 91–119.

Goldhagen, E., 'The Ethnic Consciousness of Early Russian Jewish Socialists', *Judaism* (23: 1974) 479–96.

Gordon, Mania, *Workers Before and After Lenin: 50 Years of Russian Labor* (New York, 1941).

Gordon, Milton, *Assimilation in American Life: The Role of Race, Religion, and National Origins* (New York, 1964).

Gorev, B., *Iz partiynogo proshlogo: vospominaniya, 1895–1905* (Leningrad, 1924).

—— 'Russian Literature and the Jews', A. Levin, trans., *Critique* (5: 1976 [1917]) 35–53.

Gouldner, A., 'Metaphysical Pathos and the Theory of Bureaucracy', *American Political Science Review* (46: 1955) 496–507.

—— 'Prologue to a Theory of Revolutionary Intellectuals', *Telos* (26: 1975–6) 3–36.

Gorky, M., *Autobiography of Maxim Gorky*, I. Schneider, trans. (New York, 1949).

Gramsci, A., 'The Intellectuals', *Selections from the Prison Notebooks*, Q. Hoare and G. Smith, eds. (London, 1971 [1929–35]) 5–23.

Greenberg, L., *A Critical Investigation of the Works of Rabbi Isaac Baer Levinsohn (RIBaL)* (New York, 1930).

—— *The Jews in Russia: The Struggle for Emancipation* 2 vols. (New Haven, 1944–51).

Grinfeld, Y., 'Das leben fun di rusishe politishe in oisland', *Di tzukunft* (23: 1918) 44–7.

Grunwald, K., 'Europe's Railways and Jewish Enterprise', *Leo Baeck Institute Yearbook* (12: 1967) 163–209.

Guindon, H., 'Social Unrest, Social Class and Quebec's Bureaucratic Revolution', *Queen's Quarterly* (71: 1964) 150–62.

Gurr, T., *Why Men Rebel* (Princeton, 1970).

Habbakuk, H. and Postan, M., eds., *The Cambridge Economic History of Europe*, vols. 1 to 4 and 6 to date (Cambridge, Eng., 1941–67) vol. 6, pt. 2.

Haimson, L., *The Russian Marxists and the Origins of Bolshevism* (Boston, 1955).

—— 'The Problem of Social Stability in Urban Russia, 1905–17 (Part One)', *Slavic Review* (23: 1964) 619–42.

Hall, O., 'The Canadian Division of Labour Revisited', *Canadian Society: Pluralism, Change and Conflict*, R. Ossenberg, ed. (Scarborough, 1971) 89–99.

Halpern, B., *The Idea of the Jewish State* (Cambridge, Mass., 1969 [1961]).

Hamm, H., 'Liberalism and the Jewish Question: The Progressive Bloc', *Russian Review* (31: 1972) 163–72.

Hampden-Turner, C., *Radical Man: The Process of Psycho-Social Development* (Garden City, 1970).

Hansen, A., 'Cycles of Strikes', *American Economic Review* (11: 1921) 616–21.

Harcave, S., 'The Jewish Question in the First Russian Duma', *Jewish Social Studies* (6: 1944) 155–76.

—— *The Russian Revolution of 1905* (London, 1970 [1964]).

Haupt, G. and Marie, J.-J., eds. *Makers of the Russian Revolution: Biographies of Bolshevik Leaders*, C. Ferdinand and D. Bellos, trans. (London, 1974 [1969]).

Heberle, R., *Social Movements: An Introduction to Political Sociology* (New York: 1951).

Hechter, M., 'The Political Economy of Ethnic Change', *American Journal of Sociology* (79: 1974) 1151–78.

Hedlin, M., 'Zinoviev's Revolutionary Tactics in 1917', *Slavic Review* (34: 1975) 19–43.

Hersch, L., 'International Migration of the Jews', *International Migrations*, 2 vols., W. Willcox, ed. (New York, 1929–31) vol. 2, 471–520.

Hertz, Y., ed., *Doires Bundistn*, 3 vols. to date (New York, 1956–8) vols. 1–2.

Hertzberg, A., ed. *The Zionist Idea: A Historical Analysis and Reader* (New York, 1959).

Herzen, A., *Selected Philosophical Works*, L. Navrozov, trans. (Moscow, 1956).

Hobsbawm, E., 'Economic Fluctuations and Some Social Movements Since 1800', *Economic History Review* (5: 1952) 1–25.

Hoffer, E., *The True Believer: Thoughts on the Nature of Mass Movements* (New York, 1951).

Howard, L. and Wayne, J., 'Ethnicity in Canada: A Social Structural View', *Journal of Comparative Sociology* (2: 1974) 35–52.

Hughes, E., 'Social Change and Status Protest: An Essay on the Marginal Man', *Phylon* (10: 1949) 58–65.

Ianni, F. and Reuss-Ianni, E., *A Family Business: Kinship and Social Control in Organized Crime* (New York, 1972).

Ionescu, G. and Gellner, E., eds., *Populism* (New York, 1969)

Izgoev, A., 'On Educated Youth (Notes on its Life and Sentiments)', *Vekhi (Signposts): A Collection of Articles on the Russian Intelligentsia*, M. Schatz and J. Zimmerman, trans., in *Canadian Slavic Studies* (3: 1969 [1909]) 594–515.

Jellinek, F., *The Paris Commune of 1871* (New York, 1965 [1937]).

Johnson, R., *The Nature of the Russian Working Class: Social Characteristics of the Moscow Industrial Region, 1880–1890* (unpublished Ph.D. thesis, Cornell University, 1975).

Johnson, W., *Russia's Educational Heritage* (Pittsburgh, 1950).

Junior, J., 'The Right Honourable Benjamin Disraeli', *Vanity Fair* (30 Jan 1869) 153.

Kadushin, C., 'The Friends and Supporters of Psychotherapy: On Social Circles in Urban Life', *American Sociological Review* (31: 1966) 786–802.

Kaplan, A., *The Conduct of Inquiry: Methodology for Behavioral Science* (Scranton: 1964).

Kaplan, S., *Once a Rebel* (New York, 1941).

Karpovich, M., 'A Forerunner of Lenin: P. N. Tkachev', *Review of Politics* (6: 1944) 336–50.

Katz, J., *Exclusiveness and Tolerance: Jewish-Gentile Relations in Medieval and Modern Times* (New York, 1961).

—— *Tradition and Crisis: Jewish Society at the End of the Middle Ages* (New York, 1962).

—— *The Jewish National Movement: A Sociological Analysis* (Jerusalem,

1970).

—— *Out of the Ghetto: The Social Background of Jewish Emancipation, 1770–1870* (Cambridge, Mass., 1973).

Katz-Blum, H., *Zikhroines fun a Bundist: bilder fun untererdishen lebn in tzarishn Rusland* (New York, 1940).

Katzenelson, B., *Darki la-aretz* (Tel-Aviv, 1941).

Keep, J., *The Rise of Social Democracy in Russia* (Oxford, 1963).

Khersakov, I., 'Reminiscences of the Moscow Student Movement', *Russian Review* (11: 1952) 223–32.

Kisch, G., 'The Jews' Function in the Medieval Evolution of Economic Life', *Historica Judaica* (6: 1944) 1–12.

Kochan, L., *The Making of Modern Russia* (London, 1962).

Kon, F., *et al.*, eds., *Deyateli revolyutzionnogo dvizheniya v Rossii: bio-bibliograficheskii slovar'*, 5 vols. (Moscow, 1927–31) vol. 5.

Kostka, E., 'At the Roots of Russian Westernism: N. V. Stankevich and his Circle', *Slavic and East European Studies* (6: 1951) 156–76.

Kremer, M., 'Jewish Artisans and Guilds in Former Poland, 16th-18th Centuries', *YIVO Annual of Jewish Social Science* (11: 1956–7) 211–42.

Kushnir, S., *The Village Builder: A Biography of Abraham Harzfeld*, A. Regelson and G. Hirschler, trans. (New York, 1967).

Landau, H., 'Di Yidn in ruslender neft industrye un neft handel', *YIVO bleter* (14: 1939) 269–84.

Lane, D., *The Roots of Russian Communism* (Assen, 1969).

Laqueur, W., *A History of Zionism* (London, 1972).

Lavrov, P., *Historical Letters*, J. Scanlan, trans. (Berkeley, 1967 [1870]).

Leggett, J., *Class, Race, and Labor: Working-Class Consciousness in Detroit* (London, 1968).

Lenin, V., *Collected Works*, 45 vols., C. Dutt and J. Katzer, eds. (Moscow, 1960–70 [1925–6]) vols. 1–10.

Lenski, G., 'Status Crystallization: A Nonvertical Dimension of Social Status', *American Sociological Review* (19: 1954) 405–13.

Leon, A., *The Jewish Question: A Marxist Interpretation*, E. Germain, trans. (New York, 1970 [1946]).

Leshchinsky, Y., *Der idisher arbeiter in Rusland* (Vilna, 1906).

—— *Das idishe folk in tzifern* (Berlin, 1922).

—— 'Di antviklung fun idishen folk far di letzte 100 yor', *Shriftn far ekonomik un statistik* (1: 1928) 1–64.

—— 'Yidishe vanderungen in di letzte hundert yor', *YIVO bleter* (23: 1944) 41–54.

Levin, A., 'B. Gorev and his "Russian Literature and the Jews"', *Critique* (5: 1976) 53–7.

Levin, S., *Forward from Exile: The Autobiography of Shmarya Levin*, M. Samuel, trans. (Philadelphia, 1967).

Levitats, I., *The Jewish Community in Russia, 1772–1844* (New York, 1970 [1943]).

Leykina-Svirskaya, V., *Intelligentziya v Rossii vo vtoroy polovine XIX veka* (Moscow, 1971).

Leyton, E., 'Composite Descent Groups in Canada', *Man* (97–8: 1965) 107–10.

Lichtheim, G., *Collected Essays* (New York, 1951).

Lieberson, S., 'Stratification and Ethnic Groups', *Social Stratification: Research and Theory for the 1970s* (Indianapolis, 1970) 172–81.

Lilienthal, M., 'My Travels in Russia', *Max Lilienthal, American Rabbi: Life and Writings*, D. Philipson, ed. (New York, 1915) 159–363.

Lipset, S., 'Students and Politics in Comparative Perspective', *Daedalus* (97, 1: 1968) 1–20.

—— *Agrarian Socialism: The Cooperative Commonwealth Federation in Saskatchewan* (Berkeley, 1971 [1950]).

—— and Dobson, R., 'The Intellectual as Critic and Rebel with Special Reference to the United States and the Soviet Union', *Daedalus* (101, 3: 1972) 137–98.

—— and Zetterberg, H., 'A Theory of Social Mobility', *Transactions of the Third World Congress of Sociology* (2: 1956) 155–77.

Litman, J., *Yitzchak Schipper's Contributions to the Understanding of the Economic Role of Jews in Medieval Poland* (unpublished Ph.D. thesis, New York University, 1968).

Litvak, A., *Gezamelte shriftn* (New York, 1945).

Lodhi, A. and Tilly, C., 'Urbanization, Crime, and Collective Violence in 19th-century France', *American Journal of Sociology* (79: 1973) 296–318.

Loker, B., ed. *Idisher arbeter yor-bukh un almanakh* (New York: 1928).

Loim, S., 'A. Valt (Liesin) in kheder, tzvishen di Slovodker musarnikes in Volozhiner yeshiva', *Di tzukunft* (24: 1919) 193–5.

Lunacharsky, A., *Revolutionary Silhouettes*, M. Glenny, trans. (London, 1967 [1919]).

Luxemburg, R., 'Die industrielle Entwicklung Polens', *Gesammelte Werke*, 2 vols., G. Adler *et al.*, eds. (Berlin: 1972) vol. 1, pt. 1, 113–216.

Lyadov, M., *Iz zhizni partii: nakanune i v gody pervoy revolyutzii (vospominaniya)* (Moscow, 1926).

Lyashchenko, P., *History of the National Economy of Russia to the 1917 Revolution*, L. Herman, trans. (New York, 1949 [1927]).

MacDonald, J. and MacDonald, L., 'Chain Migration, Ethnic Neighbourhood Formation, and Social Networks', *Milbank Memorial Fund Quarterly* (42: 1964) 82–97.

Macpherson, C., *Democracy in Alberta: Social Credit and the Party System* (Toronto, 1962 [1953]).

Mahler, R., 'Antisemitism in Poland', *Essays on Antisemitism*, K. Pinson, ed. (New York, 1946) 145–72.

—— *A History of Modern Jewry, 1789–1815*, Y. Haggai, trans. (New York, 1971 [1952–6]).

Maimon, S., *Solomon Maimon: An Autobiography*, J. Murray, trans. (New York, 1947 [1792–3]).

Maisky, I., *Before the Storm: Recollections*, G. Shelley, trans. (London, 1944).

Malia, M., 'What is the Intelligentsia?', *The Russian Intelligentsia*, R. Pipes, ed. (New York, 1961) 1–18.

—— *Alexander Herzen and the Birth of Russian Socialism* (Cambridge, Mass., 1966).

Malowist, M., 'Poland, Russia and Western Trade in the Fifteenth and Sixteenth Centuries', *Past and Present* (13: 1958) 26–41.

—— 'The Economic and Social Development of the Baltic Countries from the Fifteen to the Seventeenth Centuries', *Economic History Review* (12: 1959) 177–89.

—— 'The Problem of the Inequality of Economic Development in Europe in the Late Middle Ages', *Economic History Review* (19: 1966) 15–28.

Mandel, N., 'Turks, Arabs and Jewish Immigration into Palestine, 1882–1914', *St Antony's Papers* (17: 1965) 77–108.

Mannheim, K., *Ideology and Utopia*, L. Wirth and E. Shils, trans. (New York, 1954 [1929]).

—— 'The Problem of the Intelligentsia: An Inquiry into its Past and Present Role', *Essays in the Sociology of Culture*, E. Mannheim and P. Kecskemeti, eds. (London, 1965) 91–170.

Margolin, S., 'Die wirtschaftliche Lage der jüdischen arbeitenden Klassen in Russland', *Archiv für Sozialwissenschaft un Sozialpolitik* (26: 1908) 240–69.

Marmor, K., *Mein lebens-geshikte*, 2 vols. (New York, 1959).

Martov, Y. (L. Martoff), 'Das russische Proletariat und die Duma', *Arbeiter Zeitung* (24 Aug 1905a) 1–2.

—— (L. M.), 'Na ocheredi: rabochaya partiya i 'zakhvat vlasti' kak nasha blizhayshaya zadacha', *Iskra* (17 Mar 1905b). See footnote 22, Chapter 4.

—— (L. Martov), 'Der vende-punkt in der geshikhte fun der yidisher arb.-bavegung', *Arbeiter luakh* (3: 1922 [1895]) 71–90.

—— (L. Martov), *Zikhroines fun a sotzialdemokrat* (Berlin, 1923).

—— (J. Martov), 'On Party Organization', *Masters of Russian Marxism*, T. Anderson, ed. (New York, 1963 [1904]) 101–5.

Marx, K., *Pre-capitalist Economic Formations*, E. Hobsbawm, ed., J. Cohen, trans. (London, 1964 [1857–8]).

—— *Capital*, 3 vols. (Moscow, 1971 [1867–94]).

—— and Engels, F., *The Marx-Engels Reader*, R. Tucker, ed. (New York, 1972).

Masaryk, T., *The Spirit of Russia: Studies in History, Literature and Philosophy*, 2 vols., E. and C. Paul, trans. (London, 1919 [1913]).

'Materialn un dokumentn: di diskusie vegn der natzionaler frage oifn V tzuzamenfor fun "Bund" [,] Yuni [,] 1903 [,] Tziurikh (fun di protokoln fun tzuzamenfor)', *Unzer tzait* (1, 2: 1927a) 87–96.

'Materialn un dokumentn: di diskusie vegn der natzionaler frage oifn V tzuzamenfor fun "Bund", Yuni, 1903, Tzirikh [sic] (fun di protokoln fun tzuzamenfor)', *Unzer tzait* (1, 3: 1927b) 83-96.

Materialy k istorii evreyskago rabochago dvizheniya (St Petersburg, 1906).

Mathes, W., 'The Origins of Confrontation Politics in Russian Universities: Student Activism, 1855-1861', *Canadian Slavic Studies* (2: 1968) 28-45.

Maynard, J., *The Russian Peasant and Other Studies* (London, 1942).

McCagg, W., 'Jews in Revolution: The Hungarian Experience', *Journal of Social History* (6: 1972-3) 78-105.

McGee, T., 'Peasants in the Cities: A Paradox, a Paradox, a Most Ingenious Paradox', *Human Organization* (32: 1973) 135-42.

McKay, J., *Pioneers for Profit: Foreign Entrepreneurship and Russian Industrialization, 1885-1913* (Chicago, 1970).

McNeal, R., 'Women in the Russian Radical Movement', *Journal of Social History* (5: 1971-2) 143-63.

Medem, V., *Fun main leben*, 2 vols. (New York, 1923).

Meijer, J., *Knowledge and Revolution: The Russian Colony in Zurich, 1870-73* (Assen, 1955).

Mendelsohn, E., 'The Russian Jewish Labor Movement and Others', *YIVO Annual of Jewish Social Science* (14: 1969) 87-98.

—— *Class Struggle in the Pale: The Formative Years of the Jewish Workers Movement in Tsarist Russia* (Cambridge, Eng., 1970).

Menes, A., 'Di yidishe arbeter-bavegung in Rusland fun onhoib 70er bizn sof 90er yorn', *Historishe shriftn* (3: 1939) 1-59.

—— 'The Jewish Socialist Movement in Russia and Poland (From the 1870s to the Founding of the Bund in 1897)', *The Jewish People: Past and Present*, 4 vols. (New York, 1949) vol. 2, 355-68.

Merton, R., *Social Theory and Social Structure* (New York, 1968 [1949]).

Meyer, A., *The Origins of the Modern Jew: Jewish Identity and European Culture, 1749-1824* (Detroit, 1967).

Michels, R., 'Intellectuals', *Encyclopaedia of the Social Sciences*, 15 vols. (New York, 1932) vol. 8, 118-26.

—— *Political Parties: A Sociological Study of the Oligarchical Tendencies of Modern Democracy*, F. and C. Paul, trans. (New York, 1962 [1911]).

Mill, J., *Pionern un boier*, 2 vols. (New York, 1946).

Mills, C., *White Collar: The American Middle Classes* (New York, 1951).

Mishkinski, M., 'ha-Sotzializm ha-mishtarti u-m'gamot b'mediniut ha-shilton ha-tzari l'gabei ha-Yehudim', *Tzion* (25: 1960) 238-49.

—— 'Regional Factors in the Formation of the Jewish Labor Movement in Czarist Russia', *YIVO Annual of Jewish Social Science* (14: 1969) 27-52.

Morison, J., 'Educational Expansion and Revolution in Russia', *Paedagogica Historica* (9: 1968) 400-24.

Morokhovetz, E., 'Krest'yanskoe dvizhenie 1905-07 gg. i sotzialdemokratiya', *Proletarskaya revolyutziya* (39: 1925a) 41-83.

—— 'Krest'yanskoe dvizhenie 1905–07 gg. i sotzial-demokratiya', *Proletarskaya revolyutziya* (40: 1925b) 57–91.

—— 'Krest'yanskoe dvizhenie 1905–07 gg. i sotzial-demokratiya', *Proletarskaya revolyutziya* (41: 1925c) 64–95.

—— 'Krest'yanskoe dvizhenie 1905–07 gg. i sotzial-demokratiya', *Proletarskaya revolyutziya* (42: 1925d) 54–81.

—— 'Krest'yanskoe dvizhenie 1905–07 gg. i sotzial-demokratiya', *Proletarskaya revolyutziya* (43: 1925e) 5–36.

Mosse, W., 'Makers of the Soviet Union', *Slavonic Review* (46: 1968) 141–54.

Mutnikovich, A., (A. Mutnik) 'Bletlekh fun main leben', *Di tzukunft* (38: 1933) 509–13, 595–7, 664–6, 718–20.

Namier, L., *1848: The Revolution of the Intellectuals* (London, 1944).

Nedava, J., *Trotsky and the Jews* (Philadelphia, 1972).

Nettl, J., *Rosa Luxemburg*, 2 vols. (London, 1966).

Niger, S. and Shatzky, Y., eds. *Leksikon fun der naier yidisher literatur*, 6 vols. to date (New York, 1956–8).

O'Boyle, L., 'The Problem of an Excess of Educated Men in Western Europe, 1800–1850', *Journal of Modern History* (72: 1970) 471–95.

Oelsner, T., 'Wilhelm Roscher's Theory of the Economic and Social Position of the Jews in the Middle Ages', *YIVO Annual of Jewish Social Science* (12: 1958–9). 179–95.

Olson, M., 'Rapid Growth as a Destabilizing Force', *Journal of Economic History* (23: 1963) 529–52.

Orlov, V., 'Studencheskoe dvizhenie v 1901 g.', *Krasniy arkhiv* (75: 1938) 83–112.

Pareto, V., *The Mind and Society*, 4 vols., A. Livingston, ed., A. Bongiorno, trans. (New York, 1935 [1916]).

Park, R., 'Human Migration and the Marginal Man', *American Journal of Sociology* (23: 1928) 881–93.

Parkin, F., *Middle Class Radicalism: The Social Bases of the British Campaign for Nuclear Disarmament* (Manchester, 1968).

—— *Class Inequality and Political Order: Social Stratification in Capitalist and Communist Societies* (London, 1971).

Parsons, T., 'The Intellectual: A Social Role Category', *On Intellectuals*, P. Rieff, ed. (New York, 1963) 3–24.

Patkin, A., *The Origins of the Russian-Jewish Labour Movement* (London, 1947).

Perrie, M., 'The Russian Peasant Movement of 1905–1907: Its Social Composition and Revolutionary Significance', *Past and Present* (57: 1972) 123–55.

Perrot, M., 'Grèves, grévistes et conjoncture. Vieux problème, travaux neufs', *Le mouvement social* (63: 1968) 109–24.

Peskin, Y., 'Di "Grupe Yidishe Sotzial-demokratn in Rusland" un Arkady Kremer', *Historishe shriftn* (3: 1939) 544–56.

Piatnitsky, O., *Memoirs of a Bolshevik* (New York, 1933 [1925]).

Pinson, K., 'Arkady Kremer, Vladimir Medem, and the Ideology of the Jewish "Bund" ', *Jewish Social Studies* (7: 1945) 233–64.

Pipes, R., 'Russian Marxism and its Populist Background: The Late Nineteenth Century', *Russian Review* (19: 1960) 316–37.

—— *Social Democracy and the St Petersburg Labor Movement, 1885–1897* (Cambridge, Mass., 1963).

Plekhanov, G., *Selected Philosophical Works*, 5 vols., M. Iovchuk *et al.*, eds., Y. Kots, *et al.*, trans. (Moscow, 1974 [1960]) vol. 1.

Pollard, A., 'The Russian Intelligentsia: The Mind of Russia', *California Slavic Studies* (3: 1964) 1–32.

Pomper, P., *The Russian Revolutionary Intelligentsia* (New York, 1970).

—— *Peter Lavrov and the Russian Revolutionary Movement* (Chicago, 1972).

Pope, A., *Maxim Litvinoff* (New York, 1943).

Program fun der Yidisher Sotzial-demokratisher Arbeter-partai ('Poalei-Tzion') in Rusland (Lublin, 1918 [1906?]).

Raba, Y., 'Al ha-mivne ha-miktzoi shel Yehudei malkut Polin ba-emtza shel ha-me'a ha-19', *Tzion* (25: 1960) 190–211.

Rabinovich, Z., 'ha-'Rotshildim' shel Pinsk v'Karlin', *he-Avar* (17: 1970) 252–80.

Rabinowitsch, S., *Die Organisationen des jüdischen Proletariats in Russland* (Karlsruhe: 1903).

Raeff, N., *Origins of the Russian Intelligentsia: The Eighteenth Century Nobility* (New York, 1966a).

——, ed., *Russian Intellectual History: An Anthology* (New York, 1966b).

Raisin, J., *The Haskalah Movement in Russia* (Philadelphia, 1914).

—— 'Jewish Contributions to the Progress of Russia (cont.)', *The Jewish Forum* (2: 1919) 870–80.

Raizen, Z., ed., *Leksikon fun der naier yidisher literatur, prese un filologie*, 4 vols. (Vilna, 1928–30).

Rappaport, C., 'The Life of a Revolutionary Émigré (Reminiscences)', *YIVO Annual of Jewish Social Science* (6: 1951 [1939]) 206–36.

Rashin, A., 'Gramotnost' i narodnoe obrazovanie v Rossii v XIX i nachale XX vekakh', *Istoricheskie zapiski* (37: 1951) 28–80.

'O chislennosti i territorial'nom razmeshchenii rabochikh Rossii v period kapitalizma', *Istoricheskie zapiski* (46: 1954) 127–81.

—— *Formirovanie rabochego klassa Rossii: istoriko-ekonomichiskie ocherki* (Moscow, 1958).

Reddaway, M., *et al.*, eds., *The Cambridge History of Poland* 2 vols. (Cambridge, Eng., 1950).

Rees, A., 'Industrial Conflict and Business Fluctuations', *Journal of Political Economy* (60: 1952) 371–82.

Reznichenko, Y., ed., *In baginen: di tzionistishe-sotzialistishe bavegung biz der grindung fun velt-farband Poalei-Tzion (Hag, 1907)* (Tel-Aviv, 1948).

Rimlinger, G., 'The Management of Labor Protest in Tsarist Russia:

1870–1905', *International Review of Social History* (5: 1960) 226–48.
—— 'The Expansion of the Labor Market in Capitalist Russia: 1861–1917', *Journal of Economic History* (21: 1961) 209–15.

Rivkin, E., *The Shaping of Jewish History: A Radical New Interpretation* (New York, 1971).

Robinson, G., *Rural Russia Under the Old Regime: A History of the Landlord-Peasant World and a Prologue to the Peasant Revolution of 1917* (Berkeley, 1969 [1932]).

Ro'i, Y., 'The Zionist Attitude to the Arabs, 1908–1914', *Middle Eastern Studies* (4: 1968) 198–242.

Roiter pinkas: tzu der geshikhte fun der yidisher arbeter-bavegung un sotzialistishe shtremungen bei Yidn, 2 vols. (Warsaw, 1921–4).

Roscher, W., 'The Status of the Jews in the Middle Ages Considered from the Standpoint of Commercial Policy', S. Grayzel, trans., *Historica Judaica* (6: 1944 [1875]) 13–26.

Rosenzweig, R. and Tamarin, G., 'Israel's Power Elite', *Transaction* (7, 9–10: 1970) 26–42.

Rubinow, I., 'Economic Condition of the Jews in Russia', *Bulletin of the Bureau of Labor* (72: 1907) 487–583.

Ruppin, A., *The Jews in the Modern World* (London, 1972 [1934]).

Sachar, H., *The Course of Modern Jewish History* (New York, 1959).

Sapir, B., 'Liberman et la socialisme Russe', *International Review for Social History* (3: 1938) 25–88.

—— 'Jewish Socialists Around *Vpered*', *International Review of Social History* (10: 1965) 365–84.

Sartre, J.-P., *Anti-Semite and Jew*, G. Becker, trans. (New York, 1948 [1946]).

Sawer, M., 'Plekhanov on Russian History: A Marxist Approach to Historical Pluralism', *Science and Society* (39: 1975) 292–317.

Schapiro, L., 'The Rôle of the Jews in the Russian Revolutionary Movement', *Slavic Review* (40: 1961) 148–67.

Schneiderman, J., *Sergei Zubatov and Revolutionary Marxism: The Struggle for the Working Class* (Ithaca, 1976).

Scholem, G., *Shabbatai Sevi, the Mystical Messiah: 1626–1676*, Z. Werblowsky, trans. (Princeton, 1973 [1957]).

Schulman, E., 'David Shub, 1887–1973', *Russian Review* (32: 1973) 460–2.

—— 'Solomon M. Schwarz, 1883–1973', *Russian Review* (33: 1974) 118–19.

Schumpeter, J., *Imperialism, Social Classes: Two Essays*, H. Norden, trans. (New York, 1951 [1919–27]).

Schwarz, S., *The Russian Revolution of 1905: The Workers Movement and the Formation of Bolshevism and Menshevism*, G. Vakar, trans. (Chicago, 1967).

Schweitzer, A., 'Ideological Groups', *American Sociological Review* (9: 1944) 415–26.

Secord, P. and Blackman, C., 'Interpersonal Congruency, Perceived Similarity, and Friendship', *Sociometry* (27: 1964) 115–27.

Senn, A., *The Russian Revolution in Switzerland, 1914–1917*, (Madison, 1971).

Shanin, T., 'Socio-Economic Mobility and the Rural History of Russia, 1905–1930', *Soviet Studies* (23: 1971–2) 222–35.

Sharot, S., 'Minority Situation and Religious Acculturation: A Comparative Analysis of Jewish Communities', *Comparative Studies in Society and History* (16: 1974) 329–54.

Shazar, S., *Morning Stars*, S. Nardi, trans. (Philadelphia, 1967 [1950]).

Sheret, Y. and Tamir, N., eds. *Anshei ha-aliya ha-shniya* 3 vols., (Tel-Aviv: 1970–1).

Shibutani, T. and Kwan, K., *Ethnic Stratification: A Comparative Approach* (New York, 1965).

Shils, E., 'The Intellectuals in the Political Development of the New States', *Political Change in Underdeveloped Countries*, J. Kautsky, ed. (New York, 1962) 195–234.

Shub, D., 'Yidn in der rusishe revolutzie', *Di tzukunft* (49: 1944) 360–88.

—— *Fun di amolike yorn*, 2 vols., (New York, 1970).

Simmel, G., 'The Web of Group Affiliations', *Conflict and the Web of Group Affiliations*, K. Wolff and R. Bendix, trans. (New York, 1955 [1922]) 124–95.

—— 'The Stranger', *On Individuality and Social Forms*, D. Levine, ed. (Chicago, 1971) 143–9.

Singer, I., *The Brothers Ashkenazi*, M. Samuel, trans. (New York, 1937).

Slusser, R., *The Moscow Soviet of Workers' Deputies of 1905: Origin, Structure and Policies* (unpublished Ph.D. thesis, Columbia University, 1963).

Slutzky, Y., 'Tzmikhata shel ha-inteligentzia ha-ychudit ha-rusit', *Tzion* (25: 1960) 212–37.

Smith, C. and Freedman, A., *Voluntary Associations: Perspectives on the Literature* (Cambridge, Mass., 1972).

Smith, D., 'The Determinants of Strike Activity in Canada', *Relations industrielles* (27: 1972) 663–78.

Snyder, D. and Tilly, C., 'Hardship and Collective Violence in France, 1830–1960', *American Sociological Review* (37: 1972) 520–32.

Sombart, W., *The Jews and Modern Capitalism*, M. Epstein, trans. (New York, 1951 [1911]).

'Soviet Emigrant Plans to Tell of Labor Camps', *New York Times* (13 Jan 1975) 15, col. 1.

Spinrad, W., 'Correlates of Trade Union Participation', *American Sociological Review* (25: 1960) 237–44.

Stateri, G., *Death of a Utopia: The Development and Decline of Student Movements in Europe* (New York, 1975).

Stepniak, *The Career of a Nihilist* (London, 1890).

Stern, S., *The Court Jew: A Contribution to the History of the Period of Absolutism in Central Europe*, R. Weiman, trans. (Philadelphia, 1950).

Stern-Taubler, S., 'The Jew in the Transition from Ghetto to Emancipation', *Historica Judaica* (2: 1940) 102–19.

Strauss, H., 'Revolutionary Types: Russia in 1905', *Journal of Conflict Resolution* (17: 1973) 297–316.

Struve, P., 'My Contacts and Conflicts with Lenin (II)', *Slavonic Review* (13: 1934–5) 66–84.

—— 'The Intelligentsia and Revolution', *Vekhi (Signposts): A Collection of Articles on the Russian Intelligentsia*, M. Schatz and J. Zimmerman, trans., in *Canadian Slavic Studies* (4: 1970 [1909]) 183–98.

Stryker, S., 'Social Structure and Prejudice', *Social Problems* (6: 1959) 340–54.

Sverdlov, Y., *Izbranye proizvedeniya*, 3 vols. (Moscow, 1957–60) vol. 1.

Syrkin, M., *Nachman Syrkin: A Biographical Memoir, Selected Essays* (New York, 1961).

Talmon, J., 'Jews Between Revolution and Counter-Revolution', *Israel Among the Nations* (London, 1970) 1–87.

Tarnopoler, L., 'Avraham Ravotzky—itonai, khoker v'lokhem', *he-Avar* (17: 1970) 217–28.

Taylor, K. and Frideres, J., 'Issues Versus Controversies: Substantive and Statistical Significance', *American Sociological Review* (37: 1972) 464–72.

Thompson, E., *The Making of the English Working Class* (Harmondsworth, 1968).

Tidmarsh, K., 'The Zubatov Idea', *Slavic Review* (19: 1960) 335–46.

Tilly, C., 'The Analysis of a Counter-Revolution', *History and Theory* (3: 1963–4) 30–58.

—— 'Reflections on the Revolution of Paris: An Essay on Recent Historical Writings', *Social Problems* (12: 1964) 99–121.

—— 'The Chaos of the Living City', *An Urban World*, C. Tilly, ed. (Boston, 1974) 86–108.

—— *The Vendée* (Cambridge, Mass., 1976 [1964]).

—— *et al.*, *The Rebellious Century, 1830–1930* (Cambridge, Mass., 1975).

Tobias, H., *The Jewish Bund in Russia from its Origins to 1905* (Stanford, 1972).

Tompkins, S., *The Russian Mind from Peter the Great Through the Enlightenment* (Norman, 1953).

—— *The Russian Intelligentsia: Makers of the Revolutionary State* (Norman, 1957).

Trotsky, L., *Our Revolution: Essays on Working-Class and International Revolution, 1904–1917*, M. Olgin, trans. (New York, 1918).

—— 'Results and Prospects', *The Permanent Revolution and Results and Prospects* (New York, 1969 [1906]) 29–122.

—— *My Life: An Attempt at an Autobiography* (New York, 1970 [1930]).

—— *1905*, A. Bostock, trans. (Harmondsworth, 1971 [1909]).

Tugan-Baranovsky, M., *The Russian Factory in the 19th Century*, A. and C. Levin, trans. (Homewood, 1970 [1898]).

Turin, S., *From Peter the Great to Lenin: A History of the Russian Labour Movement with Special Reference to Trade Unionism* (London, 1968 [1935]).

Tzitron, S., *Drei literarishe doires: kharakteristikes un zikhroines vegn yidishe shriftshteler*, 3 vols., (Vilna, 1921-2).

Tzivyon, *Far 50 yor* (New York, 1948).

Tzunzer, E., *Tzunzers biographie: geshriben fun im alein* (New York, 1905).

Ulmen, G., 'Wittfogel's Science of Society', *Telos* (24: 1975) 81-114.

Uron, S., 'Ya'akov Sverdlov: n'sia ha-rishon shel Brit ha-Mo'atzot', *he-Avar* (15: 1968) 208-10.

Utechin, S., 'Who Taught Lenin?' *Twentieth Century* (168: 1960) 8-16.

—— 'The "Preparatory" Trend in the Russian Revolutionary Movement in the 1880s', *St. Antony's Papers* (12: 1962) 7-22.

Vallee, F., *et al.*, 'Ethnic Assimilation and Differentiation in Canada', *Canadian Society: Sociological Perspectives* B. Blishen, *et al.*, eds. (Toronto, 1968 [1961]) 593-603.

Veblen, T., 'The Intellectual Pre-eminence of the Jews in Modern Europe', *Essays in Our Changing Order*, L. Ardzrooni, ed. (New York, 1943 [1934]) 219-31.

Venturi, F., *Roots of Revolution: A History of the Populist and Socialist Movements in Nineteenth-Century Russia*, F. Haskell, trans. (New York, 1960 [1952]).

Verba, S., 'Comparative Political Culture', *Political Culture and Political Development*, L. Pye, ed. (Princeton, 1965) 512-60.

Vladimir Meden: tzum tzvantzigstn yortzeit (New York, 1943).

Volhiner, A., ed. *Idisher arbeter yor-bukh un almanakh* (New York, 1927).

Von Haxthausen, A., *Studies on the Interior of Russia*, S. Starr, ed., E. Schmidt, trans. (Chicago, 1972 [1843]).

Von Laue, T., 'Russian Peasants in the Factory, 1892-1904', *Journal of Economic History* (21: 1961) 61-80.

—— 'Russian Labor Between Field and Factory, 1892-1903', *California Slavic Studies* (3: 1964) 33-65.

—— *Sergei Witte and the Industrialization of Russia* (New York, 1974 [1963]).

Vtoroy s'yezd RSDRP, yul'-avgust 1903 goda: protokoly (Moscow, 1959 [1904]).

Walsh, W., 'Economic Conditions and Strike Activity in Canada', *Industrial Relations* (14: 1975) 45-54.

Weber, M., *From Max Weber: Essays in Sociology*, H. Gerth and C. Mills, eds. and trans. (New York, 1946).

—— *Ancient Judaism*, H. Gerth and D. Martindale, eds. and trans. (New York, 1952 [1917-19]).

—— *General Economic History*, F. Knight, trans. (New York, 1961 [1927]).

Weeks, A., *The First Bolshevik: A Political Biography of Peter Tkachev* (New York, 1968).

Weinberg, I. and Walker, K., 'Student Politics and Political Systems: Toward a Typology', *American Journal of Sociology* (75: 1970) 77-96.

Weinryb, B., *The Jews of Poland: A Social and Economic History of the Jewish*

Community in Poland from 1100 to 1800 (Philadelphia, 1972).

—— *Neueste Wirtschaftsgeschichte der Juden in Russland und Polen: von der 1. polnischen Teilung bis zum Tode Alexanders II. (1772–1881)* (New York, 1972 [1934]).

Weintraub, A., 'Prosperity versus Strikes: An Empirical Approach', *Industrial and Labor Relations Review* (19: 1966) 231–8.

Weisbord, R., *African Zion: The Attempt to Establish a Jewish Colony in the East African Protectorate, 1903–1905* (Philadelphia, 1968).

Weiss, R., 'Defection from Social Movements and Subsequent Recruitment to New Movements', *Sociometry* (26: 1963) 1–20.

Weizmann, C., *Trial and Error: The Autobiography of Chaim Weizmann, First President of Israel* (New York, 1966 [1949]).

—— *The Letters and Papers of Chaim Weizmann. Series A. Letters*, 7 vols. to date, L. Stein and G. Yogev, eds. (London, 1968–76) vols. 1–4.

Westwood, J., *A History of Russian Railways* (London, 1964).

Wildman, A., 'The Russian Intelligentsia of the 1890s', *Slavic Review* (19: 1960) 157–79.

—— 'Lenin's Battle with Kustarnichestvo: The Iskra Organization in Russia', *Slavic Review* (23: 1964) 479–503.

—— *The Making of A Workers Revolution: Russian Social Democracy, 1891–1903* (Chicago, 1967).

—— 'Russian and Jewish Social Democracy', *Revolution and Politics in Russia: Essays in Memory of B. I. Nicolaevsky*, A. and J. Rabinowitch and L. Kristof, eds. (Bloomington, 1972) 75–86.

Wirth, L., *The Ghetto* (Chicago, 1956 [1928]).

Wischnitzer, M., *A History of Jewish Crafts and Guilds* (New York, 1965).

Wittfogel, K., *Oriental Despotism: A Comparative Study of Total Power* (New Haven, 1957).

Wolf, E., 'Kinship, Friendship, and Patron-Client Relations in Complex Societies', *The Social Anthropology of Complex Societies*, M. Banton, ed. (New York, 1966) 1–22.

—— *Peasant Wars of the Twentieth Century* (New York, 1969).

—— 'On Peasant Rebellions', *Peasants and Peasant Societies*, T. Shanin, ed. (Harmondsworth, 1971) 264–74.

Wolfe, B., 'Gapan and Zubatov: An Experiment in Police Socialism', *Russian Review* (7: 1948a) 53–61.

—— *Three Who Made a Revolution: A Biographical History* (New York, 1948b).

Wood, N., *Communism and British Intellectuals* (New York, 1959).

Woodhouse, C. and Tobias, H., 'Primordial Ties and Political Process in Pre-Revolutionary Russia: The Case of the Jewish Bund', *Comparative Studies in Society and History* (8: 1965–6) 331–60.

Wortman, R., *The Crisis of Russian Populism* (Cambridge, Eng., 1967).

Woytinsky, E., *Two Lives in One* (New York, 1965).

Woytinsky, W., *Stormy Passage. A Personal History Through Two Russian*

Revolutions to Democracy and Freedom: 1905–1960 (New York, 1961).

Yanait-Ben-Tzvi, R., 'Molin', *he-Avar* (18: 1971) 199–204.

Yancey, W., *et al.* 'Emergent Ethnicity: A Review and Reformulation', *American Sociological Review* (41: 1976) 391–403.

Yaresh, L., 'The "Peasant Wars" in Soviet Historiography', *Slavic Review* (16: 1957) 241–59.

Yarmolinsky, A., *Road to Revolution: A Century of Russian Radicalism* (New York: 1962 [1956]).

Yuditzky, A., *Yidishe burzhwazie un yidisher proletariat in ershter helft XIX yorhundert* (Kiev: n.d. [1930?]).

Zborowski, M., 'The Place of Book-Learning in Traditional Jewish Culture', *Harvard Educational Review* (19: 1949) 87–109.

Zelnik, R., 'The Peasant and the Factory', *The Peasant in Nineteenth-Century Russia*, W. Vucinich, ed. (Stanford: 1968) 158–90.

―――― *Labor and Society in Tsarist Russia: The Factory Workers of St Petersburg, 1855–1870* (Stanford, 1971).

―――― 'Russian Workers and the Revolutionary Movement', *Journal of Social History* (6: 1972–3) 214–36.

Zenan, Z. and Scharlau, W., *The Merchant of Revolution: The Life of Alexander Israel Helphand (Parvus), 1867–1924* (London, 1965).

Zerubavel, Y., *Ber Borokhov: zein leben un shafen* (Warsaw, 1926).

―――― , ed., *Yidisher arbeter pinkas (tzu der geshikhte fun der Poalei-Tzion bavegung)* (Warsaw, 1928).

―――― *In onhoib: artiklen-zikhroines* (Tel-Aviv, 1938).

―――― *Bleter fun a leben*, 2 vols. (Tel-Aviv, 1956) vol. 1.

―――― *Geshtaltn* (Tel-Aviv: 1967).

Zinger, M., *b'Reishit ha-tzionut ha-sotzialistit* (Haifa, 1944).

―――― *Shlomo Kaplansky: khayav u-fe'alov*, 2 vols. (Jerusalem 1971) vol. 1.

Zinoviev, G., *Sochineniya*, 16 vols. (Moscow, 1923) vol. 1.

Index